MAKING A KILLING

MAKING

A

KILLING

The Business of Guns in America

TOM DIAZ

THE NEW PRESS   NEW YORK

Library of Congress Cataloging-in-Publication Data

Diaz, Tom.
    Making a killing : the business of guns in America / by Tom Diaz.
       p.   cm.
    Includes bibliographical references and index.
    ISBN 1-56584-470-X
    1. Firearms industry and trade — United States.   2. Firearms
ownership — Government policy — United States.   3. Gun control — United
States. I. Title.
    HD9744.F553U63   1999
    338.4′762344′0973 — dc21   98-34227
                                                       CIP

Published in the United States by The New Press, New York
Distributed by W. W. Norton & Company, Inc., New York

The New Press was established in 1990 as a not-for-profit alternative to the large, commercial publishing houses currently dominating the book publishing industry. The New Press operates in the public interest rather than for private gain, and is committed to publishing, in innovative ways, works of educational, cultural, and community value that are often deemed insufficiently profitable.

www.thenewpress.com

Printed in the United States of America

9 8 7 6 5 4 3 2

—Contents

—LIST OF TABLES   *vii*

—ACKNOWLEDGMENTS   *ix*

—INTRODUCTION: THE MESS   *3*

PART I—THE GUN BUSINESS   *17*

1—The Manufacturers   *19*

2—The Dealers   *36*

3—The Promoters   *50*

4—The Market   *69*

5—"A Little Money-Making Machine"   *85*

PART II—THE SPIRAL OF LETHALITY   *89*

6—The Deadly Role of Innovation   *91*

7—A Domestic Arms Race   *106*

8—The Rambo Factor   *120*

9—Exploiting Ties to Law Enforcement   *141*

PART III—NURTURING A CULTURE OF FEAR   *153*

10—The Self-Defense Mirage   *155*

11—Playing Soldier   *175*

12—Targeting New Markets   *184*

—CONCLUSION: CLEANING UP THE MESS   *193*

—NOTES   *210*

—INDEX   *250*

—List of Tables

Table 1.	Domestic Gun Manufacturing	24
Table 2.	Top Ten Domestic Pistol Manufacturers	25
Table 3.	Top Ten Domestic Revolver Manufacturers	25
Table 4.	Top Ten Domestic Rifle Manufacturers	26
Table 5.	Top Ten Domestic Shotgun Manufacturers	26
Table 6.	Top Ten Crime Guns Traced by the ATF	27
Table 7.	Guns Imported into the U.S. Civilian Market	31
Table 8.	Rifle Imports from China to the United States, 1987–1994	73
Table 9.	Total Imports and Imports from China, 1987–1994	74
Table 10.	Leading Handgun Exporters to the U.S., 1991–1996	76
Table 11.	Handgun Imports from Austria to the U.S., 1983–1996	78
Table 12.	Handgun Imports from the former "Iron Curtain" Countries to the United States, 1991–1996	80

—Acknowledgments

It is impossible to list all of those who played a role in the journey that led to the writing of this book. At the forefront are the victims of gun violence and their survivors whose real life testimony touched me deeply when I was counsel to the Crime Subcommittee of the U.S. House of Representatives. The stories of these ordinary people—children, fathers, mothers, sisters, brothers and just friends—put indelible human faces on the grim statistics of gun violence that shame our nation and to which we have become hardened. At a more particular level, I thank my colleagues at the Violence Policy Center whose clear strategic vision and deep knowledge of the gun industry and the violence it causes have been an unfailing source of wise guidance and help: Josh Sugarmann, Kristen Rand, Sue Glick, Marty Langley, and Bill McGeveran. Their work is woven throughout these pages. Randy Turkel, who did an excellent and creative job manhandling a mountain of detailed fact-checking, deserves special mention. Matt Weiland of The New Press did a masterful job of editing. I am indebted to his fine sense of structure and flow. This book would not have been possible without the encouragement and support of Debby Leff and the support of the Joyce Foundation. Congressman Charles E. Schumer and former Crime Subcommittee chief counsels Andy Fois and David Yassky taught me invaluable lessons about the federal law and about how public policy is really made (and not made). Finally, I would like to thank my several friends in the trenches at the Bureau of Alcohol, Tobacco and Firearms. They know who they are, I hope. The criticism I make in this book of that agency's leadership should not be confused with disrespect for the work of these men and women, who put their lives on the line virtually every day going after the "bad guys." On the contrary, they have been given a too often thankless "mission impossible"—dealing with gun violence in a topsy-turvy system that encourages more rather than less lethality on our streets. The nation owes them, and itself, a better way.

MAKING A KILLING

THE BUSINESS OF GUNS IN AMERICA

—Introduction:
The Mess

Few things arouse as much visceral passion among Americans as firearms do. To many, guns are repulsive and exceedingly dangerous, even evil. But to others, guns are venerated objects of craftsmanship and tangible symbols of such fundamental American values as independence, self-reliance, and freedom from governmental interference. This divide has made the national debate about firearms often seem to be a shouting match between people from different planets—or at least from different eras—talking about entirely different things.

Amid the heated exchanges of statistics on firearms mayhem, finely drawn constitutional arguments about individual "rights" and "responsibilities," and solemn invocations of cultural symbols from the Revolution and the frontier, any sense of firearms as a profit-making business gets lost. The ultimate fact is that the gun industry is simply a business, and nothing more. It is neither a national trust nor a repository of American values. Although the people who make, import, and sell guns often wrap themselves in ideological and nostalgic symbols of early America, they are not latter-day founding fathers. They are businessmen. They are in the game because they want to make money, and as much of it as possible.

However complicated the debate over guns, the business of selling guns is quite banal, at least on its face. In terms of the structure of manufacturers, importers, wholesale dealers, and retail outlets, the trade appears no different than the trade that brings power tools and gum balls to the hardware store around the corner. Like other consumer products, guns get to U.S. consumers through an organized market: Domestic and foreign manufacturers, large and small, make guns, which are then distributed through wholesalers and importers to local dealers, where they are first sold at retail.

Domestic firearms manufacturers, importers, and retail dealers are required to obtain a federal firearms license. And buyers of new handguns at federally licensed retail dealers are subject to a waiting period, during which a background check may be made to screen out convicted felons and others barred by federal law from possessing firearms.

But there is a substantial amount of debate about how effective such mild restrictions are in preventing felons and other prohibited persons from getting firearms, even brand new guns from licensed dealers. Even assuming that these cursory federal screening mechanisms work, the nation's guard drops entirely once a new gun has been sold for the first time at retail. Used guns frequently are resold in a variety of secondary markets, entirely unregulated in almost all states. These markets operate by means of private transactions, such as sales through classified advertising in newspapers or newsletters, contacts made through the Internet, and sales or "swaps" across backyard fences or at organized informal markets, which are sometimes called "flea markets" or "gun shows." Guns are also borrowed for use from friends or relatives, and transferred as gifts or bequests. About forty percent of all gun transfers in the United States in 1994 were made in these unregulated secondary markets, according to a U.S. Justice Department survey released in 1997.[1] With the exception of those in a few unusually strict states (like New York), these transactions are entirely free of licensing, record-keeping, waiting periods, or other regulatory oversight. In most states it is as easy to buy a gun in these secondary markets as it is to buy a pack of cigarettes.[2]

The gun industry is aided in its marketing efforts by the "gun press," a constellation of newspapers, magazines, and newsletters bonded by a common infatuation with guns and the trade in guns. The entertainment media also often serve the interests of the gun industry, intentionally or not, by portraying the use of firearms as an effective and acceptable means to resolve disputes, and by featuring specific firearms in so-called "action" films and television shows.

Finally, gun manufacturers, firearms industry associations, lobbyists, the gun press, gun importers, wholesalers, and dealers are all entwined in an interlocking network of mutual promotion. Representatives of all of these elements of the industry meet often in a variety of forums, where they plan, develop, and set into motion gun industry marketing and political strategies.

But beyond these basic facts, not much is publicly known. Peeling back the gun industry's protective veneer to get at its inner workings and basic motivations is not an easy task. All but one of the major domestic manufacturers — Sturm, Ruger & Company, Inc. — are privately held companies. A number of other major domestic gun-makers are subsidiaries of secretive foreign companies, like Beretta USA Corporation (Italy) , Browning (Japan), and Smith & Wesson (England), among others. And a major part of the U.S. gun market consists of imports — guns shipped directly into the United States from foreign manufacturers or foreign surplus stockpiles, many with undisclosed private and foreign governmental ownership interests. These companies — and the importers, wholesale distributors, and retail dealers who are the gun industry's commercial arteries — vigorously conceal information that most other U.S. industries routinely reveal. Indeed, the firearms industry is a business so secret that it makes the tobacco industry look like a model of transparency.

As a result, basic facts that would help inform public opinion and illuminate wise policy-making about the production and consumption of firearms in the United States are all closely held secrets.[3] These include:

- the breakdown by each manufacturer and outlet of guns made and sold within each product line, including specific numbers of guns made and sold by each type of gun and caliber;
- the ownership of all manufacturers, importers, and dealers, including foreign private and government interests and their financial performance, including profit margins;
- the record of specific defects in guns, steps taken, if any, to correct those defects, and resulting product liability litigation;
- specific quantities by type of firearms made by each foreign manufacturer and imported into the United States;
- *ex parte* meetings and communications between manufacturers, importers, and industry representatives with officials of the U.S. Treasury Department and its Bureau of Alcohol, Tobacco and Firearms (ATF).

This secrecy is compounded by the fact that the gun industry has never been comprehensively examined by Congress or any other national authority. Even though firearms kill tens of thousands of men, women, and children in the United States, and wound many times that every year, Congress has never subjected this lethal industry to the kind of scrutiny that it has the tobacco industry, the automobile industry, the airline industry, the funeral home industry, and the manufacturers and distributors of many other products that threaten the public health and safety.[4]

What little public information there is about the firearms industry must be gleaned from records related to the minimal federal firearm licensing requirements, Census Bureau surveys and compilations from customs declarations, cursory manufacturers' reports to the ATF, self-serving sales materials and promotional leaks from individual manufacturers, and broad summaries reported in the trade press.

But none of these provide detailed data on the production and sale of civilian firearms. Although the federal government regularly collects some data about the firearms business, it is organized into categories that overlap with other related markets, and none of it reveals details about individual companies. The U.S. Census Bureau, for example, conducts an economic census every five years in which it gathers data from virtually all manufacturers, wholesalers, and retailers in the United States about what they make and sell. But none of the Bureau's standard groupings aligns precisely with the civilian firearms market.[5]

Similar problems attend the data that the Census Bureau collects in the companion census of retail trade. For example, the Bureau does not collect or report national aggregate retail trade data specifically for firearms or ammunition. Rather, it lumps them into a composite figure for retail sales of all "sporting goods," a category that includes everything from hockey pucks to shotguns. Therefore, one cannot derive from the data either the quantity or sales figures of guns and ammunition sold at retail in the United States.[6]

Even the ATF is unhelpful beyond summary data. It is an increasingly reluctant source of even potentially unfavorable information about the gun industry. Decades of criticism from the National Rifle Association and the conservative wings of both national parties appear to have finally had a deleterious effect on the ATF, including on the public's right to know. Under its current director John Magaw, the ATF has aggressively sought détente with the gun industry, and now withholds from the public as much information as possible about the industry. The ATF stands virtually in a class by itself among federal agencies in stonewalling routine requests under the federal Freedom of Information Act for information about its dealings with the industry it regulates.

By and large, the people who make, import, and sell guns in the United States hide from the public's view, projecting only the image they wish Americans to see. Nevertheless, it is possible to sketch a rough view of the overall dimensions of the civilian firearms market. The wholesale dollar value of all firearms and ammunition manufactured in the United States in 1995 was about $1.7 billion. Of that total, about $525 million was attributed to handguns, $647 million to other firearms, and $511 million to ammunition. Some estimates put total gun and ammunition retail sales at about $9 billion, with a total economic impact (including sales of accessories and gun-related services) of between $20 billion and $25 billion.[7] The Sporting Arms and Ammunition Manufacturers Institute, Inc. (SAAMI), a gun industry trade group, claims that "the hunting and shooting sports market generates in excess of $18 billion of economic activity annually," including about $8 billion on equipment, "including firearms, ammunition, clothing, reloading equipment, optics and accessories."[8]

But these estimates are either mere guesses — a kind of "Kremlinology" of the U.S. gun industry — or self-serving statements intended to promote the industry's interests. Since a surprisingly large part of the U.S. gun market is supplied by or through foreign interests — including foreign governments like the People's Republic of China — there is also a vast lack of data about imported firearms and ammunition that is currently beyond the reach of even the U.S. government. Exactly who, or which interests, makes and sells guns to Americans remains shrouded in mystery. But it is undoubtedly safe to say that many foreigners and foreign entities are profiting from the anguish guns cause in United States.

A PUBLIC HEALTH DISASTER

Each of the millions of firearms that the gun industry produces, imports, and sells in the United States every year is lethal. Every type of gun sold in this country, from the "cutest" little derringer pistol in 22 caliber to the "ugliest" AK-47 assault rifle, can kill a human being. Some types of firearms are more efficient at killing, more lethal, than others. But there is no such thing as a "harmless" firearm.

Given the inherent lethality of firearms, it is no wonder that guns cause so much mayhem in the United States every year. The wonder is that our society has become so inured to firearms violence that we hardly pay attention to the casualties that mount steadily, day after day and year in and year out. After thirty-five people were killed by a gunman with an array of assault weapons in Port Arthur, Australia, in 1996, Australia banned all automatic and semi-automatic weapons and pump-action shotguns, paid their owners a fair price, and destroyed the lot. Britain—which already had strict gun control laws—totally banned all handguns in 1997, following a massacre at Dunblane Primary School in Scotland by a man who killed sixteen children and a teacher with four handguns.[9] The United States suffers the creeping equivalent of almost one thousand Port Arthur and two thousand Dunblane massacres every year, but its anemic gun control movement musters little effective outcry.[10]

Since 1960, more than three-quarter of a million Americans have died in firearm suicides, homicides, and unintentional injuries. In 1995 alone, 35,957 Americans died by gunfire: 18,503 in firearm suicides, 15,835 in firearm homicides, 1,225 in unintentional shootings, and 394 in firearm deaths of unknown intent. Nearly three times that number are treated in emergency rooms each year for nonfatal firearm injuries.[11] The United States leads the industrialized world in the rate at which its children die from firearms: A 1997 study by the federal Centers for Disease Control analyzed firearms-related deaths for children under age fifteen in twenty-six countries and found that eighty-six percent of them occurred in the United States.[12] Since 1962, firearms-related deaths in the United States have doubled.

Contrary to popular perception, most gun death in the United

States is not crime-related. Although the U.S. firearms homicide rate is staggering when compared to virtually any other developed nation in the world, the plain fact is that most firearms deaths stem not from homicide but from suicide. And even among those who are murdered with firearms, the majority die because of arguments between people who know each other, not as the result of some other criminal act.

The fact is that the greater part of firearms violence in the United States does not stem from "guns in the wrong hands." It stems rather from the virtually unregulated distribution of an inherently dangerous consumer product. A public policy debate that focuses solely on firearms violence as a "crime issue"—concentrating primarily, if not exclusively, on regulating access to firearms and on punishing those who use them in criminal acts—misses the greater part of the problem. Seen from its proper perspective, firearms violence is a widespread public health and safety issue. Crime is merely the most publicly recognized aspect of this broader health and safety problem.

The recent efforts to regulate the tobacco industry and to make it pay for the illness and death caused by tobacco products contrast sharply with the gun industry's freedom. Like tobacco, guns inflict a relentlessly accumulating toll of physical, economic, and emotional harm on the United States and its residents. A health and safety perspective suggests a different remedial focus, one that starts by acknowledging the inherently dangerous nature of the commodity—in short, a focus that acknowledges that all guns are lethal. Such a focus would permit exploration of ways in which to contain the risks to society that such a dangerous commodity inevitably presents, beginning with its manufacture and continuing through the entire stream of commerce and ultimate consumer use.

Aside from the direct toll in human tragedy, firearms violence imposes many other and different kinds of costs on the United States that a health and safety perspective would consider.

One of the biggest costs, and yet one that is least understood by the public—indeed hardly touched by Congress—is the sheer economic impact of gun violence. Several analysts have suggested ways to identify and measure the costs of gun violence. Perhaps the most thorough analysis is that described by Ted R. Miller and Mark A. Cohen in a chapter devoted entirely to the question of costs in the medical textbook *Penetrating Trauma*.[13] Using 1990 data and building on earlier, less exhaustive studies,[14] Miller and Cohen's comprehensive estimate is that gunshot wounds exact a staggering annual cost of $112 billion on the United States. Of this amount, $60.1 billion is the result of assaults with firearms, $41.4 billion the result of suicides and attempted suicides, and $10.5 billion the result of unintended shootings. (As might be expected, almost all of the suicide costs—$40 billion—were the result of fatalities, i.e., successful attempts. Suicide by firearm has a much higher rate of success than suicide attempted by other means.)[15]

Gun violence has a particularly perverse economic effect in the case of children. Like the tobacco industry, the gun industry underwrites large scale campaigns that specifically target children as future consumers. But in at least one way guns have a more immediate or directly insidious effect on children than do tobacco products. The cancers, heart disease, emphysema, and other ailments that tobacco products induce usually take some time to develop and eventually disable or kill their victims. Even those who begin smoking as children typically do not suffer catastrophic health effects until later, during their adult lives. Moreover, they at least have the option as they mature to quit using tobacco products and thus mitigate the damage to their health.

Children shot by firearms do not enjoy the benefit of such a delayed effect. Nor do they have a chance to mitigate injury by reforming personal behavior. A child who is struck by a bullet and killed or wounded is robbed of childhood immediately. Society is denied an even greater proportion of the productive life of a child who is a victim of gunshot than of a child of the same age who smokes and later in life suffers adverse health effects from tobacco and the consequent costs. In other words, if one child begins smoking at fourteen and another is struck by a bullet at the same age, the smoker may well not suffer adverse medical effects until middle age, whereas the victim of gun violence suffers all the effects immediately.

The impact of these costs of gun violence radiates out to affect all

Americans. For example, a much lower proportion of gunshot victims have health insurance than the general population.[16] The cost of their treatment must therefore either be absorbed by health care providers, such as trauma centers, or shifted to others in the form of higher taxes or insurance premiums. A study at a Los Angeles trauma center of patients admitted with intentional injuries during 1986 and 1988, for example, found that seventy-five percent of their costs were uncompensated.[17] Financial burdens like these are forcing some hospital centers to close their trauma care centers.[18]

Some would argue that these costs are balanced by the utility of firearms for personal defense and sporting uses. There is much disagreement about how useful firearms really are for self-defense, and about how often they are actually used for such a purpose. However, even assuming that there is any such self-defense benefit *that could not otherwise be enjoyed in a society cleansed of firearms*, that benefit is enjoyed only by a dwindling minority at the expense of a growing majority who either suffer firearms injury and death or pay the costs thereof.

According to the Justice Department survey, the proportion of households in the United States that own firearms is declining markedly, and firearms ownership is concentrated in a minority of hands. Only one-quarter of adults in the United States own a gun, and the ratio for handguns is even more striking: Only about one in six Americans (sixteen percent) own a handgun. That means that five out of six Americans do not own a handgun.

It is clear that firearms ownership is concentrated among a decided minority of Americans, and that minority is shrinking, even as the number of guns increases. Fewer and fewer Americans own more and more guns. This has profound significance for public policy discussions, since it inevitably raises the question: to what extent should the rest of the United States indulge this minority and at what cost?

THE LAST UNREGULATED CONSUMER PRODUCT

What ought to be obvious from even this cursory review of firearms violence in the United States is that firearms are an inherently dangerous product, of use only to a dwindling minority, that imposes extraordinarily high human and economic costs on our society. One would expect that in the light of these facts, a rational public policy would seek to subject firearms to health and safety regulation like that to which virtually every other consumer product in the United States is today subject.

Yet the fact is that federal law exempts firearms and the gun industry from the standard health and safety regulation that is applied to all other consumer products manufactured and sold in the United States. The ATF, the only federal agency with arguable authority to regulate the firearms industry, confines itself to such merely ministerial matters as issuing licenses and collecting excise taxes. "Gun aficionados may liken the Bureau of Alcohol, Tobacco and Firearms to the Gestapo, but in its relationship with America's gun dealers the ATF behaves more like an indulgent parent," Erik Larson wrote in *The Atlantic,* in a long article thoroughly documenting the trail of a Cobray M11/9 assault pistol eventually used in a schoolyard murder.[19]

The ATF also has primary responsibility among federal law enforcement agencies for enforcing federal criminal law relating to firearms. But for the most part the criminal law limits access to firearms (prohibiting, for example, sales to felons and children) and punishes the use of firearms in the commission of federal crimes. Except for restricting the availability of a few categories of weapons, such as machine guns and, to some extent, assault weapons, federal law does not directly regulate either the gun industry or its products.

Some would argue that the ATF has substantially more inherent power than it has ever asserted to regulate the manufacture and distribution of firearms more vigorously than the entirely ministerial course it has chosen. However, the ATF has taken a cautious view of its powers and has chosen not to assert any such authority, although a more aggressive agency might find some penumbra of powers to be logically inherent in its licensing or other powers. Creative, proactive thinking would seem to be the key to such an assertion of powers. But given the fact that the ATF has taken a brutal pounding over the last two decades from the gun lobby and its supporters in

Congress, it is unlikely that the agency will do much more in the foreseeable future than continue to keep its bureaucratic head down. In any case, it is clear that even under the most generous reading of the ATF's inherent powers, it simply does not have broad enough power to regulate the gun industry in the way that the Consumer Product Safety Commission (CPSC), for example, regulates everything else from Barbie dolls to barbecue grills.

Hard as it is to believe, guns and ammunition are free of federal safety and health regulation. No federal agency has the power to ensure that a gun is designed and manufactured in such a way as to minimize its threat to human life. Indeed, for over thirty years firearms and ammunition have been carefully and deliberately walled off from the regulatory powers of the CPSC and the laws it administers.

This exclusion dates back at least as far as 1967, when Congress created the National Commission on Product Safety and directed it to "conduct a comprehensive study and investigation of the scope and adequacy of measures now employed to protect consumers against unreasonable risks of injuries which may be caused by hazardous household products."[20] Firearms and ammunition were specifically exempted from the National Commission's jurisdiction (notwithstanding that the gun industry to this day advertises the merits of guns for home defense, and thus for use as "household products").

The report of the National Commission led ultimately to enactment of the Consumer Product Safety Act of 1972, and creation of the CPSC. Rep. John Dingell, a Michigan Democrat and until recently a long-time National Rifle Association (NRA) board member, successfully offered an amendment in committee that excluded guns and ammunition from the law's reach. An attempt to strike the exclusion was defeated on the floor of the House of Representatives. Although the Senate version of the legislation would have included firearms and ammunition within the CPSC's jurisdiction, the Senate language was dropped in the conference committee that reconciled the two chambers' differing versions.

Interestingly, one of the reasons given in the House by opponents of CPSC jurisdiction over guns and ammunition was that the

National Commission had not inquired into those two areas, and it would be "misleading" to the public to enact a law regulating firearms "without any kind of history as to what we intended."[21] In other words, Congress first excluded guns and ammunition from the National Commission's jurisdiction, and then entertained the argument that because the Commission had not studied those products there was no basis for including them in the ultimate legislation!

In retrospect, it is clear that this victory for the gun industry has had grave long-term effects. It has permitted domestic gun manufacturers to make without restraint hundreds of thousands of firearms in such a shoddy manner and of such poor materials that they are not only unreliable, but are likely to injure the user. Moreover, gun manufacturers are free of federal requirements to design safety features into their products. Thus, whereas those who design power tools and toys must meet minimum safety standards, gunmakers are free to (and almost universally do) ignore even the most rudimentary improvements in firearms design that might help ensure the safety of users and those third parties, like children, who may happen upon a firearm.

Although individual members of Congress regularly introduce bills proposing to give authority for health and safety regulation of firearms to one or another executive agency, no such bill has ever seen the light of a public hearing or moved out of committee. (Members of Congress routinely introduce legislation relating to all manner of subjects, including firearms, that they know have no chance of going beyond the files of their colleagues. Nevertheless, both the members and the gun lobby wage vociferous press release wars over such paper tigers. The "debate" serves both of their interests.)

Ironically, because of the peculiar operation of federal laws regulating gun imports, handguns imported from abroad are held to higher product safety standards than guns made at home.

LETHALITY AND PROFIT

Thus shielded from official oversight and almost entirely privately held, the firearms industry is shrouded in a veil of protective secrecy that the tobacco industry must envy. Hammered by a wave of investigations and lawsuits, the tobacco industry has gradually given up secret documents that reveal damning information about the extent to which its executives were aware of the lethality of their product and sought not only to conceal its harmful effects, but to enhance some of them. But no one has ever brought to public light the gun industry's internal documents on market strategy or the cost-benefit analyses it considers when it decides which new weapons to make, import, and sell.

This book is an attempt to get behind the veil and examine how the firearms industry produces and markets guns. The available evidence reveals a striking pattern that is frighteningly similar to the record of the tobacco industry: Over the last two decades, at least, the gun industry has deliberately enhanced its profits by increasing the lethality—the killing power—of its products. Lethality is the nicotine of the gun industry. Time and time again, the gun industry has injected into the civilian market new guns that are specifically designed to be better at killing—guns with greater ammunition capacity, higher firepower in the form of bigger caliber or power, increased concealability, or all three—and created demand for these new products with the collaboration of the "gun press" and the entertainment media.

Just as striking as this behavior itself is its repeated confirmation in statements by gun industry experts, leaders, and spokespersons in publications aimed at friendly audiences within the industry or its customers. For example, Bob Rogers, editor-in-chief of *Shooting Sports Retailer*, a major industry magazine, wrote in January 1997:

> Industry people need to consider how to make guns both safer and reliably convenient. *Firepower is increasing. So is the killing potential as guns shrink in size and concealability.* [Emphasis added]

Internal musings like these convey a very different message from that which the industry projects to the public at large. Here is an admission within the industry that guns are becoming increasingly deadly, and that the industry "needs to consider" how to make guns safer.

But that kind of admission gets little public airing. Instead, just as the tobacco industry wraps itself in the mantle of a putative "freedom of choice" to smoke or chew tobacco products known to cause cancer and other diseases of the heart and lungs, so does the gun industry wrap itself in nostalgia for a largely mythical frontier heritage and in the false flag of the Second Amendment. In the golden glow of the gun industry's public construct of itself, the lethality of guns becomes not a matter of civic concern but a virtually indispensable implement of civic duty.

The gun industry is the last supplier of consumer products in the United States to remain unregulated for health and safety. Its products kill tens of thousands of Americans every year. They injure hundreds of thousands of others. Yet its inner workings are almost entirely unknown to the public, and it stands alone among industries, free of even the most basic health and safety regulations. What follows is a description, to the greatest extent possible out of the mouths of industry members themselves, of how the gun industry operates, and how it deliberately sells more and more deadly guns to fewer and fewer Americans.

Part One

The Gun Business

1—The Manufacturers

The U.S. firearms industry has gone through cycles of boom and bust since it was born during the Revolutionary War with the founding of the Springfield Armory in Springfield, Massachusetts. The government armory at Springfield was established to give the revolutionary forces a safe place to make and store arms, out of reach of British sailing ships and the troops they brought with them.[1]

The original Springfield Armory continued to make military firearms—including such renowned battlefield weapons as the Springfield rifle, carried by Union soldiers during the Civil War, and the M-1 Garand, the standard U.S. infantry rifle of the Second World War—until the mid-1960s.[2] But the armory had a national influence that transcended its own production record, establishing a new industrial base in the Connecticut river valley and attracting hundreds of skilled craftsmen. Many of these craftsmen became the core of the new nation's gun industry.

Over the next two centuries, scores of gun manufacturing companies were created and thrived briefly in "Gun Valley," as the region in western Massachusetts and Connecticut came to be called. Many of these companies lasted only a few years, but a hardy few, often buoyed by clever invention or timely military contracts, survived. From the founding of Colt in 1836 to the incorporation of Sturm, Ruger & Company in 1949, a procession of firearms manufacturers flourished in Gun Valley. Their names became household words, often identified as implements of the nation's mythic conquest of its Western frontier.

Samuel Colt, for example, invented the revolving cylinder design and won U.S. Patent No. 138 for it in 1836. The Single Action Army Model 1873 revolver based on that design was named the "Peacemaker," but it became popularly known as "the gun that won the West." The Colt Model 1911 .45-caliber semiautomatic pistol served as the U.S. Army's standard sidearm for over half a century. And U.S. forces have carried Colt's M-16 assault rifle into action in combat since the Vietnam War.[3]

Horace Smith and Daniel B. Wesson formed a partnership in 1852 to manufacture a pistol that fired a fully self-contained cartridge. That partnership and its patents were sold to Oliver Winchester, who eventually founded the Winchester Repeating Arms Company in 1866. But Smith & Wesson reemerged in its own right as a manufacturer of revolvers. Booming business during the Civil War gave the company a healthy boost. Eventually, Smith & Wesson became known worldwide for its innovations in revolver design, including introduction of the .357-Magnum revolver, the .44-Magnum revolver, and the first American-made 9-mm semi-automatic pistol.[4]

Meanwhile, the Winchester Repeating Arms Company produced its first rifle in 1866. It enjoyed widespread publicity for its products when sharpshooters Buffalo Bill and Annie Oakley used Winchester rifles and ammunition in their touring Wild West Show, which glorified the role of the gun in "subduing" a supposedly hostile frontier. Around the turn of the century the company was purchased and integrated into the emerging ammunition manufacturing complex of Franklin W. Olin and his associates. The Olin interests became a major supplier of ammunition during the Second World War, producing over fifteen billion rounds of ammunition. According to Winchester, the company's horse and armed rider logo conveys an image of "the cowboy, the indian, the lawman, the pioneer, the mesa, the mountains, the desert, and the grandeur of the west."[5]

Other domestic companies with similar histories became equally well known as "old line" domestic firearms manufacturers. They included trademarks such as Remington, Marlin, High Standard, Ithaca, and others.

The firearms industry began changing as the nation emerged from the Second World War. New manufacturing enterprises were founded, many in states like California and Florida, far from Gun Valley but offering less costly production. Foreign gun manufacturers also discovered the vast U.S. market and devised strategies to penetrate it. These included quietly buying out a number of well-known "old line" U.S. companies, while keeping up the facade of their historic names, so that many U.S. gun buyers aren't even aware of the foreign ownership of these companies.

Some of the newer domestic enterprises went after the old-line companies head on with innovative strategies aimed at producing traditional products in more competitive ways. The premier example of such a successful modern gun manufacturer is Sturm, Ruger & Company, Inc. Founded by William B. Ruger and Alex Sturm in 1949 to produce a 22-caliber semiautomatic target pistol, the company built its early business on manufacturing "western style revolvers"—handguns imitating the classic design of the nineteenth century Colt Peacemaker.[6] Sturm, Ruger has since branched out into modern designs and long guns. It has grown to become one of the United States's most prolific producers of all types of firearms for the civilian market. Both the company and its products are universally referred to by gun enthusiasts as simply "Ruger."

The gun industry operated free of government restraint throughout most of this period. The first federal firearms law was the War Revenue Act of 1919, which placed a tax on the manufacture of firearms and ammunition to help pay costs of the First World War. The National Firearms Act of 1934 and the Federal Firearms Act of 1938 together comprised the federal government's first attempt at regulating the industry, largely through a taxation system that required manufacturers, importers, and dealers to register with the Treasury Department, pay a tax, and obtain a license. The system was largely ineffective as anything other than a revenue-raising measure, however. What few limitations it imposed on actual commerce in firearms were easily evaded and poorly enforced.

The assassination of President John F. Kennedy in 1963, the murders of Robert Kennedy and the Rev. Martin Luther King in 1968, rising rates of violent crime, and an explosion of handguns impelled Congress to pass the first truly comprehensive federal firearms law, the Gun Control Act of 1968, commonly referred to as the GCA.

The GCA somewhat tightened federal licensing requirements. Under the Act, manufacturers, importers, and dealers in firearms must obtain a federal license from the Treasury Department, which has delegated authority to administer the law to the ATF. These licenses are issued on a virtually pro forma basis—anyone who is at least twenty-one, has a clean record and a place of business, and agrees to follow all applicable laws can get a license good for three years upon paying a fee and submitting a set of fingerprints with an application form.[7]

The 1968 gun control law encouraged another change in the U.S. gun market, a change that is still playing itself out. For the first time, the nation restricted the import of so-called Saturday night specials—small, easily concealable handguns, poorly made of lower quality materials—by imposing certain size, design, and performance standards on imported foreign guns. The law did not, however, subject domestic manufacturers to any such standards. This different treatment had two long-term results: domestic companies sprang up to fill the Saturday night special gap, and foreign manufacturers created domestic manufacturing subsidiaries to evade import restrictions and get back into the lucrative U.S. market.

Southern California has recently become the center of the domestic manufacture of cheap handguns. A complex of companies founded by a handful of people related in one way or another to a single family, the Jennings, dominates the manufacture of Saturday night specials and "junk guns." The rise and deleterious nationwide impact of these companies, collectively known as the Ring of Fire companies, has been thoroughly and definitively documented in a landmark study by Northern California emergency room physician Dr. Garen Wintemute.[8]

Another class of entrepreneurs appeared in the early 1980s, the manufacturers of new designs of military style semiautomatic assault weapons for the civilian market. One of these latter-day success stories is South Florida's Intratec, founded by Cuban refugee Carlos Garcia. Intratec manufactured the infamous TEC-9, a favorite of drug lords and at least one mass murderer, and a regular on the national list of top ten guns traced in crimes, until it was outlawed by Congress in 1994. Intratec has since simply retooled and is now producing and selling a mildly modified version of the TEC-9 that it calls the AB-10. The "AB" reportedly stands for "after ban."[9]

In light of these trends and characteristics, members of the gun industry and industry observers often divide gun-makers two ways: by origin (foreign or domestic) and by perceived status — "old line" companies (such as Ruger, Colt, or Smith & Wesson) and smaller, less savory firms, like the Ring of Fire companies of Southern California. The implication of the latter classification is that the old-line companies are somehow more "responsible" than their upstart competitors.

As will be seen throughout this book, however, these traditional distinctions make little difference from the point of view of public health and safety, as expressed in terms of the ultimate consequence of gun violence. Guns made by foreign, domestic, old-line, and up-start manufacturers all turn up on the lists of guns most often used in crimes. Guns from every pedigree imaginable kill and wound Americans in homicides, armed assaults, suicides, and unintentional shootings. In this sense, every gun manufacturer sows the same seeds of violence.

Nevertheless, distinctions between foreign and domestic manufacturers are useful. Knowing the extent of the foreign contribution to the problem of guns in the United States, especially from some of our traditional "allies," for example, may help clarify the formulation of our commercial foreign policy. Accordingly, the following "snapshot" of the gun industry in the United States treats domestic and foreign manufacturers separately.

DOMESTIC MANUFACTURERS

Domestic gun manufacturing in the United States is like a pyramid in terms of companies, and an upside-down pyramid in terms of volume. That is, a few giant manufacturers at the top make most of the guns.[10] An assortment of many other small manufacturers make the rest, some as few as one gun a year.

Tables 1-5 show the structure of the domestic gun manufacturing industry in 1995, the latest year for which data is available and a more or less typical year in terms of the various companies and their relative standings. It is particularly interesting to note the vast range in the number of guns individual manufacturers produced, which in every class of firearms ranges from a single gun (likely a prototype or custom model) to hundreds of thousands.

Table 1

Domestic Gun Manufacturing

Type	No. of Makers[11]	No. Produced	Range of No. Made
Pistols	81	1,195,266	1–241,906
Revolvers	20	527,644	1–258,223
Rifles	97	1,331,780	1–407,785
Shotguns	28	1,173,645	1–426,442
Miscellaneous	65	8,607	1–3,110

Source: ATF: 1995 Annual Firearms Manufacturing and Export Report

The basic design and manufacture of firearms is by now well understood in theory and well known in process. But, as relatively simple mechanical tools, guns by their very nature invite mechanical puzzle-playing, experimentation with materials and incremental innovation. Each of the many individual parts that make a firearm work may be designed in a wide variety of ways, and the combinations in which those parts may be assembled, can alter a gun's look, performance, and "feel" in a shooter's hands. Also, since the manufacture of firearms is virtually unregulated beyond the requirement to obtain a federal license,[12] anyone who is inclined to believe that his or her new idea might fuel the rise of the next Sturm, Ruger & Company can at least make a prototype of the next "wonder gun" with little more than a modest stake and access to a decent machine shop. The gun press brims with stories about individuals who are busily devising "wildcat," or hybrid, calibers of ammunition, and guns to match them; making custom modifications to production firearms; introducing prototypical variants; and pursuing other such entrepreneurial efforts. The most enthusiastic of gun enthusiasts are never satisfied with what they can buy off the shelf.

Of course, pursuing a new idea is one thing. Success is quite another. Small gun manufacturers regularly disappear from one year to the next, but they are important to keep an eye on. Some of the most invidious and misused guns in the United States spring from such small time tinkerers. Nevertheless, by far the greater volume of civilian guns manufactured in the United States comes from a small constellation of well-known manufacturers, as the following tables demonstrate. Again, these tables are derived from 1995 production data and are fairly representative of the general standing of the companies shown.

Table 2

Top Ten Domestic Pistol Manufacturers

Company	Number Produced in 1995
Smith & Wesson	241,906
Sturm, Ruger & Co., Inc.	197,489
Beretta USA Corp.	158,858
Colt's Mfg. Co., Inc.	118,462
Lorcin Engineering Co., Inc.	83,463
Bryco Arms	56,727
Arms Technology	51,531
Phoenix Arms	48,381
Davis Industries	45,171
Wayne E. Daniel	35,711

Table 3

Top Ten Domestic Revolver Manufacturers

Company	No. of Revolvers Produced in 1995
Smith & Wesson	258,223
Sturm, Ruger & Co., Inc.	148,349
Colt's Mfg. Co., Inc.	40,085
North American Arms, Inc.	34,265
Heritage Mfg. Inc.	29,300
H&R 1871, Inc.	10,641
Wayne E. Daniel	3,488
Freedom Arms, Inc.	2,143
Mil, Inc.	893
Texas Longhorn Arms, Inc.	103

Table 4

Top Ten Domestic Rifle Manufacturers

Company	No. of Rifles Produced in 1995
Sturm, Ruger & Co., Inc.	407,785
The Marlin Firearms Co.	396,215
Remington Arms Co., Inc.	242,706
U.S. Repeating Arms Co.	158,026
Colt's Mfg. Co., Inc.	49,385
H&R 1871, Inc.	31,130
Weatherby, Inc.	12,587
Springfield, Inc.	9,068
Oregon Arms, Inc.	7,920
Survival Arms, Inc.	2,861

Table 5

Top Ten Domestic Shotgun Manufacturers

Company	No. of Shotguns Produced in 1995
Remington Arms Co., Inc.	426,442
O.F. Mossberg & Sons, Inc.	339,881
H&R 1871, Inc.	165,813
U.S. Repeating Arms Co.	153,006
Maverick Arms, Inc.	53,291
The Marlin Firearms Co.	19,575
Sturm, Ruger & Co., Inc.	7,133
Sporting Arms Mfg., Inc.	5,624
Wayne E. Daniel	2,239

As noted above, some draw a distinction in status between more established companies like Colt, Smith & Wesson, and Ruger and newer "Ring of Fire" companies like Lorcin Engineering, Bryco Arms, Phoenix Arms, and others.

Ruger itself was once an upstart. But after almost fifty years of success, it is now regarded as an old-line manufacturer and makes a stuffy point of subtly distancing itself from its competitors in the industry underclass by its marketing slogan: "Arms makers for responsible citizens." To some, this slogan implies that other manufacturers aim their products at *irresponsible* citizens, or perhaps to undocumented aliens and other foreigners who are not *citizens.*

In fact, however, Ruger and other main-line companies have in recent years also scrambled to market small, easily concealed, more powerful handguns, at prices more competitive with the Ring of Fire manufacturers. "Top manufacturers are moving down the ladder in size and price and the California companies are going up," points out Jim Waldorf, founder of Lorcin. "The line between us is blurring."[13]

These main-line guns differ from Saturday night specials in that they cost more, are made from higher quality material, and are better manufactured. But they present identical problems as ideal tools for violence, crime, and unintentional death and injury. Thus, the guns of main-line companies regularly appear as weapons of choice in such mass shootings as the Long Island Railroad massacre (Ruger), the Empire State Building shootings (Beretta), the Connecticut lottery homicides (Glock), the Jonesboro middle school ambush (Ruger, Remington, Smith & Wesson), and innumerable others.

Main-line gun companies also regularly show up on the list of guns most often traced by ATF because of involvement in crimes, as Table 6 demonstrates:

Table 6

Top Ten Crime Guns Traced by the ATF, 1989–1997

(Main-line companies are shown in **bold**)

1989	*1990*
Raven Arms P25 pistol	Raven Arms P25 pistol
Smith & Wesson 38 cal. revolver	**Smith & Wesson** 38 cal. revolver
Smith & Wesson 357 cal. revolver	**Smith & Wesson** 357 cal. revolver
Mossberg 12 gauge shotgun	**Mossberg** 12 gauge shotgun
Smith & Wesson 9 mm pistol	**Marlin** .22 cal. Rifle
Marlin 22 cal. rifle	**Smith & Wesson** 9 mm pistol
Colt 45 cal. pistol	Intratec TEC-9 pistol
Intratec TEC-9 pistol	**Remington Arms** 12 gauge shotgun

Remington Arms 12 gauge shotgun
Jennings Firearms J22 pistol

Jennings Firearms J-22 pistol
SWD M11/9 pistol

1991

Raven Arms P25 pistol
Davis Industries P380 pistol
Intratec TEC-9 pistol
Mossberg 12 gauge shotgun
Jennings Firearms J22 pistol
SWD M11/9 pistol
Davis Industries P32 pistol
Smith & Wesson 38 cal. revolver
Colt AR-15 rifle
Ruger 10/22 rifle

1992

Raven Arms P25 pistol
Davis Industries P380 pistol
Jennings Firearms J22 pistol
Mossberg 12 gauge shotgun
Intratec TEC-9 pistol
SWD M11/9 pistol
Ruger P85 9mm pistol
Stallard/Maverick JS9 pistol
Davis Industries P32 pistol
North China Industries SKS Rifle

1993

Raven Arms P25 pistol
Davis Industries P380
Lorcin Engineering L380 pistol
North China Industries SKS rifle
Mossberg 12 gauge shotgun
Jennings Firearms J22 pistol
Lorcin Engineering L25 pistol
SWD M11/9 pistol
Intratec TEC-9 pistol
Smith & Wesson 38 cal. revolver

1994

Lorcin Engineering L380 pistol
Davis Industries P380
Raven Arms MP25 pistol
Lorcin Engineering L25 pistol
Mossberg 12 gauge shotgun
Phoenix Arms Raven 25 cal. pistol
Jennings Firearms J22 pistol
Ruger P89 9 mm pistol
Glock Mod. 17 9mm pistol
Bryco Arms Model 38 pistol

1995

Lorcin Engineering L380 pistol
Davis Industries P380 pistol
Raven Arms MP25 pistol
North China Industries SKS rifle
Ruger P89 9mm pistol
Mossberg 12 gauge shotgun
Lorcin Engineering L25 pistol
Bryco Arms Model 59 9 mm pistol
Smith & Wesson 38 cal. revolver
Phoenix Arms Raven 25 cal. Pistol

1996

Lorcin Engineering L380 pistol
Davis Industries P380 pistol
Raven Arms MP25 pistol
F.N. 32 cal. Pistol
Smith & Wesson 38 cal. revolver
Mossberg 12 gauge shotgun
Ruger P89 9mm pistol
North China Industries SKS rifle
Lorcin Engineering L25 pistol
Bryco Arms Model 59 9 mm pistol

1997

Smith & Wesson .38 Special Revolver
Lorcin .380 pistol
Raven .25 pistol
Ruger 9 mm pistol
Smith & Wesson 9 mm pistol
Davis .380 pistol
Smith & Wesson .357 Magnum revolver
North China Industries SKS rifle
Colt .38 Special revolver
Mossberg 12 gauge shotgun

Source: ATF: National Firearms Tracing Center

Ring of Fire companies Raven and Lorcin held the number one spot against all comers for guns most often linked to crimes until 1997, when old-line company Smith & Wesson moved to the top. Although other Ring of Fire companies like Jennings, Davis, Bryco, and Phoenix appear regularly, old-line companies like Smith & Wesson, Mossberg, Ruger, Colt, and Marlin now also make the top ten list every year.

In sum, labeling gun manufacturers as more or less responsible based on the physical characteristics of their products — such as quality of metal, care in manufacture, or retail cost — obscures the point that the difference among manufacturers in terms of ultimate responsibility for firearms violence in the United States is one of degree, not of kind. The sheer economics of supply and demand probably propels cheap junk guns like the Raven P25 and the Lorcin L380 into the top ranks of guns that criminals use. But it is clear that a gun is a gun, and if a criminal can obtain and use a top of the line Ruger, Colt, Glock, Beretta, or Smith & Wesson, he or she certainly will.

It should be noted that these tracing figures represent only guns related to crime and reported by law enforcement authorities — primarily state or local police — to the ATF for tracing (identification of the gun's origin and commercial path, usually through the first point of commercial sale, after which the trail of unregulated and undocumented transfer in the secondary market grows abruptly cold). This leaves several gaps of unknown dimension in our overall picture of the pedigree of firearms used in violence.

As mentioned above, most crimes involving firearms are handled by state or local police, and many such police agencies do not report guns to the ATF for tracing unless a trace is seen as necessary to advance the investigation of a specific crime. This will often not be the case, as for example in a domestic shooting where the shooter is apprehended and the source and ownership of the gun is not in doubt. In addition, guns used in suicides and unintentional shootings are not included in the ATF trace data unless the gun is somehow otherwise related to a crime, and the origin is relevant and unknown. In fact, although the ATF encourages 100 percent reporting in selected cities in order to develop analytical databases with which to track illegal gunrunning operations, the agency would be overwhelmed if all crime guns were reported to it for tracing. This is largely because the gun lobby succeeded in having legislation passed forbidding the ATF to automate most records of gun sales through licensed dealers. This ban, which the gun lobby claims was needed to prevent mass gun seizures, seriously impedes the ATF in its criminal enforcement work.

FOREIGN MANUFACTURERS

For some reason, many Americans—even those in the gun control movement—think the United States is a net exporter of civilian firearms. Nothing could be further from the truth. Although there are certainly areas (e.g., Latin America) in which illicit trafficking in civilian firearms from the United States is a problem, many more civilian firearms pour into the United States than leak out of it.

The wide-open U.S. market is a powerful magnet for foreign gun manufacturers. Civilian gun imports grew dramatically between 1978 and 1994, the peak year so far.[14] Between 1978 and 1996, 20,462,605 guns were imported for the U.S. civilian market.

Handguns soared to dominate the import market over this period. In 1978, handguns accounted for only twenty-four percent of imported civilian firearms. But in 1994, handguns represented sixty-two percent of the same import market.

Table 7

Guns Imported into the U.S. Civilian Market[15]

	1978	1994	Percent Change
Handguns	180,275	1,395,320	674%
Rifles	204,401	698,907	242%
Shotguns	362,462	145,233	- 60%
Total	747,138	2,239,460	200%

Source: U.S. Census Bureau, Foreign Trade Division

Even less is known about foreign gun manufacturers than is known about domestic manufacturers. Which firms are the leading foreign manufacturers often can be deduced from annual summaries of gun imports (by country), and from bits and pieces in the press. But the details of those companies' operations and imports to the United States are hidden.

It is interesting to note that most, if not all, of the foreign gun manufacturers who export to the United States cannot sell their products to civilians at home as freely as they can here. These countries all have stricter gun control laws than the United States and much lower rates of firearms violence.[16]

For example, only 1.2 percent of Japan's 1993 gun production stayed in Japan, which has very strict gun control laws. At the same time, eighty percent of its top three gun manufacturers' production went to the United States.[17] A substantial portion of these guns are marketed in the United States under the Browning mark (other Browning long guns are made in Belgium and assembled in Portugal).[18]

For another example, the Brazilian company Taurus began shipping revolvers to the U.S. market in 1968 after the Brazilian government "imposed restrictive handgun control legislation that greatly cut into Taurus's [domestic] market."[19] According to the gun press, virtually all of the company's production of 9mm semi-automatic pistols is exported because Brazilian law forbids civilian ownership of such guns.[20]

Industry data also indicates that eighty-five percent of the value of Germany's firearms production was exported in 1990, and eighty percent in 1991.[21] It is not clear how much of that went to the United States, but Germany has been among the top five exporters of handguns to the United States for at least the last six years.

The handgun manufacturer Para-Ordnance of Canada offers another striking example. Handguns are rigidly controlled in Canada. Tourists are forbidden to bring any handguns into the country,[22] and even certain pellet guns (air-powered guns somewhat more powerful than the familiar "BB" gun) are considered prohibited handguns under Canadian law.[23] But Para-Ordnance—whose "only reason for being" is "high firepower," according to gun writer and pistol expert Jan Libourel—exports thousands of high caliber, concealable pistols to the United States every year.[24]

This image of foreign gun manufacturers shipping to the United States guns that they are forbidden to sell at home is a telling reversal of the unpleasant image of U.S. cigarette companies dumping tobacco on less regulated and less health conscious Third World markets.[25]

Another unpleasant international aspect of the U.S. gun culture is that, to some, the United States has become a kind of underdeveloped moral Third World, a place where the rest of the world can indulge its gun lust. Shooting ranges on both coasts now cater to foreign tourists, offering the opportunity to shoot guns strictly controlled everywhere in the world but here.[26] A brochure aimed at Japanese tourists, for example, offered tours to San Francisco and Los Angeles where the lucky traveler can "experience 200 types of firearms."[27] Alaska's North Pole Police Department reportedly accommodates visitors from the hamlet's "twin city," Itadori, Japan, with live fire instruction on pistols, rifles, and shotguns.[28] It is not reported whether the police department also tells its Japanese visitors that, in 1995, four out of five of North Pole's armed assaults, and four out of six of its total aggravated assaults, were committed with firearms.[29]

It may be helpful at this point to summarize for the unfamiliar reader the basic kinds of firearms sold in the U.S. civilian marketplace. (This summary will be supplemented with further description where appropriate in later chapters.)

"Firearms" refer to weapons that use a powder charge (sometimes called the "propellant") to fire a projectile. Nonpowder firearms such as BB and pellet guns use a burst of air or other force (e.g. a spring) to fire their projectiles. They are thus not considered firearms, although they are capable of inflicting severe injuries, and are beyond the scope of this book.

Traditionally, firearms are broken down into two main groups: long guns and handguns.

Long guns are weapons designed to be fired from the shoulder and include rifles and shotguns. The National Firearms Act of 1934 regulates the barrel lengths of long guns to discourage the carrying of concealable firearms such as sawed off shotguns. Under the law, rifles with barrel lengths of less than sixteen inches, and shotguns with barrel lengths of less than eighteen inches are subject to strict federal tax licensing and registration.

Handguns are firearms designed to be fired with a single hand and are usually defined as having an overall length of less than eighteen inches.

Modern ammunition consists of four parts assembled into what is usually called a "round" or a "cartridge": the projectile, the powder or propellant, a "primer" which ignites when struck by a firing pin and in turn sets off the main charge of powder, and a case or "shell" in which the powder, primer and projectile are assembled. Projectiles are either bullets (in the case of rifles and handguns) or pellets of varying standard sizes, called "shot" (in the case of shotguns). Ammunition size in the case of rifles and handguns is generally expressed in terms of the approximate diameter of the bullet, measured either in inches (as 38 caliber) or millimeters (as 9 mm). For shotguns, ammunition is expressed as a measure of the size of the diameter of the barrel and the size of the pellets in a given round (e.g., 12-gauge OO buckshot, also called "double aught buck"). The term "magnum" refers to a cartridge with an especially powerful propellant charge, usually achieved by lengthening the case in which a given diameter of bullet is seated.

There are numerous variations and combinations possible among all of these ammunition components, and gun enthusiasts obsess over them in mind-numbing detail.

Repeating firearms may be either handgun, rifle, or shotgun. They allow the shooter, by operating a mechanism on the gun, to load another round after a shot has been fired. Manually operating a bolt, lever, pump, or other mechanism extracts and ejects the empty case after the cartridge has been fired. It then reloads a fresh shell or cartridge from a storage device, called the "magazine," into the chamber and cocks the gun. Semiautomatic guns do this automatically when they fire. With each squeeze of the trigger the semiautomatic repeats the process of firing, ejecting, and reloading.

Semiautomatics fire only one cartridge per trigger pull. True "automatics"—also known as machine guns—fire more than one cartridge with one pull of the trigger. Although some automatics fire in "bursts" (e.g., three rounds) with each pull of the trigger, most machine guns will continue firing rounds as long as the trigger is depressed. Machine guns are strictly regulated under federal law but can be legally obtained by the determined civilian.

Handguns are either revolvers or pistols. Revolvers have a round cylinder that is actually the magazine and acts as a chamber when properly aligned with the barrel. In double-action revolvers, each time the trigger is pulled the weapon fires and the cylinder advances to the next chamber. Single-action revolvers require that the hammer be manually cocked before each shot. A revolver's cylinder traditionally held up to six cartridges, although, as we shall see, revolver capacity has been increasing to as many as ten rounds.

Instead of a revolving cylinder, a semiautomatic handgun (also known as a pistol) carries its extra cartridges in an ammunition magazine usually located in the handle of the handgun. Spring pressure forces the cartridges upward in the magazine. Each time the weapon is fired, a new cartridge is moved up and is loaded into the chamber. Pistols are often known as "automatics," a point of confusion since they actually require a separate trigger pull for each shot. Pistols that *are* fully automatic—that will fire more than one cartridge per trigger pull—are known as machine pistols and are regulated like machine guns.

A subcategory of handguns are Saturday night specials— inexpensive, short-barreled handguns made of inferior materials. Because of their low quality and inaccuracy, these weapons have no sporting purpose and are best suited for criminal use. Saturday night specials can be either pistols or revolvers.

Assault firearms are semiautomatic (firing one bullet per trigger pull), fully automatic (firing more than one bullet per trigger pull), or select fire (the weapon can be set to fire either semiautomatic or fully automatic) antipersonnel rifles, shotguns, and handguns that are designed primarily for military and law enforcement use. They are not particularly suitable or readily adaptable for sporting purposes. Characteristics that are often present in assault weapons include: the ability to accept a detachable ammunition magazine; folding stocks, flash suppressors, bipod mounts, and pistol grips on rifles or shotguns; threaded barrels (allowing for the easy attachment of silencers on assault pistols); and concealability relative to firearm type.

The retail sale of firearms in the United States is for all practical purposes unregulated.

Whole forests of trees disappear every year in the reams of paperwork associated with the movement of new firearms in commerce—applications, licenses, forms, and records. But throughout most of the United States little stands in law, and virtually nothing in practice, between the transfer of a firearm from a seller with a gun for sale to a purchaser with the means to buy it. The nature and quality of the firearm, the ethics of the dealer, and the good sense or even sobriety of the buyer are effectively irrelevant to the exchange of money for guns in most states.

Gun advocates often assert that the United States has more than twenty thousand gun control laws at the local, state, and federal level.[1] In their view, the United States is already overregulated and our gun violence problems would go away if only these twenty thousand laws were strictly enforced. But what they do not say is that—even assuming that there actually are twenty thousand such laws—the vast majority of them do not regulate the sale or possession of guns. Rather, most of them deal with collateral questions, such as zoning laws that regulate where gun stores and shooting ranges can be located, or that set limits on transporting and discharging firearms within city limits, and so forth.[2]

The fact is that any adult who is not a convicted felon, convicted spouse- or child-abuser, or an adjudicated "mental defective" can legally buy a gun almost anywhere in the United States. True, the person who wants a gun immediately and wants to buy it from a licensed retail dealer in the primary market will be inconvenienced by minor impediments: a waiting period imposed by the 1994 Brady Law,[3] the requirement to show a picture ID, and the few minutes it takes to check off questions on a standard federal form, to determine whether the would-be buyer is a convicted felon, an illegal alien, or a drug addict.[4] Some gun dealers claim that even these minor inconveniences hurt their business,[5] but—aside from the fact that the buyer can avoid all of this paper-pushing regulatory inconvenience by *legally* buying a used gun in the secondary market—the truth remains: Almost any adult who is legally of sound mind and has not committed a crime can buy a gun legally almost anywhere in the United States.

Who can legally sell that gun? Well, again, almost anyone with a place of business that conforms to local laws, a clean criminal record, and with a few hundred dollars to pay an application fee can get a federal license to go into business as a full fledged interstate-trafficking gun dealer.

Those with more modest ambition who are willing to keep a lower profile can simply skip the federal license and make a tidy income selling guns legally as a hobby, often at gun shows, described in more detail below.

After one prunes away the twenty thousand or so zoning, transport, and miscellaneous laws that somehow touch on the subject of guns, one is left with a few score of laws that truly control the sale of firearms. Almost all of these are at the federal or state level as opposed to the municipal level, where regulation generally sticks to zoning laws and business licensing.

Federal law preempts, or overrides, weaker state and local law. Since 1968, it has established minimum national requirements for legal gun transfers. It regulates the sale of guns in three basic ways:

1. Those who are engaged in the business of manufacturing, importing or selling firearms must have a federal firearms license.
2. Handguns, and with some exceptions long guns, may be bought or sold across state lines, or imported from abroad, only through such federal licensees. The first legal retail sale of any firearm in the commercial market is therefore always made through a licensed dealer.
3. Restrictions are placed on the sale of certain classes of firearms (e.g., machine guns and semiautomatic assault weapons).

The ATF says that it will approve federal firearm license applications if the applicant is twenty-one or older; is not legally prohibited from shipping, receiving, or possessing guns or ammunition; has not "willfully violated" the GCA; has not "willfully failed to disclose material information or willfully made false statements" on the application; has business premises; and certifies that the business complies with local laws and that the applicant has notified the local law enforcement agency of the application for a license.[6]

State regulation of firearms dealers varies wildly. Arizona has no statewide licensing provisions for gun dealers and forbids local jurisdictions from regulating the sale, possession, or use of firearms. New Jersey, on the other hand, strictly controls who may have a state gun dealer's license. In any event, a minority of states impose their own gun licensing requirements, and most of these suffer from two basic flaws that make them easy to evade: they either do not adequately define what constitutes dealing in firearms (and thus the necessity to obtain a dealer's license), or they are limited to certain types of guns, such as handguns.

Since 1994 federal authorities have more vigorously exchanged information with state and local authorities about licensed dealers, and, as is described below, this has undoubtedly helped weed out many marginal gun dealers. Nevertheless, becoming a licensed gun dealer still requires only that one conform to minimal legal procedures. Meanwhile, vast loopholes in the law condone a bustling legal trade in firearms that is wholly outside of the system of licensed dealers.

(It is important to note that this discussion does not treat the ways in which firearms are *illegally* bought and sold, a subject worthy of a book in itself. Briefly, beyond petty opportunistic theft of firearms, there is a large scale underground criminal trade in firearms in the United States that relies on diversion to organized gun traffickers from corrupt dealers; use of "straw purchasers" with clean records to buy guns for traffickers and for persons such as felons or juveniles who are barred from buying firearms; and there is organized theft from gun stores, common carriers, and manufacturers.)

In fairness, it must be said that getting a dealer's license and going into business is a wholly different matter from making a profit and staying in business. In fact, licensed dealers who actually operate from stores, known as "stocking dealers," and hobbyists are constantly at each others' throats in the gun press. Stocking dealers complain about the hobbyists' nonexistent overhead and their consequent ability to undercut stocking dealers' retail gun prices. The

stocking dealers favor stricter regulation of firearms licenses in order to level the playing field, which sometimes puts them in the
ironic position of being on the same side as gun control advocates.
Stocking dealers are also unhappy, for much the same reason, with
an intermediate class of licensed dealers who are something more
than hobbyists but do not operate from retail gun stores. These intermediate dealers sell guns out of their homes or other casual premises, sometimes as a sideline to another business, and are known
generically as "kitchen table" dealers. Hobbyists and kitchen table
dealers rebut the stocking dealers' call for more regulation by ap-
pealing to a putative Second Amendment right to sell guns, and by
criticizing the stocking dealers as poor business persons who want
government protection to compensate for their inability to compete.

Who are these people who sell guns to ordinary Americans?

IMPORTERS

In the case of foreign guns, the key group is the federally licensed
importers. As of December, 1996, 773 entities were licensed by the
federal government to import firearms, according to the ATF. Data
is not readily available to describe the structure of the import
market—e.g., how many of what types of firearms each importer
brings in, whether they sell them primarily to wholesalers or retail
dealers, and so forth. But given the number of foreign guns imported into the United States, the import market is obviously organized well enough to distribute and sell millions of firearms.

Some imported guns are sold by the importers under U.S. brand
names or under brand names inherited from former U.S. companies now owned or controlled by foreign interests. Others are simply sold as foreign guns. A few of the larger importers, such as Navy
Arms Company, Interarms, and Century International Arms, are
well known in gun circles.[7] But the vast majority of the more than
seven hundred licensed firearms importers are not known publicly.

Some importers maintain standing brand lines of new firearms;
others import batches of military surplus firearms as they become
available abroad, and some do both. Thumbnail sketches of three of

the better known companies may give some sense of this end of the business.

Century International Arms claims that it is "North America's largest importer/exporter of surplus firearms and accessories . . . dealing directly with sporting goods retailers and wholesalers worldwide through an established network of distribution centers in Montreal, Vermont and Florida." Century was started after the end of the Second World War when its founder, William Sucher, attempted to sell a typewriter through a classified ad and ended up being offered a rifle in exchange. That led him into the business of buying and selling used guns. Today, Century says that it "has agents constantly traveling the world looking to buy firearms that can be offered to the various firearms markets in the U.S."[8] Although Century carries some newly manufactured firearms, it is best known for its trade in surplus military guns, including (until recently) Chinese assault weapons.

Interarms, headquartered in Alexandria, Virginia, imports and markets relatively well known lines of new firearms, such as Rossi handguns and rifles from Brazil, Walther handguns from Germany, FEG pistols from Hungary, and Howa rifles from Japan.[9] Interarms was founded in 1953 by Samuel Cummings, until then a CIA weapons specialist. The company, originally known as the International Armament Corporation, thrived on the global trade in military small arms, and established several foreign subsidiaries. Cummings apparently did very well in the gun business. He moved to Europe in the mid-1960s, became a British subject, and died at his estate in Monaco in April, 1998.[10]

Navy Arms Company markets a mix of foreign firearms. The company was founded on the concept of importing foreign replicas of famous American period firearms, such as those used by the two sides in the Civil War. (The company's logo is the seal of the Confederate Navy.) These replicas are collected, used to outfit reenactment organizations, and fired in various target shooting activities. A substantial portion of the current Navy Arms catalog is devoted to these period replicas, many of them made in Italy.[11]

In addition to replica firearms, the company imports large quantities of surplus military arms, some of which are also featured in its catalog. These appear to be opportunistic deals made wherever large lots of guns can be secured abroad for import. For example, in 1993 Navy Arms announced it would import some eighty thousand Second World War military arms, mostly rifles of German manufacture. It also said it would import to the United States some sixty-six thousand German and Czech military rifles from the Turkish Army, Navy, and Air Force.[12]

WHOLESALERS ("DISTRIBUTORS")

There were 122 firearms distributors (not including gun manufacturers) in the United States in 1997, according to a comprehensive listing published in *Shooting Industry,* a journal catering to firearms dealers.[13]

These wholesale gun distributors practice widely different degrees of care in deciding with whom to deal. Some distributors require only that a potential customer send them a signed copy of the customer's federal firearms dealer license. Others require not only a copy of the license, but a photograph of the dealer's storefront, and copies of state sales tax permits and state and local business licenses. Still others fall somewhere between these two standards.[14]

The degree of care that a wholesaler takes could well be an important factor in criminal trafficking of firearms. A federal firearms license is a powerful piece of paper, since it gives the holder the privilege of ordering and having shipped to him, sight unseen, guns from anywhere in the country. Rogue dealers who abuse their licenses are one well known source of guns for the underground criminal trade. A single such dealer in Southern California diverted thousands of handguns to criminal street gangs in one year's time.[15] In light of that fact, one might reasonably argue that a wholesaler who regularly ships quantities of firearms to a dealer with no more knowledge than that the dealer has a license is acting negligently, even recklessly.

LICENSED DEALERS

The federal regulatory system enacted in the GCA is primarily intended to restrict the interstate sale of firearms to gun dealers, and thereby prevent individuals without licenses from running over state lines to buy guns.

Thus, federally licensed dealers may have firearms shipped to them across state lines (e.g., from wholesalers, manufacturers, or other licensed dealers). They may buy and sell both new and used guns to and from other licensed dealers regardless of the latter's location, and they may buy and sell to or from residents of the state in which they are located. A licensed dealer also may sell long guns (rifles and shotguns) to a nonresident, so long as the sale is legal under the laws both of the dealer's state and the nonresident's state. However, handguns may be sold across state lines only from one licensed dealer to another. In other words, a resident of Alabama may not legally buy a handgun in Georgia unless she has a federal firearms license.

As recently as 1993, there were nearly two-hundred-fifty thousand federally licensed dealers in the United States. Thanks largely to administrative reforms made by the Clinton administration and the passage of the 1993 Brady Law and the 1994 crime bill, that number has been dramatically reduced to less than one-hundred thousand—mainly through such simple regulatory efforts as requiring licensed dealers to specify a place of business on the application form and to notify local law enforcement authorities that they are in the gun business. Apparently, many kitchen table dealers (and some storefront dealers) who used to operate in violation of local zoning or licensing laws chose not to renew their federal licenses. In Boston, New York, and other cities, federal and local authorities paid joint calls on license holders to ensure that they were complying with all applicable laws.[16]

But the more than ninety thousand licensed dealers in the United States are still hopelessly unregulated. Although licensed dealers must keep specific records of sales of firearms, the law contains elaborate restrictions to prevent the ATF from using these records to set up any kind of national database of gun ownership. Moreover, they are simply evidence that each gun buyer filled out the federal form certifying that he or she was not in the class of prohibited persons, and documenting which guns came into and went out of the dealer's inventory and how. Since hardly anyone is ever prosecuted for lying on the purchase form, and there is little evidence that the form affects suicides or unintentional shootings, these records are useful mainly for tracing the sale of firearms that are later linked to a crime and reported to the ATF for tracing. They might be compared to the steward's records of the count of deck chairs on the *Titanic*.

In theory, the ATF monitors the conduct of licensed dealers through a program of on-site inspection. In 1997, however, the agency made only slightly more than thirteen thousand on-site inspection visits,[17] at which rate it would take more than seven years to visit each licensee only once. In fact, ATF's resources are spread thin and most of its attention in the area of firearms goes to enforcing federal criminal laws relating to guns, not dealer compliance. The result is that your local fast food outlet probably gets more regular government attention (from health, fire, and weights and measures personnel) than the average firearms dealer gets from the ATF.

Since firearms dealers operate with little regulatory oversight, their sales practices and ethics vary considerably, at least according to the gun press.

Andrew Molchan, president of the National Association of Federally Licensed Firearms Dealers, estimates that "between 50% to 80% of the stocking gun dealers cheat on their taxes."[18] This is a staggering admission, especially when compared to an IRS estimate that about eighteen percent of Americans do not fully comply with tax laws, and polls in which about twenty percent of Americans admit to cheating on taxes. That gun dealers apparently cheat on taxes at a rate of from two to four times the rate at which the general public does may not be too surprising, given the libertarian bent that pervades the gun industry. But it does make one wonder whether the people at the ATF and their counterparts at the IRS—both part of the Treasury Department—might find it profitable to compare notes.

Tax cheating has nothing directly to do with guns, but the quality of advice a gun dealer gives to a new customer does. A survey of gun dealers on the first-time buying habits of handgun purchasers indicates that suburban gun dealers tend to be more conscientious about advising first time buyers, while urban dealers concentrate on moving the product. *Shooting Industry* reported that, according to the survey, suburban dealers think it is more responsible to sell a first-time buyer a revolver, which many gun experts believe is easier and safer for a novice to learn to handle than a semiautomatic pistol. But "in larger metropolitan areas, dealers seemed more concerned with making a sale, regardless of the type of action of the firearm."[19]

The theme of making the sale taking priority over other considerations was stressed in *Shooting Sports Retailer,* a national magazine aimed at gun dealers. It advised gun dealers "to avoid discussions about the legalities or illegalities of shooting someone in self-defense or carrying a concealed weapon." This was not because the dealer might not have the right answers — "although you certainly wouldn't want someone coming back and suing you for something said in your store" — but "simply because this wastes time and is not central to the sale of a firearm."[20]

Gun dealers show no particular rush to report obvious violations of the law, either, when given the chance. Many looked the other way when tens of thousands of smuggled Chinese AK-47 assault rifles were laundered literally right through their hands and on to America's streets in the late 1980s.

According to *The Washington Post*, as many as eighty thousand AK-47s may have been smuggled into the United States between 1986 and 1989. The paper quoted one dealer as saying of the importers that "all they did was plug them [the assault rifles] into legitimate distribution centers because at that point nobody knows or cares" about the guns' origins.[21] This would indicate at best a sort of passive determination by gun dealers to "see no evil." But other gun dealers said that because the smuggled guns did not contain certain markings that are required by federal law to be stamped on all imported guns, the assault rifles' smuggled status should have been clear to any dealer who bothered simply to look at them. The *Post* summed up the gun dealers' "look the other way" attitude with the following quote:

> "You can count on one hand the number of dealers who called the ATF and told them that they were getting imported guns with no import license," said one dealer who has cooperated with the investigation.

"Most dealers didn't say anything because by the law they are not responsible . . . and everybody says, 'Well, it's not my job.'"[22]

Many dealers also feel that it is "not their job" to decline to sell guns to people who know little about them. *Shooting Industry* carried until recently a section titled "Dumb Questions," which offered anecdotes from gun dealers about customers whose questions indicated that they knew next to nothing about the lethal weapons they owned or were buying. Many of the anecdotes reported in this feature appeared to have resulted in sales of guns or ammunition to such obviously dangerous customers.[23]

A 1979 issue of the magazine analyzed the ethics of selling an unreliable gun in the following pragmatic way:

> As a dealer, you must sometimes make some decisions of conscience, rough as they might be. Should you stock a line which is not reliable? The question gets an immediate answer of "NO!" if you own a range, because as soon as the customer buys the gun and takes it downstairs or out back and tries it, he will know he has a lemon and will want to return it. . . . If you do not have a range, the answer may be a little more dubious.[24]

In short, the ethics of selling a defective firearm appeared to hinge on whether the dealer was likely to get caught by the customer.

Whatever their ethics, gun industry organizations and trade publications advise retail gun dealers to get involved in local civic and business organizations. The idea is to show, as it were, the human face of the gun business. The message is that gun dealers are just like any other small businessperson, trading in an everyday commodity that has as much right as any other good to compete in the vast U.S. marketplace.

"We cannot apologize for being in the shooting business," one speaker told seminar participants at the 1997 SHOT Show, the industry's annual trade show, while advising them to join their local chambers of commerce.[25] "Let people know that you want to be a good citizen—a good citizen of the community, a good citizen of the business community. . . . Be active. Don't apologize. Be active."

Dealers have become increasingly conscious of their growing liability under a variety of legal theories. Industry publications often suggest ways for gun retailers to insulate themselves from the consequences of sales that result in death or injury.

A 1994 article in *SHOT Business*, for example, described a number of incidents that had resulted in dealers being held liable to customers. Because of such incidents, according to the article, "It is becoming increasingly difficult for gun retailers to obtain insurance through the traditional market." The article cited cases ranging from a retailer "30 years in the business" who "shot the customer without realizing there was a round in the chamber" to another who was held liable for a death after he sold a firearm without any instructional literature.[26]

The article suggested that dealers get insurance, get assurances from manufacturers that they would defend the dealer in court, become familiar with applicable firearms laws, don't sell guns without manuals, and "size up your customers." On the latter point, it quoted Mike Sapporito, executive vice-president of a major wholesale gun outlet:

> Obviously, if a guy comes in and he's flushed and he's red and hyperventilating and he says "Give me a gun—any gun—just give me a gun and some bullets," I think that should raise some question in your mind about whether you should give this guy anything but a glass of cold water. . . . But this kind of thing sometimes escapes employees at some stores. . . .[27]

Virginia gun dealer Mike Dick, when asked how he felt upon learning that guns he had sold were later used to kill people, told *The Atlantic*:

> I did everything I possibly could have, short of compromising something I feel very strongly about. And that is, I'm not going to decide if you are a worthwhile person or not . . . I'm not gonna decide somebody's character based on my impressions of him—I'm just not gonna do it. . . . Empowering people to do that is dangerous.[28]

If licensed gun dealers like Mike Dick are less worried about "empowering" people to kill each other with a gun than "empowering" themselves to decide a potential buyer's character, what chance is there that an ordinary citizen making a casual sale to another person will worry about such niceties?

Yet gun sales between ordinary people who are both residents of the same state are almost wholly unregulated in the United States. Federal law bars sales of guns between individuals who are residents of *different* states. But federal law does not control private sales of guns within state boundaries, unless the guns are otherwise controlled under federal law (e.g., machine guns).

Thus, most gun transfers between private individuals are controlled only by state and local law. In most states, this means no control at all, since most states do not regulate private transactions. Even in states that do control gun sales between individuals, authorities will admit privately and sometimes even publicly that they don't have the resources to effectively police private sales by individuals who ignore the laws. About forty percent of all gun transfers in the United States occur through this casual, unregulated secondary market.[29]

In theory, a person could make so many "private" gun sales that he or she would be engaged in the business of selling guns under federal law, and would thus be required to secure a federal firearms dealers license. In fact, however, federal law so generously defines the right of individuals to sell guns out of their own "collections" that in practice many such unlicensed hobbyists—especially those who sell at so-called "gun shows"—are indistinguishable from licensed firearms dealers.[30]

Gun shows are held every weekend in communities all over the United States. Private citizens and licensed dealers alike sell firearms and related paraphernalia at these almost entirely unregulated events, which range from small flea markets with a handful of tables to enormous extravaganzas covering acres of ground with hundreds of exhibitors.

The boom in these gun shows can be traced directly to legislation supported by, passed under, and signed into law by NRA Life Member Ronald Reagan on May 19, 1986—the Firearms Owner's Protection Act, commonly known as McClure-Volkmer, after its Congressional sponsors. McClure-Volkmer loosened up the federal gun laws by repealing or cutting back a number of provisions of the original Gun Control Act of 1968. Most important, McClure-Volkmer:

1. allowed federal firearms license holders to sell at gun shows in their home states
2. allowed unlicensed private individuals to sell their personal guns as a hobby
3. restricted ATF inspection authority and watered down already weak gun dealer record-keeping requirements[31]

The dramatic consequence of this loosening in the laws was described in a May 1993 letter from the late Bill Bridgewater, executive director of the National Alliance of Stocking Gun Dealers, to the U.S. House Subcommittee on Crime and Criminal Justice:

> The BATF has established rules and regulations for these things they call "gun shows." The opportunity for black marketeers is that the BATF doesn't enforce those regulations and there isn't anyone else to do so. Consequently, there are literally hundreds of "gun shows" around the country where you may rent tables, display your wares, sell what you please to whomever you please and once again the sale that is made with no records, no questions and no papers, earns the highest sales price. . . . There are wide open "gun shows" the length and breadth of the United States, wherein anyone may do as he chooses, including buy firearms for children.[32]

A visit to the average gun show is an enlightening introduction to America's hard core gun culture. The typical exhibitor sets up a table and fans out an array of whatever gun-related objects he has to offer. These start with firearms of every type and vintage, from brand new guns to muskets and single shot derringers to machine guns. The displays usually also include ammunition, ammunition magazines, gun parts, hunting equipment, knives, various kinds of military surplus and memorabilia, books about guns, knives, explosives, and even bomb-making manuals.

For whatever reason, Nazi memorabilia is often prominently displayed at gun shows. I once engaged an exhibitor of such regalia in casual conversation at a small gun show on Maryland's Eastern Shore, and was soon treated to the unrolling of a huge Nazi naval battle flag. This is not to suggest that all, or even most exhibitors or participants at gun shows condone that most demented of political philosophies. It is nevertheless a singular phenomenon, since one hardly ever sees Nazi trinkets on public sale anywhere else. The grace note on these exhibits is often a display of racist and anti-Semitic material, such as the notorious *The Protocols of the Elders of Zion* and the ultra-right wing screed, *The Turner Diaries*.[33]

The ATF estimates that about two thousand of these shows are held every year, while the National Association of Arms Shows puts the number at one hundred a weekend, or more than five thousand a year.[34] But no one really knows.

What is known is that gun shows are a breeding ground for illegal gun sales. According to state, local, and federal law enforcement reports, criminals, criminal gangs, so-called "militias," and terrorists regularly secure guns illegally at gun shows that they could not otherwise acquire lawfully.[35] For example, convicted Oklahoma City bomber Timothy McVeigh and Branch Davidian leader David Koresh frequented gun shows and participated in them as exhibitors.

3—The Promoters

One cannot fully understand how the U.S. gun industry works without appreciating the role played by three powerful promoters of the industry and its products: the gun press, the entertainment media, and gun industry organizations.

Each of these institutions has helped create and maintain the unique U.S. gun culture, within which the firearm is less a utilitarian tool than an icon, so laden with implicit value that its hold over its devotees approaches the mystical. These auxiliary promoters treat guns not simply as mechanical devices to be used as means to such ends as self-defense, target competition, or hunting, but as tribal totems embodying a complex of values that includes manliness (defined in warrior terms), individual liberty (as against the state), self-reliance (as against everyone else), and the administration of peremptory justice by ad hoc personal means (shooting "bad" people).

It is no coincidence that these values embody virtues that some Americans and many gun enthusiasts believe were characteristic of a hardier cast of national forebears, namely the libertarian branch of the revolutionists who won independence from England, the pioneers who wrested the frontier from its previous owners, and generations of citizen soldiers who "fought and died" to preserve those political and territorial gains.

Gun press journalists, gun industry advertising copywriters, movie and television script writers, and gun industry apologists all appeal unabashedly in their public voices to these powerful images. If the rest of America has forgotten the minuteman and the lone cowboy making a stand with his lever action saddle rifle against a heathen horde circling the water hole, the gun industry has not—advertising art, company logos, and industry propaganda alike portray and explicitly identify with these figures. If most Americans settle their disputes peaceably, the "heroes" and antiheroes of film and television frequently do not—we are constantly shown images of these characters resorting to guns to settle the simplest of problems.

It is impossible to exaggerate the hyperbole of the appeal to idealized national mythology and *machismo* individuality that these institutions, particularly the gun press, broadcast to their audiences. Even a cursory glance through the articles and advertisements that regularly appear in the gun press is likely to provoke a sense of wonderment at these images from a culture vastly different than the world in which most of us—including most responsible gun owners—live. Those who live in the angry world of the gun press apparently believe, perhaps even hope, that someone worth shooting—whether jackbooted government agent or common thug—is at every moment of day and night poised to come crashing into their lives, and that the gun is all that stands between them and an apocalyptic dictatorship of weak-kneed, paternalistic liberalism.

As a result, a gun bought in the United States today is not simply a clever assembly of metal, plastic, and wood parts capable of propelling a certain projectile with a given amount of force, but a powerfully laden symbol that links the buyer to a perceived nobility of libertarian ideals. Indeed, in the world according to the gun press, buying, owning, and using firearms are indications of good citizenship and badges of virtue.

THE GUN PRESS: "BETWEEN THE BIBLE AND A CATALOG"

The gun press falls into two broad categories: trade publications aimed at the firearms industry itself, such as *Shooting Industry*, *Shooting Sports Retailer*, and *Firearms Business*; and publications aimed at gun owners and potential gun buyers, such as *Guns & Ammo* and *Shooting Times*. The latter include both commercial and foundation magazines (published by pro-gun organizations), some general in their coverage and others focused on specific types of guns.

The trade publications report on commercial aspects of the firearms trade, give business advice, post intraindustry gossip, and report on strategies to advance the industry's interests. They include

American Firearms Industry (circulation, 24,154)
Shooting Industry (23,549)

Shooting Sports Retailer (17,463)
Firearms Business (1,000)[1]

The major commercial gun publications focus on the putative technical virtues of specific guns and ammunition, and on the societal values of gun ownership. Those with circulations over 100,000 include:

Guns & Ammo (circulation, 575,000)
Shooting Times (189,634)
Guns (168,000)
Shotgun Sports (155,000)
Handguns (150,000)
Petersen's Rifle Shooting (150,000)
American Handgunner (133,648)
Combat Handguns (126,498)
Gun World (126,402)
Petersen's Shotguns (125,000)
Rifle & Shotgun SportShooting (107,282)

Several of the largest general-circulation magazines are the foundation publications of pro–gun organizations, sent to their members. These include:

American Rifleman (NRA), (circulation, 1,480,074)
American Hunter (NRA), (1,059,010)
North American Hunter (North American Hunting Club), (715,725)
American Guardian (NRA), (140,000)

Finally, a collateral genre of commercial hunting magazines enjoys high circulation. In addition to the foundation-supported press, these include:

Petersen's Hunting (circulation, 325,000)
Buckmaster's Whitetail Magazine (237,720)
Deer & Deer Hunting (225,000)

The commercial hunting press is for the most part less obsessively focused on firearms per se than the gun press, and more concerned with the use of guns in a specific activity (however controversial hunting may be). Accordingly, although the hunting press is clearly an important adjunct to the firearms industry, discussion of its content is left to other analysts. One may fairly point to constellations of publications aimed at enthusiasts and consumers of other consumer products and ask what distinguishes the gun press from them. The automobile industry and popular music, for example, are boosted by scores of publications. Several factors distinguish the gun press from these and other areas of enthusiast journalism.

First is the gross degree to which the gun press is directly involved in the structure of the firearms industry, and participates in its strategy and planning. Gun press executives often sit on the boards of firearms industry trade organizations. They regularly attend industry political and marketing strategy sessions as working participants (as opposed to neutral journalist observers). And they openly promote in their publications specific actions decided upon as industry objectives in these strategy sessions.

Second is the extraordinary ideological bond between the gun press and the industry. A sense of "us against them" wagon-circling pervades the gun press. This is expressed in constant and repetitive propagandistic reaffirmations of the supposed individual right to keep and bear arms, interminable exposés of the latest schemes of the "gun-grabbers" in Washington, D.C. to violate that right, and panegyrics hailing one or another gun manufacturer or grand patron of the industry. As central as the automobile is to U.S. culture today, nothing about the industry or the often obsequious press that reports on it comes close to the emotion or strength of this ideological bond between gun industry and gun press.

Third is the issue of inherent lethality. Although automobiles are clearly capable of causing death and mayhem, they are not designed for lethality. On the contrary, today's motor vehicles incorporate dozens of life-saving features and minimum safety standards from safety glass to seat restraints. Many of these features were either mandated or inspired by the kind of product health and safety regulation from which firearms are exempt.

Finally, virtually all publications of the gun press serve as unabashed cheerleaders for the industry and its products. Although some automobile magazines seem partial to almost any automobile, critical reviews of "lemons" are not unheard of. And popular-music critics routinely flay what they perceive to be poor performances or subpar products.

The gun press, on the other hand, stands in a class by itself for self-congratulatory, smug toadying up to the industry it reports on. As journalist Erik Larson wrote in his 1993 *Atlantic* article, "The Story of a Gun":

> Gun writers . . . help orchestrate the mood that so infuses the gun culture. . . . To the gun writers, no firearm is unworthy of praise, not even the Saturday-night specials made by the now defunct RG industries, one of which was used by John Hinckley to shoot President Ronald Reagan and permanently disable James Brady, his press secretary.[2]

Gun writer Dick Williams's folksy account in *Shooting Industry* of his 1993 visit to Ruger's manufacturing plant in Prescott, Arizona, illustrates the cheerleading tone so prevalent in the gun press. Williams recounts that when he was invited to visit the facility, "I accepted faster than a New York cabbie honks his horn when the light turns green!"[2a]

"Unabashedly" counting founder William Ruger, Sr., as one of the "damn few" living "handgun manufacturing legends," Williams lavishes on the praise, overlooking or sugarcoating problems that a more objective journalist would have criticized.

Williams writes that "Ruger . . . doesn't buy insurance. If you know your product's good, why pay someone who knows nothing about it to confirm your belief?" By contrast, The *New York Times* reported fully ten years before Williams's trip to Prescott that Ruger actually stopped buying insurance because its rates had gone through the roof on account of product liability suits:

> Sturm, Ruger is defending itself in 60 product liability cases, including one in Alaska where it is appealing a $500,000 award. "Our insurance premiums, when we stopped being insured, reached five percent of sales," Mr. Ruger said.[3]

Williams also glowingly describes Ruger's operating "philosophy" as follows:

Mr. Ruger seems to cling to three basic philosophies: Don't offer it to the public until you're sure it works properly; don't fix it/change it if it ain't broke; and don't borrow money to make something new and/or different.[3a]

In fact, Ruger offered to the public a handgun that didn't "work properly" because of a fundamental safety defect, the Ruger Old Model Single Action revolver. He continued to sell the unsafe handgun after numerous civil liability judgments against it, refused for many years even to add a simple one dollar safety feature that would have prevented deaths and injuries from the defective product, and to this day refuses to recall hundreds of thousands of the same gun still in consumer hands.* Moreover, by Ruger's own account his marketing philosophy is to "change it" as often as the market will bear in order to generate new sales (as described in Chapter Five).

Product "reviews" offer another regular example of the gun press sucking up to the firearms industry. The degree of sycophancy for the industry that these reviews reflect may be unrivaled in the commercial and trade publishing world. For example, *Guns & Ammo* magazine, the five-hundred-pound canary of the gun press, runs a monthly feature called "Proof House," which purports to test objectively firearms and related products. Out of a random sample of 175 "Proof House" reviews of guns (not other products) in various *Guns & Ammo* issues, 164 (or ninety-four percent) were clearly favorable to the firearm reviewed and eleven were favorable but qualified because of concern about one or more features of the gun. But absolutely none—zero out of 175—were unfavorable.[4]

The dearth of criticism is not surprising. Several gun writers have flatly told their readers that they won't write a bad word about guns. For example Bob Milek, a writer for *Guns & Ammo*, wrote the following in reply to readers who wanted a "critical piece about a particular product that, due to design and manufacturing flaws, failed to make muster with the shooting public":

---

*"Ruger Gun Often Fires If Dropped, but Firm Sees No Need for Recall," *The Wall Street Journal* (June 24, 1993), p. A1; Violence Policy Center, "Lawyers, Guns, and Money," 1996.

> Sorry folks, you won't see such a piece from me. I'm one who finds that it's fun to write a positive, up-beat piece about a product and pure drudgery to write a negative piece. If a product fails to make the grade, I prefer to return it to the manufacturer with a note as to what I find wrong. If he sees fit to correct these things and return the product to me, I'll be happy to test it again. And I'll certainly write about it if it proves to be good. If not, you'll see no story from me. No one or nothing is ever served by a negative piece of writing.[5]

Milek's colleague, handgun expert Jan Libourel, informed his readers that "I seldom encounter a really 'bad' handgun. Even most of the very cheap zinc-alloy guns fulfill their intended missions surprisingly well."[6] Libourel is now editor of *Handguns* magazine.

Garry James, another *Guns & Ammo* writer, concluded a favorable review of a Colt assault rifle with this comment on journalistic standards and practice:

> We were told in journalism school that, for veracity's sake, a good reviewer should include brickbats as well as laurels. Well, I'm just going to have to disappoint my old professor.[7]

James was recently named editor of the magazine.[8]

One publication stands out, however, as a real "straight shooter" among the gun press—*Gun Tests*. Published by Belvoir Publications, the same house that publishes *Firearms Business*, *Gun Tests* lives up to its billing as "the consumer resource for the serious shooter." The small circulation monthly accepts no advertising, presents its tests of firearms in much the way *Consumer Reports* reviews other consumer products, and pulls no punches in reporting the results of its evaluations.

Handguns and *Guns & Ammo* are among the products of the Petersen Publishing Company, the largest and most successful of the nonfoundation commercial gun press. Petersen provides an excellent example of how closely the gun press and the industry are intertwined. Through a partnership with the National Shooting Sports Foundation (NSSF), a major gun industry trade association, Petersen took over publication of *SHOT Business*, a periodical NSSF started in 1993. *SHOT Business* described itself at the time the partnership was announced in 1997 as "dedicated to helping the sporting arms and ammunition retailer succeed and profit in a highly competitive market." A Petersen spokesman said combining the "expertise" of the NSSF and the "professionalism" of the Petersen Company would "create a partnership that will benefit manufacturer, retailer, and consumer alike, pulling the industry together for the common good."[9] The magazine, now beefed up and more slickly produced, serves not only as a Petersen trade publication but also as "the official publication and newsletter" of the NSSF.[10]

Pulling the industry together for the "common good" is also the goal of Wally Arida, publisher of *GunGames,* a magazine introduced at the 1995 NRA convention (circulation as of early 1998: 80,000). According to *Firearms Business,* Arida "sees his magazine as a route for the industry to take a new direction in promotion and marketing." He is quoted as saying, "I'm trying to publish a magazine and build a whole industry around it."[11] Arida dismissed other gun magazines as aimed at the "Rambo" market, and unduly focused on "Which gun is better for self defense? What bullet design causes the biggest wound channel?"[12]

Arida is right that much gun press writing focuses on the morbid subject of which guns and ammunition cause the greatest damage to human flesh, a concept often discussed in pornographically detailed descriptions of "wound channels," the size and shape of the holes bored through human beings. But Arida's opinion of such reviews misses the mark of their importance to the industry. Gun manufacturers rely on reviews in gun magazines, in addition to advertising, to draw attention to new products, as Glock official Paul Jannuzzo told *The Palm Beach Post* in 1996. (Jannuzzo was helping to explain the decision of local police officials to buy new Glock .40 caliber pistols.)[13]

The gun press abounds with other examples that aptly illustrate how manufacturers use enthusiastic gun "reviews" to boost gun sales. For example, in his column aimed at retail gun dealers, *Shooting Industry* writer Massad Ayoob wrote that "plenty of play in the gun magazines" was "sure to get some of your customers interested" in the Beretta M9 pistol on its 10th anniversary. "The bottom line," he wrote, "is the heavy publicity . . . will sell a lot of Beretta . . . pistols."[14]

Among the articles to which Ayoob was referring was *Guns &*
Ammo's contribution to the anniversary celebration: "M9 Beretta,
Ten Years of Combat: America's Latest Warhorse Is Proving To Be
Another Tough Battle Gun!" by Sheriff Jim Wilson.[15] The long-
winded praise heaped into that article's bulging headline is characteristic, and may even fall on the modest side, of the unabashed
boosterism typical of gun press reviews.

A 1996 Kahr Arms ad aimed at retail gun dealers explicitly cited
favorable gun reviews as a reason to stock its guns. The Kahr ad
explained that among a "truckload of reasons" to stock the company's subcompact K9 9-mm pistol were that "Kahr advertising has
more than doubled . . . in the major handgunning and shooting
magazines," and that "the major gun magazines have pre-sold the
K9. . . . Every major firearms magazine has told your customers
how much they love the Kahr K9."[16] Among articles the Kahr ad
implicitly referred to was a *Guns & Ammo* article boasting that the
"diminutive, all-steel 9mm Parabellum eight-shooter works as good
as it looks and may just prove to be the ultimate hideout package."[17]
Another aspect of the close relationship between gun manufacturers
and the gun press is the increasingly blurred distinction between
advertising and content. The February, 1993 issue of *Shooting In-*
dustry, for example, featured a front page cover advertisement for
Jennings Firearms, and an inside "news" story that sympathetically
reported Jennings's efforts to rehabilitate its "negative image" as a
maker of "gang guns" and "crime guns."[18]

But the relationship between the gun press and gun manufacturers goes even deeper. Gun writers actually advise gun manufacturers on the design and marketing of specific guns. This practice
raises an obvious journalistic question concerning the writers' ob-
jectivity and impartiality. Openly disclosing the link could help reduce the ethical dilemma, but another issue remains—the writer
and publisher's potential liability if a manufacturer were successfully sued on grounds related to the writer's advice. For example,
Guns & Ammo's Libourel reported in January 1997 that "G&A has
played some role in the development of" a Canadian handgun designed for export to the United States, the Para-Ordnance P10. Libourel described in detail how the magazine's staff advised the gun

manufacturer to make changes, based on models given them for tests.[19] "I think that when these little pistols hit the shelves a few weeks after I write this, you will find that they are extremely reliable with quality ammo, and I am pleased to have had a hand in this," wrote Libourel.[20] More than ten years earlier, Libourel reported giving advice to Brazilian manufacturer Taurus about revolvers "I thought would appeal to American shooters."[21] Some more aggressive tort lawyers might think that by going beyond mere reporting to giving specific advice on gun design and sales, Libourel and *Guns & Ammo* had opened the door on themselves for damages should Para-Ordnance or Taurus ever be held liable regarding the guns involved.

Gun manufacturers like Ruger, Glock, Brazil's Rossi, and Para-Ordnance often invite members of the gun press to tour their plants and to try out new guns. Afterward, the writers typically produce enthusiastic accounts of the merits of manufacturers and guns alike.[22] *Guns & Ammo* writer Jim Grover described the conduct of the gun press at one such junket, when Glock introduced its new "pocket rocket" miniguns: "Soon after, the pistols were passed out, and like a greedy bunch of kids pawing at the candy jar, we all dug in."[23]

The popular gun magazines have virtually perfected a system of hyperpromotion of the gun industry's latest models. They run feature articles promoting specific firearms, both new and old, in virtually every issue. Writing about the same guns or type of gun month in and month out obviously presents its difficulties. How many times, for example, can one write glowingly and freshly of the virtues of .45 caliber semiautomatic pistols small enough to fit in the palm of one's hand, and thus easy to conceal for "serious social purposes" (a popular gun writer's euphemism for civilian combat)?

After one reads enough gun magazines, it becomes clear that the gun press, like the supermarket tabloid press, has developed a system for dealing with this problem. It is the "variant" article. One common variant is the "first look" article about "hot new" guns. Affecting to have scooped an imaginary world of investigative gun journalism, "first look" writers describe the merits of new firearms sent to them for testing by gun manufacturers under breathless headlines.[24] Another common promotional variant is the comparative "test" of similar guns or ammunition.[25] Finally, "buyer's guides" that present several options for a particular use are yet another staple for showcasing specific guns.[26]

In short, the gun press and the industry work closely and cooperatively. At minimum, the industry provides advertising revenue and the gun press provides uncritical praise in the form of favorable product reviews.[27] These reviews clearly have an effect on consumers, as evidenced by the comments of industry officials and advertising quoted above, and exemplified by this letter to the editors of *Guns & Ammo*:

> You guys have cost me a bundle of money. Every time I open a new issue, there's another great gun I've got to have. . . . Honestly, my wife tells me I treat the magazine like a cross between the Bible and a shopping catalog.[28]

Moreover, the gun press serves as a kind of militant watchdog, its scribes pillorying in the most abusive terms responsible gun control advocates or those who dare criticize the gun industry on any level, for any reason.

THE SILENT PARTNERS

The entertainment media, and especially the movie industry, have also significantly influenced America's fascination with guns. "TV and motion picture guns create powerful, unforgettable images that have had a measurable impact on the shooting world," according to *Guns & Ammo*.[29] One of these effects is helping promote the sale of specific firearms, *Fortune* magazine found:

> Like any market, the gun market has fads and trends, many driven by movies. After Dirty Harry's .44 Magnum first cleared its throat, everybody wanted one. Before Rambo, who'd ever heard of an assault rifle?[30]

Erik Larson noted the same influence in his in-depth study of the life of an assault weapon used in a murder:

> America's entertainment media provide the last ingredient in the perverse and lethal roux that keeps the body count climbing even as the

domestic arms industry shrinks. Just as McQ promoted the Ingram, Dirty Harry promoted the Smith & Wesson Model 29 and *Miami Vice* such assault weapons as the Uzi, Bren 10, and members of the Ingram family. Park Dietz, a California forensic psychiatrist, studied the effect of *Miami Vice* on gun prices and demand, and found that the appearance of the Bren 10 in the hands of Sonny Crockett (Don Johnson) in early episodes of the show immediately boosted demand for the weapon.[31]

The *Miami Vice* television series apparently even caused the move of an assault-weapon shotgun from TV fiction to street fact, a rare event according to *American Rifleman's* account:

> The Mossberg Model 500 Bullpup appeared at trade shows in prototype form several years ago and made a more widely noticed appearance on the TV series *Miami Vice*. It has now become one of the relatively few items of exotic weaponry from that program that has become available to the general public.[32]

It is worth noting that Mossberg 12-gauge shotguns (not necessarily the Bullpup variant from *Miami Vice*) have appeared among the top ten crime guns traced by ATF every year since 1989, the earliest year for which data is available.

The entertainment media's role in promoting firearms as tools of violence has even been questioned by industry patriarch William B. Ruger, Sr., as a 1994 *Los Angeles Times* story on fallout from the Long Island Railroad massacre with a Ruger pistol revealed:

> Ruger blames Hollywood violence for twisting America's conception of firearms. "Movies and TV these days have sold the idea of the shootout as though that were the purpose of firearms, " he said.[33]

If this is true, or even if Ruger simply thinks it's true, it raises this problem: The nation's leading firearms manufacturer believes (by his own admission) that Americans have been "sold" on the idea that the very purpose of firearms is to be used in a "shootout." Yet he continues to manufacture and sell firearms designed precisely for this use.

Press profiles of major gun companies often include commentary on how gun sales have been helped by media exposure. For example, a 1995 *Baltimore Sun* profile of Beretta, whose U.S. plant is located in Maryland, said:

Sales have also been helped over the years by publicity, much of it on the silver screen. James Bond carried a Beretta before most people in this country ever heard of the weapon, and Bruce Willis brandished one in the "Die Hard" movies, as did Mel Gibson in the "Lethal Weapon" series.[34]

According to the same article, employment at Beretta's Maryland handgun plant grew from 120 workers to 500 between 1985 and 1995, with sales (at $120 million in 1994) growing at annual rates of between ten percent and twenty percent. It is impossible to sort out how much of Beretta's growth in the United States is attributable to media exposure and how much to the access it gained to the U.S. civilian market after its successful forays into the defense and police markets (a subject discussed later in this book). But the experience of other firearms manufacturers indicates that media exposure helps.

Likewise, according to *American Rifleman*, Smith & Wesson's Model 29 .44 Magnum revolver "enjoyed a massive burst of popularity in the 1970s when it was featured in *Dirty Harry*," and "commanded premium prices."[35] (When Eastwood switched from the big revolver to a .44-magnum semiautomatic pistol in a later movie, *Sudden Impact*, fans tried to revive the manufacture of the by-then out of production pistol.[36]) After Smith & Wesson fell on hard times in the 1980s and into the 1990s, handgun expert Phil Johnston recalled the potential power of movie exposure to revive the company's fortunes:

> If Smith [& Wesson] could tie into one of these Bruce Willis-type movies and have the good guy win shooting one of these Smith & Wesson revolvers, that would do a lot to bring them front and center.[37]

The use of firearms as "co-stars" in movies and television shows raises two levels of questions, similar to those raised by the use of cigarettes as props.

First, of course, is the example set when popular idols use guns to solve disputes or even just to get their way in an otherwise uncooperative world. It seems fatuous to suppose that such depictions, no matter how commonplace they are today, have no effect on the attitudes or behavior of those who, for whatever reason, see movie

and television stars as their role models. In fact, it is well known that
the promoters of consumer products from cigarettes and alcoholic
beverages to sneakers and automobiles believe there is an effect.
They angle fiercely (and spend a great deal of money) to "place"
their product for even seconds of exposure in movies or television
shows.

Which raises the second question: How do specific brands of
guns get placed in movies? The deals through which guns get tied
into movies are not publicly discussed. But the gun industry's overall efforts to win favor in Hollywood and some hints about how tie-
ins happen can be gleaned from occasional articles in the gun press.

For example, *American Firearms Industry* editor Andrew Molchan reported in 1992 on his self-described "pro-firearms lobbying
with the major movie studios":[38]

> I'm out West talking to many of the executives from [sic] Hollywood. We
> ARE making progress. . . . Little by little we are persuading people to
> our side.
>
> It took a little while to learn who really runs Hollywood. **A sure hall-
> mark of a public relations amateur is anyone who thinks "stars" run
> Hollywood.** 95% of the people who really run Hollywood are unknown
> to the public. (emphasis in original)[39]

Molchan's article suggests that "behind the scenes" lobbying
with the "people who really run Hollywood" is a major reason behind the widespread appearance of guns in the movies.

A glimpse of how a specific gun is promoted was provided in
another magazine's profile of John Risdall, president of Magnum
Research, purveyor of the "Desert Eagle" line of magnum pistols.
The article described Risdall's activities at the 1994 SHOT Show in
Dallas, Texas, including a visit with people who supply the guns
used in movies:

> While the foreign dealers and manufacturers are soaking up the West,
> Risdall's inside with Hollywood prop suppliers. There's a woman from
> Burbank, Calif., who reps for a manufacturer of rubber guns that are used
> as props and a gun supplier who gives directors almost any model they
> need.
>
> If *Dirty Harry* started the Magnum machine running, then Arnold

Schwarzenegger and his pals put the rocket fuel in it. The Desert Eagle has found its way from one violent scene to another in such movies as *Last Action Hero, Cliffhanger, Red Heat, Menace II Society, RoboCop* and *Commando.*[40]

The description of Risdall's chats suggests a more direct connection with a specific line of guns than Molchan's behind-the-scenes lobbying. And it appears to have paid off. As of March, 1998, the Magnum Research Web site on the Internet listed sixty-two films and television shows, including thirty-six "feature films," under the topic "Film Credits for the Desert Eagle Pistol and Other Magnum Research Firearms." A few among the feature films listed were *Eraser, Assassins, Get Shorty, Natural Born Killers, The Mask, Pulp Fiction, I'm Gonna Git You Sucka,* and *Beverly Hills Cop II.* Television credits listed included *Melrose Place, The Stand, Alien Nation, Beverly Hills 90210,* and *Saturday Night Live.*

Movie stars who appeared in these movies and who may have unwittingly contributed their names to the gun lobby read like an all-star cast. They include, among others, Pamela Anderson Lee, Sean Connery, Alec Baldwin, Sylvester Stallone, Antonio Banderas, Steven Seagal, Wesley Snipes, Patricia Arquette, Eddie Murphy, Teri Garr, Jennifer Jason Leigh, Keenen Ivory Wayans, and Patrick Swayze.

If getting products placed on the silver screen is good for business, Hollywood has been at least as good to the firearms industry as it has been to the manufacturers of cigarettes, soap, sneakers, automobiles, and other consumer products.

INDUSTRY ORGANIZATIONS

The gun industry is accompanied by a quiet phalanx of industry-financed trade and lobbying organizations, and a much noisier entourage of "gun rights" organizations. Among the latter, the giant National Rifle Association (NRA) is the best known and most active nationwide, although it has been riven for decades by a succession of costly internal fights over strategy and personality. A favorite foil of gun control advocates, the NRA has stumbled in recent years and at times appears to be a wounded dinosaur hell-bent for bankruptcy. Yet the NRA's more thoughtful opponents concede that it

has effective nationwide and state-by-state grassroots organizations, which it can usually mobilize more effectively than any existing gun control organization can. As a result, the NRA's mouth
often roars at a volume far out of proportion to its body, if only because it is the only voice legislators hear.

The lesser known, smaller, and more militant Gun Owners of
America (GOA), is a relentless critic of the NRA. Headed by Larry
Pratt, often credited as one of the founders of the militia movement,
GOA in recent years has proven itself adroit at lobbying Congress in
Washington. Pratt's GOA forges coalitions with liberal civil libertarian groups, like the American Civil Liberties Union, to stop so-
called "omnibus" packages of legislation that contain many
different provisions, or as one wag observed, "something to offend
everyone." Thus, for example, although GOA and ACLU opposed
different parts of a recent antiterrorism bill, by joining forces they
were able to lobby both conservative and liberal members of Congress.

A cluster of small advocacy groups, like the Citizens Committee
for the Right to Keep and Bear Arms, Jews for the Preservation of
Firearms Ownership, and The Firearms Coalition, bring up the ca-
cophonous rear.

Since the NRA and the other advocacy groups claim to represent
the interest of gun owners, rather than the gun industry, these gun
rights groups are beyond the scope of this book. However, further
study of the relationship between such groups and the industry is
warranted. The Violence Policy Center has documented financial
links between the NRA and the industry,[41] and the NRA and others
are active participants in industry planning sessions. The following
conclusion from a 1993 *Boston Globe* series on the NRA summarizes
well what is known about the NRA and the firearms industry:

> The bond between the gun manufacturers and the NRA involves direct
> financial contributions, almost-always-favorable reviews of newly devel-
> oped products in NRA publications like *American Rifleman*, and includ-
> ing NRA literature in the packaging of new guns.[42]

Although the NRA's claim may be a bit like trying to separate the
dance from the dancer, the gun industry suffers no lack of organiza-

tions that exist solely to support its interests. The industry supports several organizations that, however less well known to the general public they may be, aggressively represent its interests in various forums. These include the National Shooting Sports Foundation (NSSF), the American Shooting Sports Council (ASSC), and the Sporting Arms and Ammunition Manufacturers Institute (SAAMI). There are also a number of other more specialized trade organizations, such as the National Alliance of Stocking Gun Dealers.

These organizations are so thoroughly intertwined with gun manufacturers, the gun press, and other components of the firearms industry that there is little light between them on most issues. They share common strategies, often share common officers, and frequently meet to plan coordinated action.[43]

The NSSF holds itself out as "the shooting industry's trade association" and says its mission is to "promote a better understanding of and more active participation in the shooting sports."[44] It is funded by dues from more than 1,200 members, according to its literature. The foundation sponsors the annual SHOT Show, an industrywide extravaganza at which products are revealed or promoted, and a variety of other promotional programs designed to "educate and support new shooters and encourage those who already enjoy the sport to participate more often."

According to its tax returns, the NSSF's board of governors is made up mostly of senior executives of major firearms and ammunition manufacturers, sprinkled with executives from gun magazine publishers and hunting organizations.

SAAMI, located at the same address as NSSF, claimed for nearly seventy years to be devoted only to technical and safety matters regarding the industry. But in 1994, SAAMI came out into politics. Robert Delfay, its executive director (and also president of NSSF), announced that SAAMI would "take on an expanded role as spokesman for its members and the industry in general." It hired a Washington lobbyist and planned to coordinate activities with other organizations, including the ASSC (SAAMI already being a close cousin of the NSSF, there was presumably no need to reach out to it).[45] Tax returns show that SAAMI's board, like NSSF's, is dominated by executives of the gun manufacturing business.

ASSC is the industry's self-proclaimed voice, representing the industry "before every level and branch of government," according to its promotional literature. The group sponsors an annual "Congressional fly-in" to Washington, bringing industry pashas to "fly the flag" in Washington, and hires public relations firms to push the industry's interests. It publishes congressional candidate ratings, and takes members of the news media and Congressional staff to shooting ranges "to experience first hand exactly what we mean when we proudly speak of 'the American firearms tradition.'"

ASSC's members include the publishers of major gun magazines and enterprises from all levels of the gun industry, including foreign and domestic manufacturers, importers, wholesalers, and retailers. It gets grants from gun manufacturers and trade groups; its current board is made up of gun industry executives and has in the past included gun magazine executives. In 1991, ASSC announced a joint program with the National Rifle Association under which retailers who signed up new NRA members were rewarded with a $10 commission,[46] and it operates a Washington office, staffed by a Director of Governmental Affairs.[47]

Many of the major gun rights and industry organizations network with each other and most have formal or informal working contacts with state, local, and federal government legislatures and executive agencies. The extent of this networking should not be underestimated. As will be seen, federal and state wildlife and natural resource agencies can be and often are powerful supporters of gun industry interests, able to provide direct taxpayer subsidies to assist them.

These organizations are not a monolithic front. There is some hostility and occasionally outright war among some of the groups or their leadership—usually disagreements about strategy, sometimes the clash of egos and ambitions. But by and large, the gun industry and its constellation of supporting organizations are cooperating more to develop a common strategic plan, in the sense of having agreed-upon strategic goals (such as increasing the number of shooting ranges in the country, and targeting women, children, and minorities as consumers), hashed out in large public symposia and in private meetings in board rooms and government offices, and implemented by getting the word out through the gun press and taking active stands through the organizations and their networks of contacts.

4—The Market

The United States is the world's greatest market for civilian firearms. Between 1899 and 1993, nearly 223 million firearms were brought onto the U.S. civilian firearms market, according to the ATF.[1] A comprehensive survey of American firearms ownership in 1994 found that about 192 million guns were actually in civilian hands. The difference between the two figures seems reasonable, given natural attrition and the vagaries of estimation.

As vast as the U.S. gun market is, it has grown dramatically over the last twenty-five years. Almost half of the guns made available to civilians between 1899 and 1993 (forty-six percent) were produced between 1974 and 1993. The national firearms ownership survey estimated that eighty percent of all guns in private hands in 1994 had been acquired since 1974.

Foreign gun companies have increasingly exploited the U.S. gun market since the 1970s, either by exporting guns to the United States, or by setting up U.S. subsidiaries. Foreign imports accounted for only about 4.6 percent of all guns brought on to the U.S. civilian market between 1899 and 1945. But during the 1990s, between a third and a half of guns sold to that market every year were imported from abroad.

Guns imported to the United States are held to a slightly higher standard than the products of domestic gun manufacturers, since federal law allows only guns that meet a "sporting purposes" test to be imported.[2] As interpreted by the ATF in its administrative "factoring criteria," however, the practical effect of the law has been only to block the import of some small, cheaply made Saturday night specials and some versions of assault weapons. Even in those cases, several foreign companies have simply shifted production to U.S. subsidiaries to get around the import restrictions, and others have modified their firearms just enough to squeeze past the import restrictions. In any case, a vast array of gun types are imported into the United States in huge numbers.

The U.S. market attracts foreign gun manufacturers not only because of our lax national gun laws, but because of the consistent demand for guns in the United States. "You can make good sales in an African or Asian country one year, then the next year, nothing," a Beretta executive said in 1978 explaining why the company wanted to pursue the "safe" U.S. market.[3] America, according to industry analyst Frank James, is "the last great market."[3a] Industry observers expect the foreign import market to continue thriving, unless U.S. policy changes significantly. There is little evidence that it will.

Foreign gun imports have a double effect on the United States. Obviously, foreign imports add significantly to the number of guns on America's streets. In addition, foreign imports stimulate domestic demand, according to firearms industry experts:

> "Usually the imports, for the most part, have a positive effect on domestic production," said Bob Lesmeistser [of *American Firearms Industry*]. "They just seem to spur peoples' interest in guns all the more."[4]

Foreign imports have grown steadily over the last two decades, from 747,138 in 1978 to a peak of 2,239,460 in 1994. More than twenty million guns were imported for the civilian market between 1978 and 1996. The swift growth of foreign imports and their sale in some cases under U.S. brand names (sold away in corporate acquisitions) rankled a few domestic observers, notwithstanding the overall silver lining that others saw. Thus, the NRA's *American Rifleman* magazine commented in 1986, midway through the period of foreign growth:

> Thirty years ago . . . all guns with familiar American brands were usually assumed to be of American make. Today the situation is far different, and even, perhaps especially, if a gun were to be marked Washington Arms Co., Mt. Vernon, Va., one would probably look for the "Made in Japan" (or Italy, Spain, Germany, Brazil, etc.) rollmark on barrel or receiver.[5]

Since then, imports and foreign-owned domestic companies have claimed a robust share of the U.S. gun market. Ammunition is also imported from abroad. Korea's PMC prompted an "open borders" (for ammunition) observation from *Guns & Ammo*'s Jan Libourel:

Although their ammunition is made in South Korea, I tend to regard PMC as "naturalized Americans," so well established and widely distributed have their products become.[6]

Foreign companies do not simply ship standard product lines to the United States. The American market's pull is now so great that foreign manufacturers design guns *specifically* to appeal to the U.S. market. For example, when East and West Germany were reunited, the German firm of Heckler & Koch was suddenly faced with a stagnant market for domestic military arms. According to *American Rifleman*, "Both the German manufacturer and [its subsidiary] U.S. importer needed a pistol that could establish a strong presence in the U.S. police and civilian markets. . . . Given the importance of the U.S. market, especially police sales, the manufacturer wisely took American tastes into account in the design phase."[7]

One cannot fully understand the U.S. gun market without having a sense of the degree to which foreign manufacturers and owners influence it. For example, foreign imports now account for one-third of all handguns offered in the U.S. market.[8] That percentage, as high as it seems, actually understates foreign influence on the U.S. market since it does not include handguns of nominally domestic manufacture produced by companies like Smith & Wesson and Beretta USA that are owned by foreign parents.

It is virtually impossible to reconstruct any specific foreign company's share of the U.S. market, since import data are aggregated only by country and not by company. But the following three brief case studies—one involving assault weapons, another involving high capacity handguns, and a third involving cheap Cold War handguns—illustrate the extent to which other countries have been dumping firearms on the United States.

MILITARY-STYLE ASSAULT GUNS: THE CHINA CONNECTION

The People's Republic of China jumped aggressively into the U.S. gun market in the late 1980s. China—which prohibits most of its citizens from owning guns of any kind—dumped millions of cheap military-style assault weapons and handguns, and tons of ammunition, on the United States to get hard currency it badly needed. This eruption of Chinese imports caused one of the greatest single escalations of civilian firearms lethality in the history of the United States.

China's paramilitary exports were fueled by rivalry between two government-owned companies, China North Industries Corp. (Norinco) and PolyTechnologies, who locked horns in battle over the U.S. market.[9] In addition to seeking hard currency, the companies wanted U.S. sales in order to keep production lines open, "because you have to keep that capability in case of war," according to an arms dealer interviewed by *The Washington Post*.[10] The *Post* said analysts compared the Chinese government companies to "rival private U.S. companies who sell jet fighters and other military equipment abroad."[11] (Some analysts, however, thought the two companies, as part of the same Chinese military establishment, were actually colluding to saturate the U.S. market.[12]) In either case, *Guns & Ammo* writer Garry James described the Chinese impact on the U.S. market as follows:

> In the firearms trade, if this decade can be noted for anything (other than perhaps the emergence of the "wondernine" auto pistol), it would have to be the introduction of the large number of products coming from The People's Republic of China. Besides the fact that the Chinese have all but made the assault rifle business their own . . . they have brought in handguns, target .22s and original "broomhandle" Mausers [pistols], to name just a few items.[13]

Before 1982, China exported only a handful of guns to the United States. Between 1982 and 1986, its firearms exports grew slightly, but its rifle exports to the United States never exceeded six percent of total American rifle imports.

That changed in 1987, when Chinese rifle imports surged to twenty-two percent of total U.S. rifle imports. The surge was reflected in an explosion of assault rifle imports. According to ATF figures published in 1989, only 8,131 AK-47s were imported into the United States in the two years ending in 1986. But AK-47 imports soared to 40,379 in a fourteen month period during 1988 and 1989, and ninety percent of those were Chinese.[14] The number may actually have been much greater, however. ATF officials estimated that "tens of thousands" additional AK-47s may have been smuggled into the country between 1986 and May 1989 and a dealer cooperating with ATF investigators said that the number of smuggled AK-47s could have been has high as five hundred thousand.[15]

China accounted for forty-two percent of all rifles imported into the U.S. civilian market between 1987 and 1994, the year in which President Clinton finally blocked the Chinese gun dumping (see Table 8).

Table 8

Rifle Imports from China to the United States, 1987-1994

	Total Rifles Imported	Chinese Rifles Imported	Percent Chinese
1987	452,059	100,897	22%
1988	484,976	182,935	38%
1989	350,012	141,382	40%
1990	273,102	31,370	11%
1991	339,966	115,902	34%
1992	420,085	164,271	39%
1993	764,498	490,399	64%
1994	698,907	344,648	49%
Total	3,783,605	1,571,804	42%

Source: U.S. Census Bureau, Foreign Trade Division

This flood of Chinese weapons was so great that it not only affected the U.S. rifle market, it strongly boosted the overall import of guns to the United States: Chinese rifles and handguns accounted for fifteen percent of all firearms imported for the civilian market in six of the eight years between 1987 and 1994, and in 1993 accounted for more than a quarter of all such guns imported (see Table 9).

In other words, if the Chinese had not started dumping guns on the United States, the total number of guns imported, sold and out on our streets—especially semiautomatic assault weapons—would have been significantly smaller.

The domestic gun industry did not see the flood of Chinese competition as all bad: Cheap guns would not only stimulate U.S. interest in firearms generally, it would also mean that some who

Table 9

Total Imports and Imports from China, 1987–1994

	Total Guns Imported	Chinese Rifles and Handguns	Percent Chinese
1987	1,138,806	106,618	9%
1988	1,240,581	203,643	16%
1989	1,100,789	149,182	14%
1990	1,025,476	39,520	4%
1991	1,084,891	126,880	12%
1992	1,541,706	186,272	11%
1993	2,081,266	560,385	27%
1994	2,239,460	387,248	17%
Total	11,452,975	1,764,650	15%

Source: U.S. Census Bureau, Foreign Trade Division

bought cheap Chinese guns would eventually "trade up" to higher quality U.S. firearms.[16]

In the meantime, however, Chinese assault rifles like the SKS showed up in criminal hands on the streets. As one ATF expert put it in 1993:

> The difference is this, and it is important. Instead of a police officer going into some house where some wacko is holed up with a smaller rifle like a .22 . . . now the guy's got a Chinese army gun; a real rifle. . . . The officer is walking into a much more dangerous situation . . . A .22 won't penetrate his bulletproof vest. But a 7.62 by 39mm — that these SKSs shoot — will. It'll penetrate a vest fairly effectively up to 250 yards. That's the difference.[17]

The problem was compounded when it was discovered that some Chinese SKS and MAK-90 rifles that were being imported ostensibly as semiautomatics were actually entering the United States capable of firing fully automatically — in other words, as illegal machine guns — and some ammunition being imported from China was of the illegal armor-piercing variety.[18]

These incidents underscore the difficulty of controlling foreign imports. The system in the United States for controlling the import of firearms is based on the belief that government paperwork, namely an import license granted to an importer for a certain number of specific guns, will match the ultimate on-the-ground reality.

In fact, the system depends almost entirely on the foreign exporter actually shipping guns and the domestic importer faithfully conforming to the terms of the paper, since neither customs inspectors nor ATF agents examine every or even most gun shipments from abroad.

Import of Chinese guns was effectively stopped in 1994 when President Clinton imposed a ban as a condition of renewing China's "most favored nation" trading status.[19] Gun importers complained about the decision and set up a new front group, the Firearms Importers Roundtable Trade Group (FAIR) to contest it.[20] The group opened diplomatic relations with the ATF and announced "a new era of better communications" with the regulatory agency, whose director reciprocated with overtures to the industry at large.[21] By 1996, FAIR was able to announce in an open letter that "by quietly working with the Congress, the Department of State, ATF, and foreign governments, we have been able to maintain the availability of guns and ammunition which earn good profits for the Dealer."[22] Meanwhile, the gun import industry looked to Russian firearms as potential replacements for the Chinese guns, setting off yet another battle, described below.[23]

China's image as the irrepressible bad boy of U.S. gun importers was further enhanced in 1996, when a number of Chinese gun manufacturer's representatives in the United States were charged in a sting operation with conspiring to illegally import firearms, and also offering to provide antiaircraft missiles, hand-held rocket launchers, silencers and full-size battle tanks, among other things.[24]

HIGH-CAPACITY HANDGUNS

What China did for the military-style semiautomatic assault rifle, a handful of European and Latin-American companies have done for the high-capacity, high-powered handgun—brought it to America's streets. Five countries—Brazil, Germany, Italy, Spain, and Austria—have shipped of millions of handguns to the United States over the last several decades. A large number of these guns have been high-capacity semiautomatic pistols, guns that carry as many as fifteen rounds in a single clip. These five countries have been the top five exporters of handguns to the United States for the last eighteen years, with the exception of only a few years when interlopers like Belgium, Luxembourg, and France slipped briefly onto the lower rungs. Table 10 illustrates the relative stability of the Big Five market in the 1990s.

Table 10.

Leading Handgun Exporters to the United States, 1991–1996

1991		*1992*		*1993*	
Brazil	218,382	Brazil	316,160	Brazil	319,281
Austria	115,430	Italy	178,318	Austria	184,283
Germany	90,842	Austria	164,034	Germany	155,374
Italy	71,616	Germany	114,032	Italy	120,055
Spain	68,706	Hungary	72,253	Spain	112,473
1994		*1995*		*1996*	
Brazil	372,003	Brazil	213,859	Austria	213,387
Russia	215,585	Austria	202,259	Brazil	182,775
Austria	209,820	Germany	181,711	Germany	113,632
Germany	165,302	Italy	74,650	Italy	57,149
Spain	95,014	Spain	53,849	Spain	22,476

Source: U.S. Census Bureau, Foreign Trade Division

Brazil rested at the top of the Big Five handgun import heap until 1996. From 1985 through 1995, Brazil—through its two handgun companies, Amadeo Rossi Municoes, and Taurus—ranked first among foreign countries shipping handguns to the United States.

"The American market today represents 40 percent of our production," Luciano Rossi told the *New York Times* in 1992.[24a] According to *American Rifleman*, as late as 1988 Rossi's guns were the most profitable lines in the trade of its U.S. importers, first Firearms International and then, following the former's demise, Interarms.[25] Brazil supplied one-third of all handguns imported into the United States in 1990.[26] In 1994 the company's total sales were about $30 million, $20 million of which was exports, mostly to the United States.[27]

In 1996, however, a decade of growth by Glock, Inc., an Austrian firm, culminated in Austria knocking Brazil into second place.

The history of Gaston Glock, an Austrian entrepreneur, and his handgun manufacturing company strikingly illustrates the impact that a single foreign gun manufacturer can have on the United States.

Gaston Glock never made a gun before the mid-1980s. He began his career as an engineer, and in 1963 formed the company of Glock Ges.m.b.H in his hometown of Deutch-Wagram, near Vienna. The company started out making doorknobs and hinges, then moved into military and police hardware (grenades, entrenching tools, etc.), combining high quality synthetic materials and special steels. In 1980, the Austrian Army announced a competition for a new standard sidearm. Gaston Glock assembled a panel of experts and produced a prototype Glock Model 17 9-mm pistol, a distinctive combination of "polymers" (also known to most of us as "plastic") and steel. That pistol won the Austrian Army competition in 1982, and Glock was airborne on the wings of the ensuing contract.[28]

Gaston Glock soon turned his eyes to the United States, opened Glock, Inc., "the company's United States beachhead" in the Atlanta, Georgia, suburb of Smyrna, and went after the American law enforcement market.[29]

Glock's pursuit of U.S. law enforcement agencies was central to its deliberate strategy first to gain the prestige of such sales, and then to use them in its marketing campaign to sell to civilians. "It was a conscious decision to go after the law enforcement market first," Gaston Glock said. "In marketing terms, we assumed that, by pursuing the law enforcement market, we would then receive the benefit of 'after sales' in the commercial market."[30]

The strategy worked so well that by 1995 the company was downplaying advertising and was chronically back-ordered.[31] According to the company, in that year there were half a million Glock pistols in use throughout North America (meaning mostly in the United States). Twenty thousand of these were issued by law enforcement agencies—eighty percent of Glock, Inc.'s production was going to civilians and twenty percent to law enforcement.[31]

Glock's rise to a commanding position in the foreign handgun import market can be seen clearly in the Austrian handgun import data, starting in 1983, two years before Glock established its "beachhead" in the United States. (See Table 11).

Table 11.

Handgun Imports from Austria to the U.S., 1983–1996

Year	Handguns From Austria	Austrian Share of Handgun Imports
1983	668	1%
1984	2,291	1%
1985	3,769	1%
1986	21,118	4%
1987	13,500	3%
1988	37,750	6%
1989	96,621	15%
1990	120,277	18%
1991	115,430	18%
1992	164,034	16%
1993	184,283	16%
1994	209,820	15%
1995	202,259	23%
1996	213,837	30%

Source: U.S. Census Bureau, Foreign Trade Division

As will be seen, Glock's rise has been accompanied by controversy, including allegations that its guns are unsafe and its marketing practices to law enforcement too aggressive.

CHEAP HANDGUNS FROM BEHIND THE "IRON CURTAIN"

The collapse of the former Soviet Union and the end of the Cold War have opened U.S. markets to gun-producing countries, such as Russia, Poland, Hungary, Czechoslovakia, and East Germany, that were formerly barred by U.S. import restrictions from shipping to the United States.[32] *American Firearms Industry* described the matter in 1993:

When the liberal press and the even more liberal lightweights in this country hailed the fall of the Berlin Wall and the democratization of Russia, little did they realize that free enterprise would open up a whole new area of firearms import/export, both to and from our two countries.[33]

According to *Shooting Sports Retailer*, sudden access to the vast U.S. market opened up a source of badly needed hard currency for these countries:

As communist countries collapsed, they were forced to look for a source of foreign currency. Most . . . had little to offer the West. We don't need their food, their technology is behind ours, they can't make a good computer, and their cars are twenty years behind even the Korean cars. But they do have guns. Lots of guns.[34]

The United States was a pot of gold for its former adversaries. The foreign suppliers were no babes in the woods dazzled by the gold, either. Far from being easy prey for sharp U.S. importers, they knew the value of the U.S. market. Val Forgett, Jr., the president of Navy Arms Company, a major importer of recycled foreign military weapons, told *American Firearms Industry*:

. . . the Ukrainians know what they have and how much it's worth. . . . No matter where you go over there, if you enter an official's office, there's a copy of *SHOTGUN NEWS* on his desk. They know what the going price is for firearms in the United States.[35]

U.S. importers jumped on the opportunity,[36] and the number of guns they shipped to the United States increased immediately and dramatically. According to ATF data, the number of rifles imported from Russia grew from less than three thousand in 1993 to more than a quarter of a million in 1994.[37] As Table 12 illustrates, handgun imports also grew significantly in the early 1990s, peaking in 1994.

The tide of guns from behind the former Iron Curtain crested in 1994, when U.S. importers sought permits that would have allowed them to import from Russia more than seven million guns and seven billion rounds of ammunition, staggering by any measure. Revelation of the pending permits generated fresh controversy in Washington, especially since the proposed Russian imports came on the

Table 12.

**Handgun Imports from the Former "Iron Curtain" Countries
to the United States, 1991 – 1996**

Year	Czechoslovakia/ Czech Republic	USSR/ Russia	Hungary	Total
1991	759	14	14,071	14,844
1992	21,177	16	72,253	93,446
1993	9,857	43,160	51,998	105,015
1994	21,973	215,585	49,368	286,926
1995	7,781	4,171	6,355	18,307
1996	23,311	0	22,019	45,330
Total	84,858	262,930	216,064	563,852

Source: U.S. Census Bureau, Foreign Trade Division

heels of the China import issue. The Clinton administration initially denied the Russian gun import requests while it studied the issue.[38]

The matter simmered behind the scenes until 1996, when the Clinton administration resolved the question for the short term by negotiating voluntary gun and ammunition import restrictions with the Russians. The voluntary restrictions blocked SKS assault rifles and cheap Makarov pistols from import, allowing in only "collectors' items" or rifles at least nominally described as having "a purely hunting or sporting purpose." Gun industry spokespersons criticized the restraints on foreign imports as "an alarming precedent in gun control."[39]

It remains to be seen how effective the voluntary restraints would be in keeping military-style rifles and cheap handguns from Russia out of the United States. The Clinton administration was reported to be negotiating with other countries to limit the import of "inexpensive, easily concealable handguns and military style semi-automatic weapons that are easily converted to machine guns."[40] But there is little evidence that either the White House, the Congress, or the Washington bureaucracy are interested in grappling with the import issue in anything more than a reactive way, dealing serially with especially egregious import proposals if and when they become publicly known.

*   *   *

Mushrooming gun imports from overseas have been only a part of the foreign scramble for the U.S. firearms market. Restrictions on imports of cheap handguns in the 1968 Gun Control Act and a weak dollar combined in the 1970s to encourage foreign manufacturers to move gun production facilities from their home countries to the United States.[41] By 1992, according to gun writer Don Shumar, writing in *American Firearms Industry*, it was:

> . . . getting hard to define just what a 'domestic company' is because so many foreign firms have manufacturing facilities in the United States. And it's no secret that several big American companies (so called at least) are controlled by international conglomerates that are based overseas.[42]

The history of Beretta, U.S.A. Corporation, the preeminent foreign-owned company in the U.S. firearms market, best demonstrates the calculation that these foreign gun manufacturers put into how to most profitably enter the U.S. market. Beretta is well known for its 1985 coup when it won a contract to supply the Defense Department replacement to the Colt Model 1911 .45-caliber pistol. The U.S.-made Model 1911 had been the military's standard sidearm since before the First World War.[43] Beretta's success shocked the U.S. gun industry, which managed to delay but not halt the final award through the application of fierce behind-the scenes Congressional pressure.

Since then, Beretta has been among the most successful companies in the U.S. market. A centuries-old Italian gun manufacturer, the company deliberately used the publicity surrounding the Defense Department contract as a wedge to enter the broader U.S. market. Beretta first began manufacturing in the United States in the 1970s in order to circumvent the 1968 federal gun control law banning import of Saturday night specials. The pistols Beretta was shipping to the United States in those days would have failed the 1968 law's size restrictions. But because the import standards do not apply to domestically made guns, Beretta opened a manufacturing plant in Accokeek, Maryland. The U.S. production base allowed Beretta to keep selling handguns in the United States, which the fiscally conservative company deemed a "safe market."[44] Although the U.S. plant is run by Americans, the company's Italian owners keep close rein on operations, frequently sending its executives back and forth from Italy for advice and consultation.[45]

In a 1993 interview, the head of the U.S. subsidiary explained the long range expansion strategy that prompted the company to pursue the Army contract: Beretta really wanted the military contract not so much for the immediate sale as to win domestic acceptance and thus a place in the more lucrative U.S. civilian market:

> The company's favorable position is no fluke, [Robert] Bonaventure [head of Beretta U.S.A. Corp.] said. It's part of a carefully planned strategy dating back to 1980. . . . The plan was to win the military contract and use it to make Beretta a household name in the United States in hopes of tapping into the larger law-enforcement and commercial markets. That's why, Bonaventure said, the company has been selling pistols to the military for about $225 each — close to production cost.
>
> By comparison, Beretta charges police departments $385 to $450 for basically the same weapon. . . . For civilians, the suggested retail price is $625. . . .
>
> The biggest market — about twice the size of the police and military business combined — is the commercial market.[46]

The success of the Beretta strategy was demonstrated in 1995, after its main contract to supply the Army expired. Bonaventure said then that there was "no slowdown whatsoever . . . The assembly line kept moving right along."[47]

Like another foreign-owned company in the top three pistol makers, Smith & Wesson, Beretta is now pushing small, concealable handguns.[48] And Beretta's overall strategy is strikingly similar to that which the Austrian company Glock used to break into the U.S. civilian market.

The ultimate ownership of some foreign subsidiaries is murky at best. For example the British *Sunday Telegraph* newspaper reported that Justin Moon, the son and putative successor to the Rev. Sun Myung Moon, founder and head of the controversial Unification Church, is president of Saeilo, Incorporated, a Delaware company that manufactures the Kahr K9 compact 9-mm pistol, designed to be the most concealable 9-mm semiautomatic pistol on the market.[49] But a spokeswoman for Saeilo, a Delaware corporation, denied that the Unification Church owns or controls it.[50] (The Unification Church also founded and controls through surrogates *The Washington Times*, a newspaper unfailing in its opposition to responsible gun control.)

The U.S. gun market has changed radically in the half century since the end of the Second World War. At midcentury, it was a pretty stodgy business. Its product mix featured a relatively stable line of utilitarian long guns aimed principally at supplying hunters and sport shooters. Handguns were a comparatively small part of the market. The gun press was positively sober when compared to the hyperpromotional style of today's magazines.

Although hunters and sport shooters still make up a significant part of the market, the industry's growth has been concentrated in the design and production of powerful handguns and military-style long guns, or assault rifles. Today's gun market is dominated by what Gary Anderson, the NRA's executive director for general operations, called the "Rambo factor" at a 1993 symposium on shooting ranges. "American shooting activities place a predominant emphasis on large caliber arms that can be fired rapidly," Anderson said. "If you look at the key words in arms and ammunition advertising, they are not skill, accuracy or marksmanship. The key words are 'power,' 'speed' and 'firepower.' "[51]

The change from a market dominated by guns designed for killing deer and pheasant and punching holes in paper to a market obsessed with guns designed principally to kill people more effectively has been dramatic. From 1946 through 1950, handguns accounted for slightly less than thirteen percent of domestic firearms production.[52] After deducting exports, only ten percent of the guns available to the civilian market in those five years were handguns, and of those less than five percent were foreign imports. Hunting guns — shotguns (forty-five percent) and rifles (forty-three percent) — dominated the market. Handgun domestic production and imports grew somewhat during the 1950s. Handguns accounted for twenty-three percent of all guns made available to the domestic market during that decade, but shotguns (forty-four percent) and rifles (thirty-two percent) still dominated the civilian market.

During the 1960s, however, the market was transformed. The sale of guns in general soared, and handguns captured a larger and larger share. In 1968, domestic production of handguns outpaced domestic production of shotguns for the first time, and since 1970, domestic handgun production has consistently outpaced domestic rifle production by wide margins. Handgun imports exploded in 1967 and 1968 as importers sought to beat the new import restrictions enacted in the 1968 Gun Control Act. Foreign imports accounted for forty-eight percent of all handguns on the U.S. market in 1967 and fifty-two percent in 1968. Over the entire decade, handguns grew to thirty-six percent of the market, whereas rifles and shotguns fell to thirty-two percent each.

The mix has never gone back—handgun share of the market has steadily risen, while rifles and shotguns have fallen.

5—"A Little Money-Making Machine"

Despite the colder realities of the business, the gun industry packages firearms in the sepia tint of nostalgia, conjuring up the Western frontier, fathers and sons hunting at the turn of the century, and grand moments of martial history.[1]

A collage on a recent Marlin catalog, for example, featured the company's generic cowboy with a rifle on horseback, Wild West showgirl Annie Oakley, and a pastiche of clippings from period catalogs. A bronze sculpture of a cowboy reining in a spirited horse dominates Ruger's catalog for the same year. Winchester's rifle catalog shows a bearded man on horseback splashing across a ford, blanket rolled behind saddle, leading another horse. A Savage Arms catalog displays a new rifle in a setting of antique cleaning materials, brass desk accessories, and an old photograph of a mustachioed man who could be anyone's grandfather. The cover of Colt's catalog is a photograph of parts Samuel Colt carved from wood while inventing his revolver. "Marketing the past is not a bad idea," *Shooting Sports Retailer* coolly advised gun dealers.[2]

For decades, the gun industry has portrayed itself in this way as a repository and guardian of fundamental U.S. cultural values. Indeed it is difficult to think of another industry—with the possible exception of professional sports—that has so successfully transformed its image from profit-making business to national institution. But however grandly the gun industry may portray itself, the plain truth remains that the gun industry *is* simply a business. For some, like patriarch Bill Ruger, it has been a very good business: Sturm, Ruger & Company earned a net profit of $34.4 million on $223.3 million in sales in 1996 and $27.75 million on sales of $209.4 million in 1997.[3]

The gun industry aims to sell more of its products to Americans at better profit margins. Individual companies want and fight for better market shares. And the storefront dealers, kitchen table dealers, and hobbyists who scrum at the retail level are scrapping over profit, not who gets the most credit for preserving "heritage." Profit determines which guns and ammunition the industry develops, which guns and ammunition it markets, and which guns and ammunition it sells to the United States.

In a 1981 article documenting a running battle between then "up-and-coming" Charter Arms and old-line Smith & Wesson to secure market share of small, "snub-nosed" revolvers, a former president of Smith & Wesson, James L. Oberg, bluntly explained this concept. When he was asked about the battle for market share of short-barreled revolvers, which statistics showed were used disproportionately in violent crimes, Oberg declared that:

> . . . we are focusing on dollars more than anything else. Most of our motivation of what we do here is to supply dollars to our stockholders. For us, a great deal of the motivation is to run a profitable company.[4]

The piece explained the respective rationales of the two company's executives for marketing guns used in violent crimes at rates much higher than their overall presence in the civilian market. It was an early—and eerily prescient—example of today's eroding difference between cheap Saturday night specials and more expensive "Cadillacs" of crime guns.

A 1992 *Forbes* magazine profile of Ruger—who started his company in 1949 with a $50,000 stake from a friend—summarized his view on the power of profitability as follows:

> By 1959, Ruger's sales hit $3 million. Around that time, Ruger recalls telling himself, "We have a little moneymaking machine here. All we have to do is keep introducing the correct new products. . . . We operate on a philosophy that you have to have new stuff, and you have to have it annually."[5]

Ruger has not hesitated to fight other companies to protect his "little machine." *Forbes* reported that in 1986, for example, reasoning that his main competition in revolvers was Smith & Wesson, Ruger refused to sell to wholesalers who also sold Smith & Wesson products. This is the behavior more of a capitalist battling for market share than of an altruistic preservationist selflessly conserving national heritage.

The money-making machine has been good to those who run it.

In 1992, *Forbes* reported that Bill Ruger and his family owned Ruger shares worth over $100 million.[6] In 1996, *The Hartford Courant* reported that Ruger was hauling down an annual salary of $333,000, and that he and his son owned 3,719,448 shares of Sturm, Ruger, at a price of $46.87 per share, worth more than $174 million. Ruger's lifestyle was reflected in his reported membership in the Rolls-Royce Owner's Club, the Bentley Drivers' Club, Ltd., the Pequot Yacht Club, and the New York Yacht Club.[7]

Gun magnates in the United States are secretive about their wealth. Ruger is an exception because his is a public company. But Samuel Cummings, the expatriate founder of the Interarms firearms importing company, was reported to be a billionnaire at his death in 1998.[8]

Making money is the common goal of all industry in the market system. But the firearms industry makes and sells products that are inherently and without exception lethal. Even the tamest low-caliber target pistol is perfectly capable of killing a human being.[9] More than thirty-five thousand Americans die by gunfire every year, and about three times as many are wounded.[10] At the same time, unlike any other industry making consumer products, the gun industry is free from health and safety regulation, and is required to disclose little about its operations.

This is doubly ironic because—even though it has vigorously fought against subjecting firearms to product safety regulation—the NRA has stressed the fundamental similarity between firearms and all other consumer products when it served its interests. Thus, arguing against critics of the eruption of semiautomatic handguns, the NRA appealed to the virtue of progress that these guns supposedly represent: "The development and improvement in firearms are similar to all of the technological progress that Americans have experienced in a wide range of products applicable to any facet of American life."[11]

The absurdity of this situation is evident. That it continues in the face of relentless carnage can in large part be explained by the confusion inherent in how our national debate over firearms has proceeded. Instead of seeing guns as the deadly commodities of a profit-making industry, we have been conditioned to imagine them as artifacts of our very freedom. While our politicians continue to recycle the same old arguments, and invoke the same old political symbols, gun manufacturers—as the following chapters show—have been coolly cranking out more and more deadly innovations.

Part Two

THE SPIRAL

OF LETHALITY

6—The Deadly Role
of Innovation

Despite its incredible profitability, the gun industry has faced serious problems in the last twenty years or so. Foremost among these is the fact, that given minimal care, guns don't wear out. A reasonably well made revolver, for example, will last a lifetime, and it will serve its purpose just as well on the last day of that lifetime as on the first. In the words of *Shooting Industry* writer Massad Ayoob:

> Who owns their grandfather's icebox or 1950 Plymouth? However, many of us have inherited our grandparents' firearms. These are durable goods in the truest sense—gifts that truly "last forever."[1]

Few other consumer products present such a marketing dead end. Sooner or later, automobiles, hair dryers, drills, grills, toys, and computers wear out. Even without considering the effect of fads or advertising-generated demand, consumers can be counted on to buy replacements for worn out goods. But guns don't need to be replaced, in the absence of extraordinarily heavy use or accidental damage. There is rarely a utilitarian reason to buy a replacement gun. In fact, consumers can just as well have a gunsmith repair or upgrade a used gun—adding "after market" equipment like better barrels, springs, sights, and stocks, for example—as buy a new one.[2] Or, they can simply buy a used instead of new gun.[3]

Moreover, the industry has increasingly had to deal with a saturated market. The boom in the sale of handguns during the 1960s and 1970s, which created enormous profits and made millionaires of many of its owners, led to a glut. In 1978 *Business Week* found the industry "mired in problems . . . a business with tired blood."[4] In 1981, C. Hugh Fletcher, the president of U.S. Repeating Arms Company, declared, "The market is basically static." Major companies like Repeating Arms [Winchester], Ruger, and Colt were "not growing except for the home-defense portion."[5] In 1984, the handgun market was said to be so saturated that, according to *Discount Store News,* all but a few discount chains bailed completely out of selling handguns because of falling prices and poor profit margins.[6] According to Cameron Hopkins of *American Handgunner* magazine, the gun business "peaked in the late 1970s, early 1980s . . . [then] started tapering off."[7] Bill Ruger acknowledged in a *New York Times* interview that the market was saturated because gun products last too long.[8]

To compound these problems, fewer and fewer young people are growing up into the "traditional" hunting and sport shooting markets. As *Shooting Sports Retailer* explained:

> An important element lacking in the growth of traditional hunting values is the familiar sight of generational experience being passed on to youthful hunters. . . . Hunting and shooting in the eyes of many in the "Vietnam" and "Me" generations became linked to violence and uncontrolled materialism.[9]

This is serious business for the gun industry. The Justice Department's 1994 survey of firearms ownership found that "one of the best predictors of gun ownership was the presence of firearms in the respondent's childhood home." People whose parents possessed guns were three times as likely as others to own one themselves.[10] And for centuries, hunting has been the reason for guns in the home, the lifeblood of the shooting industry. Hunting has not only provided its own market for guns, it has been the means by which fathers have traditionally handed the gun culture down to their sons.

Even pro-gun experts acknowledge that hunting's days are numbered in the United States. For example, Conley L. Moffett, deputy assistant director for ecological services of the U.S. Fish and Wildlife Service, reported to a National Shooting Range Symposium in 1993 that research shows "that hunting could end in this country as early as the year 2020. The most optimistic . . . date for that to occur is the year 2050."[11]

In 1996, Glock vice-president and general counsel Paul Jannuzzo told the *Financial Times* that the gun industry worries about market saturation "because grandpa or dad isn't taking the kid out into the field to teach him how to shoot any more." Other industry concerns include a decline in the number of country dwellers, who tend to have more space for shooting, and growing curbs on the discharge of lead.[12] Combined, these factors mean that there will be fewer new customers to make even a first gun purchase, and that means the lifelong loss of potential customers in the gun market.[13]

Finally, guns—and particularly handguns—have proven to be just plain bad business for a number of major retailers, especially discount chain stores, which are a major source of revenue for firearms manufacturers.[14] Some have decided that the potential liabilities and the overall bad image associated with selling guns outweigh the revenue from sales, and others are reviewing their policies on guns.[15] The loss in whole or in some part of outlets like K-Mart, Wal-Mart, and Target has exacerbated the industry's marketing problems:

> The mass merchants play an important role in the shooting sports because they sell a lot of firearms to first-time gun buyers . . . the loss of mass merchants removes a source of new gun owners who traditionally shy away from shopping in specialized stores until they feel comfortable with a particular type of product.[16]

Thus the gun industry's chronic problem over the last several decades has been figuring out how to deal with saturated or declining markets, in which "more and more guns [are] being purchased by fewer and fewer consumers."[17]

It is for this reason that innovation—Bill Ruger's "new stuff"— has become central to virtually everything the industry has done over the last two decades. The gun press discusses the subject with surprising candor. "Convincing people they need more guns is the job of innovation," a panel of industry experts reported in a 1993 *Shooting Industry* forum. The innovation need not be real—even perceived innovation will do the job, according to Jon Sundra, one of the experts on the magazine's panel. He cited as an example beltless rifle ammunition cases, which he said "won't do anything different, but it has no belt, so they're supposed to be better."[18]

Guns & Ammo writer G. Sitton addressed this gap between the need for gun products and the engine of innovation in a 1996 article about the emergence of the .50 Action Express pistol cartridge, a round whose "physical dimensions implied previously undreamed-of power":

> One citizen asked me why the world needed a .50-anything, and I had no ready answer. Now that the .50 AE has been around for five years . . . I'm still not sure the world needed it. Need, after all, is rarely a factor in the design of or demand for a sporting cartridge.[19]

The National Rifle Association's own gun writers similarly described the disconnect between need and innovation in a 1987 review of the then-newly introduced Ruger P-85 9-mm pistol:

> It could be said, with much justification, that we just don't need another staggered magazine, double-action, 9-mm pistol. But we have one and, considering its source and price, it could be with us for some time.[20]

This is the same type of Ruger pistol, incidentally, that now regularly crops up among the top ten guns traced in crimes. Five years after the NRA review of the P-85, a 1992 *New York Times* profile quoted Ruger explaining his view of the role of innovation and the irrelevance of need:

> "We've woken up to the fact that these guns are not wearing out, and used guns are competing with our new production. . . . People are buying guns for half the money. I think that hurt sales of a lot of companies in the 1980's."
>
> Gun critics might say leave well enough alone. But for Mr. Ruger . . . part of the solution to market overload is "planned obsolescence." By that he does not mean making guns designed to fall apart . . . but rather adopting innovative designs that would appeal to the technological lust inside every gun fancier.
>
> "We need to get new products and new models out there."[21]

Forbes magazine summed up Ruger's approach by saying that, "In a way Ruger operates on the philosophy that Detroit once used with much success: Keep customers spending by continually obsoleting old models."[22] Or as Andrew W. Molchan, publisher and editor of *American Firearms Industry*, put it in 1993:

> Without new models that have major technical changes, **you eventually exhaust your market.** You get to the point where 90% of the people who might want one have **one already.** This is the fundamental problem with the classic rifle and shotgun market.

Handguns during the last twenty years have sold better than long guns, mainly because of the innovation. A lot of 1993 handguns are very different from what was around in 1933. This innovation has driven the handgun market. (Emphasis in original.)[23]

But Bill Ruger is by no means alone in his pursuit of innovation. "Innovation abounds within the industry, as makers come up with new ideas to help sell guns," *Handguns '98*, a comprehensive review volume, reported in its tenth annual edition.[24]

Smith & Wesson officials recently described how consumer demand was not a factor when they designed several new "home grown" revolvers. "The project started out in a combined brainstorming session," said Smith & Wesson handgun product manager Herb Belin. "We didn't conduct any special consumer research surveys before we developed it," said Bob Scott, Smith & Wesson vice president for sales & marketing.[25]

Reliance on innovation and developing new guns has influenced the way guns are sold in the United States. In an earlier era, "the first-time buyer bought the gun his father used," according to the manager of public relations for Smith & Wesson. "Now we're seeing a lot more advertising-driven buying."[26]

This process of first creating more lethal products through innovation and then selling them through advertising and gun press reviews is seen by many in the industry—such as *Shooting Industry*'s Massad Ayoob—as a model of free enterprise. "Find a market, show them something they need and why they need it, give 'em a good price, and they'll buy it from you. Capitalism in action."[27]

The firearms industry's innovative quest, or "capitalism in action," could have taken any number of paths. The industry might, for example, have chosen to develop safer firearms—e.g., guns with passive safety devices such as childresistant locks and load indicators to show when they are loaded—or to have diversified into other, less lethal recreational products. Ruger, for example, makes golf clubs as a sideline of its casting business.

But gun industry executives deliberately chose to take exactly the opposite direction. Just as tobacco industry executives loaded cigarettes up with addictive nicotine and flavor enhancing additives, so have gun industry executives steadily increased the lethality of guns and ammunition. They have made guns to hold more rounds, increased the power of those rounds, and made guns smaller and more concealable. They have developed ammunition to cause ghastly wounds rivaling the worst carnage seen on battlefields. This in turn has made guns more suitable for use in crime, because they are more concealable, and more likely to kill or seriously injure because of their greater power, whether used intentionally or unintentionally. Bob Rogers, editor of *Shooting Sports Retailer*, described the situation pithily in 1997: "Firepower is increasing. So is the killing potential as guns shrink in size and concealibility."[28]

Some observers have seen the rise to dominance of handguns as an indication of social breakdown.[29] Social breakdown may be a likely consequence of the increased lethality on America's streets. But the one constant force driving the industry has been a need for innovation. The industry's need for new products and new models to stimulate stagnant markets—not consumer need or demand for more lethal products—has driven the gun industry's conduct over the last several decades.

Innovation to stimulate gun industry profits led to a dramatic change in the kind of guns sold in the U.S. handgun market during the mid-1980s as the U.S. market turned away from revolvers to high-capacity semiautomatic pistols.

By the late 1970s, revolvers had been the overwhelming favorite of the U.S. handgun market for over a century, since Sam Colt patented and marketed his repeating gun concept. Simple in design and sturdy in construction, revolvers are essentially a rotating ammunition cylinder suspended on a frame from which a barrel projects. They are sometimes referred to as "wheelguns" because of the characteristic multichambered cylinder.

Single-action revolvers, an older design, require that the gun be cocked and the cylinder rotated for each round by pulling the hammer back with the thumb. Only after the hammer is thus cocked is the trigger pulled, as a result of which the hammer falls and the round is fired. Pulling the trigger of a single-action revolver merely allows the cocked hammer to fall forward. It neither rotates the cylinder nor cocks the hammer for the next round.

In the case of modern double-action revolvers, each pull of the trigger simultaneously cocks the hammer and turns the cylinder, thereby advancing a new chamber and thus a new round into place. The cylinder is locked into position, and, at the end of the continuous trigger pull, the hammer falls and the round is discharged. The now-empty shell casing remains in the firing position until the trigger is pulled again. The capacity of most revolver cylinders is six rounds—hence the term "six-shooter" or "six-gun." After the sixth round is fired, the empty cases must be manually ejected (by means of a spring-loaded rod and star apparatus that pushes all of the rounds out of the cylinder at once) and a new round loaded into each of the cylinder's chambers.[30]

In short, the double-action revolver shooter's trigger finger does the mechanical work of loading and firing, through the gun's "lockwork" or "action," and that work must be done by pulling the trigger separately for each round.

Semiautomatic pistols have long been popular in Europe but have taken a back seat historically to revolvers in the United States.[31] In 1973, for example, about half as many pistols were produced in the United States as revolvers. Excepting the standard military sidearm, the .45-caliber Colt Model 1911, most U.S.-market pistols were in smaller calibers, such as .22 and .32. There are several reasons for the pistol's slow acceptance in the United States. In part, pistols were thought to be less reliable than revolvers, as illustrated by the following response to a *Guns & Ammo* reader's question by the magazine's handgun expert, Bill Jordan: "Where the targets shoot back, some 98 percent of law enforcement officers join me in preferring a revolver."[32]

Pistols are more complicated in design and function than revolvers, despite often being more compact; the ammunition is contained in a rectangular "magazine" (often called a "clip") which is inserted into the base of the pistol grip. A horizontal slide moves ammunition from the magazine to the barrel and cocks the firing pin by a system of springs and projections.

Like revolvers, pistols may be single action, double action, and double action only.

In single-action pistols, the slide must be manually pulled back and released to cock the hammer (or "striker") and chamber the first round before the gun can be fired. After the trigger is pulled and the first round is fired, the firearm itself takes over the work of reloading and cocking. Recoil and spring forces move the slide back, eject the discharged round, cock the hammer, then move the slide forward and chamber a new round from the magazine. At that point the gun is ready to fire again. Pulling the trigger simply releases the hammer to strike the firing pin and start the cycle over again, until the magazine is empty. The term "semiautomatic" refers to the pistol's self-loading and spent-shell ejecting action. (In spite of their own fussiness about correct use of firearms terms, manufacturers and gun experts cloud the semantic issue by referring to such self-loading pistols as "automatic," a term otherwise reserved for machine-guns.)[33]

Single-action pistols present the question of when to operate the slide, and thus cock the gun, for the first round. One cannot always anticipate the need to fire the gun, and the time taken to manually operate the slide and fire the first shot could be crucial, especially in a self-defense situation. On the other hand, carrying a cocked gun presents an obvious safety hazard. Despite various safety mechanisms and recommended gun-handling regimens intended to prevent accidental firing, unintentional firings of cocked single-action pistols happen, often when one is attempting to take the gun in or out of a holster, or otherwise store it on the person.[34]

Double-action pistols overcome this dilemma to some extent. Although the first round may be chambered in a double-action pistol, the pistol is not yet cocked. The gun therefore is not ready to fire. In order to cock and thus fire the pistol, the trigger must be pulled through its entire range for the first shot. The gun is designed so that this inevitably requires a significantly stronger pull to operate the cocking mechanism than is required to simply release the hammer of a cocked single-action pistol. Thereafter, the gun functions as described above for single-action pistols, with subsequent shots requiring only a lighter trigger pull comparable to that of a single-action pistol. The double-action feature also increases the speed with which the first shot may be fired, since there is no need to manually operate the slide to cock the gun.

Finally, double-action-only pistols self-load but do not self-cock after the first round. They thus require the stronger and positive pull of the trigger through its entire range of motion to cock and fire the gun for *all* rounds, just as in the case of the double-action re-volver. The extra effort (stronger trigger pull) required for the cock-ing motion is a safety measure, intended to reduce the likelihood of accidental firing by unintentional pressure on the trigger of a cocked pistol.[35]

Pistol magazines range in general from eight to fifteen rounds, although higher capacities are available in some models and in the "after market." Older "single column" or "single stack" magazines held a single column of rounds, usually totaling eight or nine. More modern "double column" or "double stack" high-capacity maga-zines, the grandfather of which was the 9-mm, thirteen round, single-action Browning Hi Power introduced in 1935,[36] are fatter. They are designed to hold two columns of rounds, stacked in a sort of zigzag or staggered pattern within the magazine.

Whether single or double stack, a magazine when empty is easily slipped out of the pistol grip and a loaded magazine inserted in its place. Thus, many more rounds can be fired from a semiautomatic pistol, with less effort, than from a revolver, and the empty pistol can be reloaded more quickly than the empty revolver.[37]

The market relationship between revolvers and pistols suddenly changed in the United States in the 1980s. Domestic pistol produc-tion began to rise in the late 1970s, then soared in the middle 1980s. Conversely, revolver production began to plummet in the early 1980s. The two trend lines crossed in 1987, when domestic pistol production surpassed revolver production.

Two forces drove the new American pistol market in the United States. One was the emergence of companies at the low end of the market specializing in small, cheaply made, and easily concealable pistols in lower calibers, widely known as Saturday night specials or "junk guns." Leaders at this end of the market included the Ring of Fire California companies, manufacturing and marketing pistols like the Raven .25 and the Davis .380, which—priced at $60 to $100—were among the best selling guns of the 1980s.[38] "Old-fashioned revolvers are just that, old fashioned," Ring of Fire magnate Bruce Jennings said. "The semiautos for this day and age are far superior. They are modern firearms."[39]

The second force was the emergence, initially at the higher end of the market, of new pistols in higher calibers that combined double-action operation with high-capacity magazines. *Guns & Ammo* described the trend in a review of the "top ten" gun trends of the 1980s:

> No class of handgun ever received the torrent of attention and developmental effort as did the modern, high-capacity, double-action 9mm pistol—the so-called wondernine. In 1979, there were only a few models available in the American marketplace and they weren't particularly popular. . . . Then somebody opened the floodgates, because in short order we had a couple dozen new and interesting pistols in this category.[40]

No single event opened the floodgates, but a combination of circumstances clearly contributed. The publicity surrounding the competition for the Army's sidearm contract, and Beretta's winning it with a 9-mm, gave the high-capacity pistol both visibility and cachet in the U.S. gun market. Other companies that had developed designs for the competition offered them on the civilian market. And the gun press found a bunch of new toys to enthuse over.

Ultimately, the two ends of the market began to merge, with the cheaper gun manufacturers increasing the caliber of their guns, and the high quality manufacturers producing cheaper pistols. Exploiting the pistol fad was good news for the gun industry, which benefited from booming sales. "The semiautomatic pistol is the only part of the gun business that has grown in recent years," David M. Guthrie, an industry analyst, said in 1992.[41] Writing in 1994 for *Guns & Ammo* magazine, Bill O'Brien described how the change had affected the consumer gun market in the early 1980s:

> . . . more and more shooters, looking for something new and egged on by the gun press, were turning to high-capacity double-action 9mms and otherwise jumping on trendy bandwagons.[42]

If O'Brien's tone in 1994 seemed to dismiss the gun press and its "trendy bandwagons," it was either ironic or self-lacerating: *Guns & Ammo* was as culpable as any other periodical. Its handgun writer Jan Libourel, for example, reviewed the Astra Model A-80, a Spanish fifteen-shot 9mm pistol import in 1982:

> Recent years have witnessed the emergence of a new breed of autoloading pistols. . . . In the eyes of many, the combination of DA [double action] first-shot speed coupled with the great firepower of the double column magazine represents the present state-of-the-art in a heavy-duty defensive sidearm.[43]

The state of the art of high-capacity, double-action pistols represented a major escalation in firepower and thus lethality. The new pistols carried more rounds in the newer high-capacity magazines than earlier pistols, and many more rounds than revolvers. Those rounds could be fired faster and reloaded more quickly than revolvers. Beretta advertised the enhanced lethality of its "D" Model double-action-only pistols as compared to revolvers this way:

> It all adds up to the best of two worlds: the familiar features of the revolver combined with the life-saving 15+1 firepower of the 92D 9mm, and 10 + 1 for the 96D .40 cal.[44]

This increase in magazine capacity was demonstrated in a recent Justice Department study that compared magazine capacity of guns acquired in 1993 and 1994 with the capacity of handguns acquired before 1993. Only about fourteen percent of all handguns acquired before 1993 (which included all the decades of revolver dominance and single stack pistols) had a magazine capacity of ten or more rounds, the average being 7.6. But nearly thirty-eight percent of the handguns acquired in 1993 and 1994 (predominantly newer model pistols) had a magazine capacity of 10 or more rounds, with the average handgun acquired having a capacity of 9.5 rounds.[45] As dramatic as this twenty-five percent increase in average magazine capacity is, it significantly understates the effect on gun violence. For one thing, it almost certainly understates the magazine capacity of guns used in crime. Guns used by criminals tend to have a comparatively short "time to crime" interval (the time between original retail sale and use in a crime). Accordingly, that pool of guns would tend to be newer than the overall pool of firearms reported in the survey.

In any case, the deleterious effects of this increase in magazine capacity are well known and widely acknowledged, even within the gun industry itself. High-capacity magazines exceed the needs of the well-trained, competent shooter and increase the danger to all involved. For example, Jeff Cooper, known as the "gunner's guru," wrote in a 1987 article for *Guns & Ammo*:

> If a man loses his composure and shoots a revolver dry without settling anything, it would seem unlikely that he would settle anything further with six more rounds. . . . It is hard to come up with an example in which a large-capacity magazine made a real difference in a gunfight. . . . [46]

High-capacity magazines also make possible and encourage the so-called "spray and pray" shooting technique, which further increases the danger to intended victims and innocent bystanders alike. Or, in Cooper's words, "When one has a whole sackful of rounds in his piece, he has a tendency to load on Sunday and try to shoot all week."

In addition to increasing magazine capacity, manufacturers at all price levels began marketing pistols for domestic civilian sales in higher (bigger) calibers than the smaller-bore 22- to 380- caliber workhorses that had characterized the old pistol market. Starting from the "wondernine," gun manufacturers have worked their way up through the calibers to the highest power that pistols can handle and still function with at least minimum reliability, through the .44-magnum to the ".45 Super," described by *Guns & Ammo* as "a supercharged 'magnum' version of the .45 ACP cartridge."[47]

Some observers argue that the trend to pistols was inspired by foreign imports, especially the Beretta, after the company won the U.S. military sidearm competition and supposedly left U.S. companies flat-footed. It is true that the military competition stimulated interest in 9-mm pistols,[48] but if the Americans were ever behind in the pistol arms race, they caught up with a vengeance. (In fact, Smith & Wesson had introduced the first American "wondernine" in 1971, the 9-mm, fifteen-shot, double action M-59, which enjoyed modest success in the law enforcement market.)[49] By 1993, according to one count, of some sixty 9-mm models on the market, at least 32 had been introduced since 1988.[50]

Ruger, America's preeminent gun manufacturer, disclosed how this new, more lethal "stuff" had helped its bottom line in a 1989 filing with the SEC:

> From 1986 to 1989, unit sales of firearms products increased significantly due in part to the successful introduction of new products such as the P85 nine-millimeter semiautomatic pistol.[51]

By 1993, Ruger was cranking out 300,000 pistols a year, or 1,600 each work day. This represented more than a third of the company's total 1993 production of about 800,000 firearms.[52]

The consequence of the industry's shift to marketing semiautomatic pistols was inevitable (and had been foreshadowed during the 1960s and 1970s by the Saturday night special experience): — Criminals snapped up the more lethal pistols. By 1991, seven of the top ten handguns used in crime were semiautomatic pistols, ranging from the cheaply made guns of Raven Arms and Davis Industries to higher quality pistols by such "responsible" manufacturers as Ruger, Colt, Smith & Wesson, and Beretta.[53]

Moreover, the 9-mm pistols quickly became the favorite of the more dangerous criminal element. "The 'nine' is the No. 1 choice of gang members, drug dealers and career criminals on the street," Jerry Singer, spokesman for the ATF said in 1993.[54] A study by the Boston Police Department and the ATF of guns recovered by police between 1989 and 1992 found that forty-two percent were pistols and the top four manufacturers of guns taken from criminals and children were, in descending order, Smith & Wesson, Colt, Raven Arms, and Ruger.[55]

Increased magazine capacity had a direct effect on the level of violence. Many more victims were shot multiple times. "It seems like we never see just one shot anymore," Andrew Burgess, an orthopedic surgeon at the University of Maryland's shock trauma center in Baltimore, told *U.S. News & World Report* in 1996.[56] Fewer victims of such multiple gunshot wounds survive, and greater damage is suffered by those who do survive, raising treatment costs and long-term-care costs. The street level effect of the so-called "nines" was evident in Chicago, where more people were murdered with 9-mm pistols during 1992 than were slain with the same gun during all of the 1980s. "They [semiautomatics] are the reason we see multiple gunshot wounds in so many cases," Chicago Detective Cmdr. Frederick Miller said during the surge of violence.[57]

In short, pistols began killing more people than revolvers had, and their enhanced firepower (especially more rounds) was directly reflected in more lethal injuries on U.S. streets. The number of pistols U.S. gun manufacturers made increased by ninety-two percent from 1985 to 1992, and deaths by handguns increased forty-eight percent, from 8,902 to 13,220.[58] The number of juveniles arrested for weapons violations more than doubled between 1985 and 1993, according to a Justice Department report.[59]

Texas Magazine compared this carnage to other supposedly violent eras, such as the frontier that gun manufacturers evoke in advertising as part of the U.S. "gun heritage":

> The Wild West? The most violent year in Dodge City, Kan., was 1878 when there were five homicides—a weekend's carnage in Washington, D.C., or Los Angeles. Gangsters in the 1920s? In 1929, the nation was horrified by the Valentine's Day Massacre in Chicago—an infamous event in which four mobsters shot and killed seven other mobsters. Last Feb. 14, there were 12 homicides in New York City alone.[60]

As *The Chicago Tribune* reported, modern firepower trends were compounded by an alarming escalation in use of firearms by and against children.[61] And Erik Larson in *The Atlantic* summed up the real-world effects:

> A relatively new phenomenon, originating in the 1980s, is the appearance of young children on the list of urban gunshot casualties. In 1987 a team of researchers from the UCLA School of Medicine and King/Drew Medical Center in Los Angeles found that King/Drew hadn't admitted a single child under ten for gunshot wounds before 1980. From 1980 to 1987 the center admitted thirty-four.[62]

As bad as it was, the rise of the "wondernine" was only the first turn in a spiral of lethality that gun industry innovation was to bring to the United States. While the nation's attention was focused on the potential for escalation from hot to cold to nuclear extinction in international relations, casualties exceeding any shooting war quietly mounted at home.

7—A Domestic Arms Race

The conversion from revolvers to high-capacity "wonder-nine" pistols in the early 1980s set in motion a spiral of lethality in the civilian pistol market that continues unabated today. Although the international arms race has cooled down, a domestic arms race almost unnoticed by the media has heated up. Similar to the international arms race in its mechanics, the domestic arms race is significantly different in its result—high-capacity pistols have killed more Americans since 1980 than all the weapons in all of the arsenals of the Eastern bloc.

Ironically, U.S. law enforcement agencies are one of the major forces driving the escalation of firepower on our streets. Just as governments on both sides of the Cold War saw every real—and imagined—arms development on the other side as reason for raising the stakes with newer and more deadly weapons, so have U.S. police agencies seen the appearance of the new wonder pistols as urgent cause for increasing their own firepower. And just as a complex of arms manufacturers profited by developing and selling new weapons to the Pentagon, so have pistol manufacturers profited by developing and selling more powerful guns to police agencies.

A key fact distinguishes gun manufacturers from defense contractors, however. Some defense contractors profit from "spin-offs" to the civilian market, but none sell the latest bombs, missiles, or high performance aircraft to U.S. civilians. Gun manufacturers, on the other hand, routinely sell their newest and most powerful guns on the civilian gun market. In fact, the civilian gun market is always the ultimate target, because it is larger and more lucrative than the law enforcement market. Sales to police agencies may be profitable stops along the way, but the big money lies in the civilian market. By working both sides of the arms race, selling new firepower to police and civilians alike, the gun industry feeds an endless cycle of escalation.

The next major turn in the lethality spiral came in the late 1980s and accelerated into the 1990s. Through most of the twentieth century, the six-shot double-action revolver was the standard sidearm

Making a Killing — 107

of almost all of state, local, and federal police agencies in the United States. The standard barrel length was four inches, but this varied under special circumstances. For example, detectives, who generally carry their guns in concealed holsters were often issued revolvers with two- or three-inch barrels. Some rural police agencies preferred the longer six-inch barrel. (All else being equal, accuracy and power for a given cartridge increase with barrel length.) The standard police ammunition was the .38 Special, although a few agencies fielded the more powerful .357-Magnum cartridge. A tiny minority carried semiautomatic pistols. In 1981, the NRA asked police schools if they issued guns to their officers, and, if so, what kind. Of those departments that issued sidearms, ninty-nine percent said they issued revolvers.[1]

As the new 9-mm pistols appeared on the civilian market and became more common in the hands of criminals in the early 1980s, some law enforcement officers began to complain that they were being "outgunned" by the new pistols. Encouraged by pistol manufacturers, more and more police agencies demanded conversion from their six-shot revolvers to the new 9-mm semiautomatic pistols.[2] Lt. Tommy Merritt of the Citrus County, Florida, sheriff's office, expressed a view common in 1988, saying, "The bad guys are using these guns. We know that. So why should policemen not be as up to date on weaponry as the bad guys?"[3]

The new police market was a godsend to the foreign and domestic arms manufacturers who had supplied the "bad guys" with the new pistols in the first place, through civilian market sales. Gun manufacturers joined in a pitched battle for the lucrative law enforcement contracts,[4] generating new demand as they fought it out for market share. The gun industry's sales pitch to police agencies was helped by the NRA and the U.S. Marine Corps, among others. The NRA's Law Enforcement Activities Division hosted a series of NRA semiautomatic pistol seminars at various locations around the country during the late 1980s. Companies like Heckler & Koch, Smith & Wesson, Sigarms, and Glock pitched the merits of their respective 9-mm pistols at these seminars, and provided samples for participants to shoot.[5] The first NRA seminar was held in October, 1987, at the U.S. Marine Base at Quantico, Virginia. The sold-out class of state, local, and federal law enforcement officials was welcomed by the commanding officer of the Marine Corps's Weapons Training Battalion.[6]

The martial welcome from a Marine Corps officer was an appropriate symbol. Drug arrests by state and local police doubled between 1981 and 1988, at about the same time the new pistols became popular with resurgent street gangs fighting for control of local turf and drug markets. Police officials and popular culture began to treat America's streets as combat zones, where winning the drug war justified new rules of engagement between citizens and police. "Police work on inner city streets is a domestic Vietnam," *U.S. News & World Report* said in 1990, "a dangerous no-win struggle fought by confused, misdirected and unappreciated troops."[7]

A few skeptics, however, questioned whether police really needed the 9-mm pistols and worried about the consequences of escalating lethal force on the streets. The skeptics raised three basic issues: How often do police actually get into gun battles? How much difference would a pistol make in such a gun battle? What new dangers to police and innocent civilians would the new pistols bring with them?

How Many Gun Battles?

Americans take for granted that sworn police officers, and many private security guards, carry guns and often use them. Indeed, if television shows and movies accurately portrayed real life, gun battles would be a daily occurrence in most police officers's lives. In fact, however, the chance of a police officer being involved in gun play is relatively low. Most gun carnage in the United States happens between civilians, and occurs before the police arrive. American University professor James Fyfe, for example, stated in 1990 that most officers never fire their guns on duty, and "the average big-city cop is involved in a fatal shooting every 450 years."[8]

There were 691,738 sworn police officers in the United States in 1993, the latest year for which data is available.[9] During that year, 67 officers were feloniously slain with a firearm and 4,002 were assaulted with firearms (another 5 officers died from unintentional shootings, such as training accidents or police crossfire, and suicide).[10] Assuming that any gun battle involving police either resulted in a felonious police fatality or a charge of assault against an officer, and ignoring any incidents involving the same officer more than once or incidents such as ambushes that were not actual gun battles, that works out to about 1 in every 170 police officers having been involved in some kind of shooting incident.

It would be foolish to deny that the possibility of a gun battle is always present in U.S. law enforcement. Gun battles do happen, usually unexpectedly and sometimes in spectacular fashion, like the July, 1998 assault that left two U.S. Capitol police officers dead, and the shooter and a tourist wounded. And some law enforcement officers in specialized duties—like those who investigate violent gangs and traffickers in drugs and guns—face a real daily risk of sudden armed violence. But the hard fact remains that most police officers will never use their gun in a fire fight. Thus, the question is whether arming every police officer in America for an event faced by a very few is wise, in light of the enhanced risk that greater firepower brings to the nation's streets. Wisely or not, most police agencies in America answered that question by opting to equip each of their officers with enough firepower for a shootout that less than one in every hundred would face.

How Much Difference Does the Pistol Make?

Even if one assumes that some police officers are going to get into gun battles, and decides that all police officers should be armed well enough to handle the worst case, the question still remains: How much firepower is enough? The argument in favor of arming police with semiautomatic pistols focused primarily on the pistol's magazine capacity. The twelve to fifteen rounds in a single loading of the pistol would seem to offer a clear advantage over the six rounds in the cylinder of a standard revolver. It is also easier to replace an empty pistol magazine with a full one than it is to reload a revolver, even though "speed loaders" have been developed so that all six rounds in a revolver's cylinder can be replaced at once. An officer with a pistol who reloads only once brings to the gunfight four to six times the number of rounds she would have reloading a revolver once.

But the matter isn't quite that simple. As it turns out, the number of shots exchanged in police gun battles are rarely so many as to exhaust a revolver's six-round capacity. The NRA reported in 1981 that the average exchange in a gunfight involving a police fatality lasted just 2.8 seconds, and only 2.5 shots were fired.[11] In other words, even less rounds were fired than the capacity of the revolver with which most officers were then equipped.

Little had changed twelve years later during the conversion frenzy. The director of firearms training for the Cook County, Illinois, sheriff's department, Patrick Costello, told the *Chicago Tribune* in 1993 that according to FBI statistics most police gun battles "occur within 10 feet, 2.1 rounds are fired, and it happens within a second and a half."[12]

These circumstances—the rapid exchange of a few shots at close range—make the pistol's greater ammunition capacity moot. Handgun expert Libourel reviewed the police conversion frenzy for *Guns & Ammo* in 1994. Libourel wrote that although "the auto pistol has a decided edge over the revolver . . . such firepower is rarely needed." In fact, "Quite a few revolver-armed police agencies have reported that they have *never* had an incident in which an officer had to reload under fire during a gunfight." Libourel continues:

> During the heyday of the police switchover . . . I would occasionally be contacted by firearms training officers about aspects of the transition. Invariably, I would ask if there had been any incidents in which the revolver had been found wanting or in which officers had suffered injury or death because of the limited firepower of their service revolvers. Without fail, I always got a slightly sheepish "no" in reply.[13]

But could the pistol's greater capacity save officers' lives if they *did* have to reload? Not very often, according to experts who pointed out that most police officers killed on duty are killed in circumstances of surprise.

"Most of our officers who have been killed never got off a round," said Maj. Jimmy Hall, then-chief of training for the Atlanta Police Department. "If you have a pistol, it's there more for confidence than anything."[14]

The question of officer confidence may in the end have decided the issue. Police officers simply felt better being armed with the same pistols the "bad guys" had, and few politicians or career police officials were willing to contradict them. (Deference to the officers's sensibilities had its limits, however: Officers at one police department wanted to be armed with Uzi submachine guns — their proposal was rejected.)[15] By 1989 so many police departments had converted to the pistol that the NRA officially changed the name of its annual police marksmanship competition from the long-standing National Police Revolver Championships to National Police Shooting Championships. The *American Rifleman* explained, "No longer do revolvers hold a monopoly on competitive equipment. Semi-auto pistols are rapidly coming into their own as competitors's tools, just as increasing numbers of officers and departments switch to them for duty use."[16]

What New Dangers?

Whether or not the new pistols make police officers safer, they make citizens less safe.[17]

In some cases, police argued that conversion to the 9-mm pistols would make streets safer. An Escondido, California, police spokesman claimed that 9-mm rounds were safer because — for some unexplained reason — the rounds supposedly would not pass through the bodies of persons shot with them.[18] But experts agree that, putting aside random effects such as the bullet striking bone, whether or not a bullet passes through a person depends on the shape, composition, and velocity of the bullet, not merely the caliber of the gun.

As it happened, controversy arose in Escondido within two years after the department switched to the "wondernine," when an officer fired fourteen rounds into a seventeen-year-old boy allegedly fighting for control of the officer's gun. "People assume that's overkill," said a police spokesman, "but if your life is threatened, you keep shooting until you neutralize the threat."[19] Or as one Chicago police official said in 1990, "If you've got more rounds, there's a temptation to use them. . . . The capacity to shoot innocent people is greater."[20]

Officers apparently yielded to the understandable "temptation" to use more rounds. Libourel reported in 1991 that the average number of shots fired by police "has begun climbing because of 'spray and pray' shooting by officers armed with high-volume nines."[21] New York City police officers were reported to have fired more rounds, with fewer hits, as the NYPD began converting to pistols from revolvers.[22]

At least one pistol, the Glock, appeared to make both police and citizens less safe, as an alleged design defect caused numerous accidental firings, killing or injuring innocent bystanders or police officers. According to Lars-Erik Nelson, unlike conventional double action and double action only, in which "the trigger must be pulled back an inch or more, against increasing resistance, to cock the hammer and fire each shot," the Glock model in question "is always about 70% cocked. Squeezing the trigger moves it back an imperceptibly short distance, against no resistance. Then the finger encounters pressure from a spring 4 to 8 pounds or more, depending on the setting and the gun goes off. And, too often, goes off and goes off and goes off as tense officers empty their magazines with virtually no effort."[23] A District of Columbia police officer's three-year-old daughter accidentally killed herself with her father's Glock pistol, and by the end of 1996, at least thirty-five suits had been filed against Glock alleging the 9-mm pistol discharges too easily.[24]

In the end, the semi-automatic pistols swept the field, "dictated more by fashion than by real need," in the words of *Guns & Ammo*'s Libourel.[25] His colleague Evan Marshall worried whether police officers were getting adequate training after switching from revolvers to pistols: "Changing weapons just to be trendy is a mistake that can have fatal results," he wrote.[26] *Guns & Ammo* expert Sheriff Jim Wilson, concluded that "too often the high-capacity feature is seen as a substitute for training, tactics and marksmanship," and lamented that "police departments around the nation have fallen victim to this fallacy and issued high-capacity autos when all they really needed was an increase in the amount of training. . . ."[27]

But even as the tide of police conversion to the 9-mm pistol was rising in 1986, a bloody shoot-out in Miami started a series of events that would set off another round of increased lethality in law enforcement and civilian armament. That spiral continues today and, ironically, struck back where it started with the 1997 murder of designer Gianni Versace in Miami.

The 1986 gun battle in Miami between an FBI team and two heavily armed felons left two FBI agents dead and five more wounded before their assailants were killed. The carnage shook the FBI to its core and ignited heated debate both in and out of the law enforcement community over whether the FBI team was "outgunned" by superior weapons or simply displayed poor tactical judgment.[28]

The two felons, wanted for a series of violent crimes, were armed with a Ruger Mini-14 223-caliber assault rifle, .357-Magnum revolvers, and a Smith & Wesson Model 3000 riot gun in "assault format," i.e. with a pistol grip and extended magazine. The agents were armed with a variety of weapons, including then standard-issue Smith & Wesson .357-Magnum revolvers loaded with .38 Special high-pressure ammunition, 9-mm pistols, and a Remington 870 riot shotgun. Due to a series of mishaps, not all of these firearms were deployed. In addition, only one of the agents wore body armor, although they knew the felons were heavily armed. Over a hundred rounds were fired by the FBI agents in the gun battle, which started as agents in several different cars attempted to stop the felons in their car.[29]

Central to the ensuing debate was the fact that early in the gun battle—apparently before any of the FBI agents was seriously wounded—one of the felons was shot in the chest with a 9-mm Winchester Silvertip jacketed hollow-point round that stopped about two inches short of his heart. Although by all accounts the wound severed an artery and would have eventually been fatal in any case, the felon was able to continue fighting effectively. Both seriously wounded felons were eventually despatched by a wounded agent who shot and killed them with a 38 caliber revolver as they prepared to drive off in an FBI car.[30]

Notwithstanding criticism of the agents's tactics from some quarters, the FBI concluded that the major problem was the inadequacy of its agents's firepower. "All other things aside, Miami was an ammunition failure," the chief of the FBI's firearms training unit was quoted as saying in 1990.[31] In short, the 9-mm was suspected, at least in the FBI's eyes, of not being good enough for a serious firefight if it could leave a man with a mortal wound standing long enough to still fight and kill others.

This conclusion led the FBI to conduct an extensive series of tests on a variety of handgun rounds, searching for a round that would most reliably and immediately incapacitate an assailant with a reasonable hit.[32] These tests put the FBI right in the middle of a heated and long-running debate in the gun community about the adequacy of the 9-mm round for armed combat.

One school, typified by gun writer Jeff Cooper ("the gunner's guru"), favored big rounds like the .45 Auto used in the old Colt Model 1911 pistol, the military's erstwhile standard sidearm, for "serious" pistol work. They dismissed the 9-mm as too "puny" a caliber for the military and the police, work to which it was increasingly being assigned with the Pentagon's switch to the Beretta pistol and the wave of police conversion to wondernines. "The hopelessly underpowered 9-mm Parabellum cartridge is fine for practice and demonstration," opined Cooper in 1987, "but quite unsatisfactory for use in a fight."[33]

The other school favored the 9-mm overall. It generally conceded the .45's power without conceding ground on the 9-mm's lethality. But it cited the greater ammunition capacity, lighter recoil, and thus easier handling of 9-mm pistols over .45 Auto pistols. Typical of this school was the remark of Libourel that, "Left to my own devices, I would choose the extra capacity, light recoil and abundant ammo of the nine."[34] Some accused Cooper and others of unreasonably clinging to the past and of being unwilling to fairly judge the 9-mm. This school dismissed putative failures attributed to the 9-mm—including the FBI disaster—as poorly documented anecdotes that, if real, were caused by poor tactics, bad marksmanship, or improper loadings.

It is important to understand that no one seriously disputed the capability of either round—indeed a round in any caliber—to kill. Police reports are full of homicides successfully effected with the lowly 22-caliber rimfire round, about as puny a firearms round as one can get. And the mounting death toll accompanying the proliferation of wondernines on America's streets was evidence enough of the 9-mm's lethality. What was at issue in this debate was stopping power, or the ability of a reasonably placed bullet to end a gun fight immediately by completely incapacitating the opponent.

Given the Pentagon's decision to switch to the 9-mm for the standard military sidearm, the debate was to some extent academic. But the gun industry continued to experiment with handgun ammunition more powerful than the 9-mm round, and with compact handguns to fire that ammunition. These experiments, which still continue, eventually led first to the development and marketing of the modern 10-mm auto round, and then to its near twin, the 40-caliber Smith & Wesson.

Resurrected and modernized from a defunct turn-of-the-century loading, the modern 10-mm auto round first appeared in the late 1970s when a Swedish ammunition company, Norma, was persuaded to manufacture the cartridge for a new American-produced 10-mm semiautomatic pistol to be known as the "Bren Ten."[35] The 10-mm auto bullet is both heavier and wider than the 9-mm bullet. Equating to 40 caliber, the 10-mm bullet comes close to the .45 Auto in size. The standard Norma powder loading exceeded the standard .45 Auto loading, giving the 10-mm Auto bullet greater velocity, both from the muzzle and down range. Since the momentum of an object like a bullet equals its mass times its velocity, the 10-mm was a suitable successor to the Colt Model 1911 .45 pistol, its higher velocity making up for its somewhat lesser mass.

Cooper and other fans of the "big round" enthusiastically endorsed the Bren Ten in the gun press. Cooper allowed the logo of his Gunsite Raven Corporation—a stylized Raven with spread wings, not dissimilar in appearance from the infamous spread eagle used in various Nazi insignia—to be stamped on the guns as a sign of his endorsement.[36] The Bren Ten was also featured on the popular *Miami Vice* television show. But the gun quickly sank from the market, apparently because the manufacturers could not make and deliver the gun complete with magazines in any quantity.[37]

This left Norma with a potentially popular ammunition round but no guns to shoot it in. Colt stepped into this breach by redesigning the Model 1911 pistol to handle the 10-mm round and marketing it as the Colt Delta Elite.[38] In 1987, Cooper introduced the Delta Elite to the market in a "first look" article, again enthusiastically endorsing the 10-mm round and the gun. He explained the 10-mm's appeal to his big bullet school, noting its key drawback:

> The .45 ACP cartridge is excellent for short-range self-defense, but lacks range and penetration. The 10, using a proper bullet shape, is theoretically slightly superior to the .45 in stopping power, and demonstrably superior in reach. Its drawback is that it is a high-pressure cartridge and calls for stronger machinery than most pistol actions afford.[39]

Colt's Delta Elite sparked a renewed wave of serious interest in the 10-mm. By 1989 all of the major ammunition manufacturers were producing 10-mm cartridges and a number of handgun manufacturers, including Smith & Wesson, were marketing guns to shoot the round.[40]

This was the state of affairs when the FBI weighed in after the Miami disaster. Its intercession gave the debate greater importance than mere internecine sniping in the pages of the gun press. "The FBI enjoys enormous prestige among American law enforcement agencies, and their disenchantment with the 9-mm led many departments to hold back on a decision to go to the 9-mm," according to Libourel.[41]

The FBI conducted an exhaustive series of tests, putting 9-mm, .380-auto, .38-Special, .357-Magnum, 10-mm, and .45-Auto rounds through a variety of conditions (shooting through clothing, automobile window glass, wallboard, etc.)[42] The agency finally announced in September 1989 that it was converting to 10-mm semi-automatic pistols, replacing its long-standard .357-Magnum revolvers with Smith & Wesson Model 1076 pistols. The ammunition would be a reduced charge version of the 10-mm round. "Full-charge 10-mm ammunition performed extremely well in the testing," explained *American Rifleman*, "but staffers agreed that recoil and muzzle blast were too severe for everyday use."[43]

The FBI decision did not settle the debate about the merits of the 9-mm,[44] but it had two significant effects that have helped boost handgun lethality over the long term.

First, the FBI decision to go to pistols provided strong incentive for any local departments that might have been wavering on the fundamental issue of conversion to switch from revolvers to pistols (in whatever caliber).[45] Second, it ignited another round of lethal escalation in both police rearmament and civilian market trend-setting, as the gun industry hastened first to market the now officially favored more powerful 10-mm pistols, and then their near twins, the 40-caliber pistols:

> Since the 1930s, the Bureau has been a trend-setter in law-enforcement equipment and procedures. Whatever the Bureau uses, lots of agencies will likewise use. That extends to handguns and ammunition. It also follows that defensive handgunners of other sorts may be influenced by what the Bureau is doing.[46]

The gun industry quickly focused on marketing the new developments to those "defensive handgunners of other sorts," i.e., civilian shooters. Smith & Wesson, for example, immediately put a civilian version of the FBI 10-mm on the market. The civilian gun differed from the FBI model only by the addition of a magazine safety.[47]

But in an ultimately more far-reaching move inspired by the FBI trials, Smith & Wesson entered into a joint venture with ammunition manufacturer Olin/Winchester to develop an entirely new round—the .40 S&W—and a new gun to go with it. "The .40 Smith & Wesson bandwagon started rolling on January 17, 1990 when S&W announced their new cartridge and Model 4006 handgun at a SHOT Show press conference," *Guns & Ammo* reported in 1990. "It is essentially a combat handgun cartridge."[48]

The .40 S&W was developed plainly and simply as a means to mass market lethality. It was compelled by a few fundamental facts of handgun design. Although the 10-mm cartridge was powerful enough for the FBI, its high pressure also demanded a relatively big gun to handle its potent recoil forces, even in reduced charge. The cartridge's size also did not lend itself well to double-stacked high-capacity magazines. The .40 S&W cartridge overcame both of these objections, thus making it possible to develop and market handguns more powerful than the 9-mm pistol while preserving its concealability and high ammunition capacity. Gun writers enthused about the new cartridge:

Compared to 9mm handguns and their best ammunition, a .40 S&W holds almost as many shots, but they're better, harder-hitting shots. Compared to the .45 ACP, a .40 S&W holds more shots, and they strike with enough gusto as to compare favorably with the legendary old .45 cartridge.[49]

This is a compact little round shooting a hefty slug at respectable velocities—a cartridge which S&W and Winchester know will fit into a compact pistol and which they hope will catch the fancy of law-enforcement, defensive and competitive shooters.[50]

In short, the .40 S&W ratcheted lethality up several notches, and, according to a 1991 article in *American Rifleman,* it came not a moment too soon for the industry:

With the 9-mm market pretty thoroughly glutted with single-actions, double-actions, decockers, trigger-cockers, compacts and even revolvers, manufacturers have had to diversify to find something new. Last year's solution was the .40 S&W. . . . [51]

Glock announced its .40 S&W model within less than two months.[52] The new cartridge "experienced phenomenal acceptance," another *American Rifleman* reported. Within one year "every major American ammunition manufacturer had one or more loads either in production or scheduled, and gun companies adding it to their lines were almost too numerous to count."[53] Manufacturers such as Spain's Star also immediately developed "ultra-compact" 40-caliber models for maximum concealability.[54]

After noting the .40 S&W's success in 1990, a 1991 *American Rifleman* article predicted that "big action for 1991 and beyond seems to be the double-action and/or large-capacity .45."[55] At about the same time, *Guns & Ammo* noted that "the tendency in current automatic-pistol design is toward a pistol the size of and near the capacity of a 9mm, but with increased power."[56] Indeed, Glock, Smith & Wesson, Ruger, Star, and others were already marketing new .45 Autos in increasingly "compact" sizes with higher-capacity magazines by the early 1990s,[57] and Canada's Para-Ordnance offered a kit to convert the old seven-round Colt Model 1911 to a fourteen-shot (13 + 1) high-capacity pistol.[58] In sum, the gun industry was designing and making guns that were smaller, held more rounds, and fired more powerful cartridges than ever before.

In 1997, the 40-caliber story came full circle. Andrew Cunanan committed suicide in Miami by shooting himself in the mouth with a 40-caliber Taurus pistol. It was the same gun with which he had allegedly ambushed and killed fashion designer Gianni Versace in Miami, and shot to death two other men in a spree of cross-country murders.[59]

8—The Rambo Factor

The gun industry learned from the "Wondernines" that lethality in guns is like nicotine in cigarettes—an addictive hook set deep into the irrational side of its customers. Accordingly, the industry has loaded up its products with greater firepower, military innovation, and deadly concealability since the 1980s. The gun industry projects fantasies of the good, or "virtuous," use of guns to sell this lethal mix. These fantasies—conveyed by advertising and through collateral marketing in the gun press—exploit images of macho warriors like "Rambo," standing alone against a sinister and sold-out state, and the good father (or mother) quietly arming to defend the peaceable family against a vague but ubiquitous evil "other" stalking America's landscape.

As a result, two of the most lethal marketing trends in the U.S. gun industry's history began in the 1980s and continue well into the 1990s: the invasion of semiautomatic assault weapons, and so-called "pocket rockets."

THE INVASION OF ASSAULT WEAPONS

Semiautomatic assault weapons are slightly modified versions of guns designed for military use where it is desired to deliver a high rate of fire over a less than precise killing zone, a procedure often called "hosing down" an area.[1] (The exact opposite of the assault weapon would be the sniper rifle, designed to deliver precisely a meticulously aimed round to a single, carefully selected target. The gun press and some manufacturers, by the way, have shown chilling enthusiasm lately in marketing sniper rifles to civilians.) By employing cosmetic design changes and cleverly splitting legal hairs, the manufacturers and importers of these deadly military-style guns have successfully evaded all efforts to regulate their products. Like stubbornly resilient weeds, artful mutations of "banned" assault guns creep back on to the civilian market within weeks of every new law or regulatory reform aimed at restricting their sale.

There is virtually no civilian market for military assault weapons.

Because they have fully automatic fire capability, military assault weapons are machine guns. Federal law has barred the sale of new machine guns to civilians since 1986, and heavily regulates sales of older models to civilians. (Nevertheless, many civilian semiautomatic assault weapons can easily be converted to fully automatic fire using only simple tools well within the grasp of a competent hobbyist, guided through each step with "how-to" books and videotapes available through mail order catalogs.)[2] Manufacturers simply developed semiautomatic versions to get around this obstacle and sell assault guns to civilians. As one industry expert observed, "While a full-automatic weapon has only a limited market, one manufactured in both auto and semi-auto only will often enjoy handsome profits, thanks to a free society's inexhaustible compulsion to purchase firearms."[3]

Although civilian assault guns do not have fully automatic capability, they retain the generic design features that make them ideal for rapidly laying down a wide field of fire. Principal among these features are the ability to accept high-capacity magazines, capable of holding from twenty to more than a hundred rounds of ammunition, and devices that make it easier to simply point (as opposed to carefully aim) the gun while rapidly pulling the trigger. These pointing devices include pistol grips — or magazines that function like pistol grips — on the fore end of the gun and barrel shrouds, which are ventilated tubes that surround the otherwise too-hot-to-hold barrel, providing an area that is cool enough to be directly grasped by the shooter even after scores of rounds have been fired. Such features make it easier for the shooter to "point and shoot" (as from the hip), and help the shooter control recoil. A *Guns & Ammo* review of the Partisan Avenger .45 assault pistol noted, for example, that when the gun "is fired rapidly from the hip, its swivelling front grip makes for easy and comfortable control of the recoil," and that the "forward pistol grip extension of this powerful assault pistol not only helps point it instinctively at the target but goes a long way to controlling the effects of recoil."[4] The NRA and other reviewers have commented favorably on the hip-firing capabilities of many other assault weapons.[5]

Taken together, these features make it possible for the shooter of the civilian assault gun to "hose down" a relatively wide area with a lethal spray of bullets, and to do it quickly. The NRA tested one such gun, the Calico M-100 rifle, in 1987 and reported that "the full 100 rounds were sent downrange in 14 seconds by one flicker-fingered tester."[6] Put another way, the semiautomatic assault gun sprayed a standard revolver's entire capacity—six rounds—in less than one second, and did it fourteen times over. This increase in lethality makes semiautomatic assault weapons particularly dangerous in civilian use, and explains why terrorists, mass killers, and violent criminals prefer them. It also distinguishes them from true hunting or target guns.

Some defenders of assault weapons have argued that because the civilian semiautomatic versions are not fully automatic machine guns, they are less lethal than the military guns they are patterned after. But Army tests and expert opinion have shown that automatic fire is significantly less accurate than semiautomatic fire, both because the shooter is less disciplined with a machine gun and because the muzzle of an automatic gun tends to "creep" upward dramatically in all but the most well-trained hands.[7] Semiautomatic fire is more effective over a longer range than automatic fire (e.g., six hundred meters for the AK-47 in semiautomatic fire compared to 300 meters for the same gun in full auto.)[8] "Rapid semi-auto fire was to be used in preference to full-auto," a *Gun Digest* expert said in discussing the design of the Sturmgewehr 44, a Second World War German gun often singled out as the model military assault rifle. "This is the most effective way to get hits in combat."[9]

In other words, civilian semiautomatic assault weapons are potentially *more lethal* than their fully automatic military kin—more effective "to get hits in combat"—and they are often cheaper. As *Guns & Ammo*'s review of the Partisan Avenger noted, fully automatic submachine guns like the MAC-10 machine pistol upon the design of which the Avenger was based "are rarely used full-auto anyway . . . [so] for vastly less money, guns like the Partisan Avenger allow you to have your cake, eat it too and still afford to eat again."[10]

Gun manufacturers have iced this cake of civilian assault guns with other features, derived directly from military service needs, that make them more lethal than ordinary sporting guns. For example, some assault rifles feature folding or telescoping stocks. The "stock" is the long end of a rifle or shotgun that the shooter rests against shoulder and cheek when firing the gun. In a sporting rifle or shotgun, the stock is usually made of wood, and in an expensive model may be made of exotic wood and may be intricately carved or "checkered" with a cross-hatched design. Military stocks are more often made of plastic or other synthetic material without embellishment. Folding stocks were developed primarily for use by paratroopers and other special forces who needed more compact firearms than standard military rifles. A stock that can be folded or collapsed reduces the size of the gun considerably. In a military context, this makes the gun less likely to tangle in shroud lines or other gear.[11] In a civilian (or special police such as the U.S. Secret Service) context, it makes the gun more concealable while being carried clandestinely. A folded stock also makes it easier to hold the firearm close to the body in a from-the-hip spray firing position.

Other features of dubious civilian value include grenade launchers[12] and threaded barrels that make it possible to add accessories such as silencers to reduce the gun's noise or "report" (purists call these devices "suppressors" on the ground that no gun can be made truly silent),[13] "flash suppressors" (or "flash hiders"), which reduce the visibility at night of the flash from the burning gases that erupt from the barrel's muzzle,[14] and bipods to support the front of the barrel while firing in a prone position. The *Ruger Carbine Cookbook*, an "operational manual and accessory guide," says about bipods and flash suppressors: "While of little if any use for the average shooter," they could have practical applications under certain survival conditions, such as sniper work against occupation forces.[15]

Owners of civilian assault guns can buy these features through the mail as custom accessories to convert their weapons to military clones. One "after-market" supplier advertised an accessory package to "upgrade your Ruger Mini-14s classic WWII design and make it look and function like a modern combat weapon should." Among the features in the package were pistol grips and a telescoping stock that could be closed "for transport and fast 'in close' work."[16] Another mail order supplier, Gander Mountain, regularly offered accessories "that will convert your present Ruger 10/22 into a handsome rapid fire survival or S.W.A.T. weapon."[17] The source of these accessories was Ram-Line, which advertised its "banana clips" in the NRA's *American Rifleman* as giving "the thrill of 50 continuous rounds of .22 firepower!!!"[18] *American Rifleman* enthusiastically reviewed a Ram-Line device that made it possible to load a fifty round 22 caliber "banana clip" in about one minute.[19] *Guns & Ammo* noted that, with these "aftermarket add-ons," one could convert the Ruger 10/22 "to a military configuration."[20]

Assault weapons in .22 caliber, by the way, present an interesting introduction to the ATF's anemic enforcement of firearms import restrictions. The agency has ruled that the statutory sporting-purpose test, which it applies halfheartedly to other foreign assault guns proposed for import, is automatically met by firearms in .22 caliber, even if they are in an assault configuration. The ATF's putative rationale is that since .22 caliber is traditionally viewed as "sporting" ammunition, any weapon that uses it must be a "sporting" weapon. Although the relatively small and inexpensive .22 round is indeed often used for many sporting purposes (just as are some other popular calibers), the ATF's ruling misses an obvious point. It is the overall configuration of the firearm that makes assault weapons, including those in 22 caliber, so lethal:

> Some people tend to regard the .22 rimfire as a toy. Yet in experienced hands, a .22 can be a very effective hunting arm as well as a weapon. With the right accessories for the given application, its effectiveness can be greatly increased.[21]

A writer reviewing the domestically produced Intratec TEC-22 Scorpion, a .22 assault pistol, described the essence of such 22-caliber effectiveness in 1989:

> For quite some time now, savvy shooters have been aware of the fact that rapid, multiple hits with a .22 have more than a simple additive function. If a large number of .22s are concentrated in a given target area fast enough, they can have devastating effect.[22]

In whatever caliber, assault weapons caught on big in the United States. Gun magazines in the 1980s featured a steady stream of favorable reviews of various types of assault weapons.[23] A 1989 *San Diego Union-Tribune* article detailed the "surging interest" in assault weapons during a period of general decline for the gun market and declared that "manufacturers have been quick to cash in on the craze."[24] A 1992 *New York Times* survey of the industry summed up the assault weapons phenomenon as "popular toys for shooting-range commandos, and tools of swagger and intimidation for drug lords."[25] Several domestic manufacturers (such as Florida's Intratec) built their business solely on assault guns, and a number of foreign manufacturers—including the Israeli maker of the Uzi submachine gun and the British maker of the Sten submachine gun—specifically redesigned their military guns to cash in on the U.S. import market.[26] Even Chinese air rifles imported into the United States feature the "assault rifle look."[27]

Many factors combined to help the emergence of assault weapons in the civilian market during the 1980s. The gun industry capitalized on all of these factors by flooding the market with new designs, and promoting their sale through advertising and gun press puffery. During the 1980s, popular television shows like *The A-Team* and *Miami Vice,* and movies like the *Rambo* series, *Commando*, and others prominently featured assault weapons. The military service of Vietnam veterans also resulted in familiarity with such weapons among a significant part of the general population.[28]

But one of the most sinister factors boosting assault weapons was the parallel emergence during the 1980s of the so-called "survivalist" movement. This movement encompasses a wide spectrum of thought, but much of it has been closely associated with the political paranoia and extreme racial and cultural views of the far right that eventually mutated into the militia phenomenon of the 1990s. The adherents of survivalism subscribe to various theories predicting cataclysmic political, economic, or military disasters. These range from a millennial apocalypse, through the "sell out" of the government to a foreign power or new world order, to the rise of a domestic police state (invariably controlled by undesirable aliens or racial, ethnic, and religious minorities). In general, the theories of these extremists declare that there inevitably will be either widespread collapse of civil order (as in a race war), severe suppression of civil liberties, or both, and they advocate that prudent persons heavily arm themselves for "survival" under such extreme circumstances.

In 1982 *Guns & Ammo* listed the "success of military assault rifles in the civilian market, together with the 'survivalist' movement they represent"[29] as one of the "10 Unlikeliest Ideas in the Shooting Sports Which Have Succeeded." And in a 1989 article on the "top 10 gun trends of the decade," one writer opined, "Ten years ago, black guns [assault weapons] were fairly rare. Then interest in survival-oriented items increased tremendously, and these interests included guns."[30] Assault weapon manufacturers specifically emphasized the utility of their firearms as "survival" guns.[31] Gun writers also noted the survivalist connection in gun reviews. As *Guns & Ammo* commented in a 1981 review of the Volunteer Enterprises Commando Mark 9, "Call it Walter Mitty-ism, an increasing concern over 'urban survival,' or whatever you like, but the fact that shooters are becoming more interested in modern military and military look-alike guns cannot be denied. Sales of assault rifles, auto-pistols and accessories have soared over the past few years. . . . [32] Another *Guns & Ammo* writer explained that "to survivalists, these compact carbines combine a wealth of firepower into a small package."[33] Gun magazines during this period carried advertising for "survival knives,"[34] for books effusing a generalized nostalgia for the "action" of the Vietnam war era,[35] and for military style clothing and gear.[36]

It was not a coincidence that David Koresh's millenarian Branch Davidian compound in Waco, Texas, was well-stocked with assault weapons, a number of which had been converted to fully automatic fire and were used as machine-guns against federal agents. Nor is it unusual for members of other extremist groups apprehended in the course of terrorist activities to be found in possession of these military-style weapons.

The question of what to call this uncomfortable class of firearms has become increasingly important in the debate over efforts to control them. The linguistic war over nomenclature is an illustration of how the gun industry and its supporters use semantics to obfuscate reality and control damage to their image.

Originally, the gun industry had little doubt about what to call civilian semiautomatic assault weapons. The gun press enthusiastically and flatly used military terms and the word "assault" to describe these guns when they first became popular in the early 1980s. Gun writers freely called them "assault rifles," "assault pistols," or "military assault" weapons and candidly discussed the features that distinguish assault weapons from such other semiautomatic guns as the ordinary hunting rifle.[37] Likewise, gun manufacturers actively used the military character of semiautomatic assault weapons and their lethality-enhancing features as positive selling points. The German company Heckler & Koch published advertisements stressing the military lineage of its civilian "assault rifles."[38] Intratec boasted that its TEC-9 "clearly stands out among high capacity assault-type pistols."[39] Magnum Research advertised that the Galil rifle system to which it had import rights "outperformed every other assault rifle."[40] And a cottage industry of after-market suppliers sprang up, including one aptly named Assault Systems, posting ads aimed at owners of civilian "assault weapons."[41]

The industry and its friends frantically backpedaled in later years, however, when assault weapons fell into wide disfavor among the general public and legislative proposals were floated to regulate them. Gun writers suddenly complained that a "real" assault weapon had to have the "selective fire" capability (i.e., the ability to switch between semiautomatic and fully automatic fire) that only military weapons have.[42] Thus, in the conveniently revised orthodoxy of the firearms establishment, there suddenly was no such thing as a civilian assault weapon, since all civilian guns were by definition semiautomatic only. If semiautomatic assault weapons don't exist, what's all the fuss about? Writers also pooh-poohed the utility of the same distinctive design features that they had earlier praised, and claimed that civilian assault rifles were getting a bad rap just because they "looked" evil. By thus denying the distinctive nature of civilian assault guns, the NRA in particular and others in general could disingenuously claim that anyone who proposes to regulate them is really going after *all* semiautomatic firearms, even hunting rifles. (The NRA's stand in favor of assault weapons is no surprise. The organization has named repeal of the 1986 federal ban on production of *machine guns* for civilian use a top priority.) This obfuscation alarmed many owners of traditional semiautomatic hunting rifles.

Unfortunately for these assault weapons advocates, however, one of their own had already poured a different mold. Leading firearms expert, prolific gun writer, and hard-core proponent of assault weapons Duncan Long—who believes that "every family should own an assault weapon or two and should be permitted to carry concealed weapons"[43]—dismissed this line of argument in his definitive 1986 publication, *Assault Pistols, Rifles and Submachine Guns*. Long wrote at length on the issue:

> The next problem arises if you make a semiauto-only model of one of these selective-fire rifles. According to the purists, an assault rifle has to be selective fire. Yet, if you think about it, it's a little hard to accept the idea that firearms with extended magazines, pistol grip stock, etc. cease to be assault rifles by changing a bit of metal. . . . I think the manufacturers are on the right track when they call all these rifles "assault rifles" rather than distinguishing between assault rifles, battle rifles, and semiauto, former assault rifles, or however a purist would classify a semiauto assault rifle.[44]

In fact, the early gun press is so laden with examples explicitly treating semiautomatic versions as assault weapons that it is clear the industry and its supporters are now trying to make a public relations problem disappear by defining civilian assault weapons out of existence.[45]

One is compelled to a similar conclusion when the industry's "ugly looks" rationale is examined. Defenders of assault weapons accuse those who wish to regulate them of simply not liking the guns' "ugly" looks. These defenders characterize the guns's physical appearance as merely irrelevant "cosmetic features," arguing that a semiautomatic is a semiautomatic, regardless of what it may look like.[46] *American Rifleman*, for example, dismissed as "fevered scribblings" editorials criticizing as assault guns weapons with the characteristics of firearms like the AA Arms AP-9.[47]

In fact, however, enthusiastic reviewers and advertisers alike made a positive selling point of the power of assault weapons to intimidate precisely through their cosmetics, i.e., their martial looks. For example, *Guns & Ammo* expert Garry James noted in his review of Colt's 9-mm AR-15 that "the intimidation factor of a black, martial-looking carbine pointing in one's direction cannot be underestimated,"[48] and Howard French of the same magazine said of the HK-94 9-mm Paracarbine that "you would not get much static from an intruder eyeballing its rather lethal appearance."[49] C.A. Inc. advertisements for the Mark 45 and Mark 9 tommy-gun-style carbines also explicitly made the point that "a show of force can be stopping power worth having":[50]

> Some have been shocked by their appearance, which is not merely cosmetic, but a result of highly practical design which, incidentally, added a great deal to their look of authority. This proved to be a big plus since they were originally designed as a deterrent weapon for law enforcement.[51]

And police officials have testified that criminals use the threatening look of these guns for their intimidation effect.

It is ironic, not to mention contradictory, that the NRA should have smugly dismissed as "fevered scribbling" a criticism of the looks of the A.A. Arms AP-9. An earlier *Guns & Ammo* review of precisely the same gun touted the appeal of its "wicked looks" to the less than mature personalities of *teenagers*:

> . . . it is one mean-looking dude, considered cool and Ramboish by the teenage crowd; to a man, they love the AP9 at first sight. Stuffed to the brim with Nyclad hollow points, the pistol is about as wicked a piece as you can keep by your pillow, or hiding 'neath your car seat (where legal of course). . . . Take a look at one. And let your teen-age son tag along. Ask him what *he* thinks. (Emphasis in original).[52]

Marketing appeals like this to teenagers and even younger children are common in the gun industry at large and have often appeared in articles and ads about assault weapons in particular. For example, in a January 1987 *Guns & Ammo* cover story on .22 assault rifles, the author relates how he "demonstrated to teen-age friend Scott Hancock how to achieve machinegun-like firepower by rapidly flickering his trigger finger" inside the guard of one of the guns highlighted.[53] The article was illustrated with photos of what were described as "youngsters" brandishing a variety of assault rifles, including a militarized Ruger 10/22. A caption advises that "military-style .22 . . . are handy guns for youngsters." The cover of the 1991 Feather Industries catalog features a boy—who appears to be at best in his early teen years—holding one of the company's assault rifles and beaming up at an adult man. Another assault rifle, ammunition, and various accessories lie on a table behind the boy.[54] An advertisement for Fleming Firearms showed an infant girl in a playsuit, about two years of age, in a three-quarters rear profile, holding an assault weapon while standing in front of an array of assault guns mounted on a pegboard wall. The caption reads "Short BUTTS From FLEMING FIREARMS!!!"[55] The word play might be inappropriate in any context, but in the context of assault weapons it approaches the pathological.

The gun industry has also changed its tune regarding the sporting uses of assault weapons as they have come under fire. The NRA, for example, originally found assault guns to be of limited utility. In a review of the Calico M-100, the NRA's writer concluded that "The M-100 is certainly not a competition gun, hardly a hunting gun, and is difficult to visualize as a personal defense gun."[56] A 1983 *Guns & Ammo* review of the HK-94 reported similarly that "You certainly aren't going to enter any serious, formal matches with it."[57]

A few years later, however, when the guns were under attack, the NRA and others claimed that assault weapons were in fact useful for each of those same three categories—competition, hunting, and personal defense. A 1992 article in *American Rifleman*, for example, highlighted the Colt Cup target competition with the military M-16 and its civilian derivative, the AR-15, as if the fact that a gun could be used for target shooting erased its fundamental character as a weapon designed and suitable for war.[58] In candid contrast, the assault weapon's true basic utility was captured in a 1990 *Guns & Ammo* review of another Calico model, the 900 carbine:

> In a military or police setting, where there's a premium on a compact firearm that delivers a maximum of firepower, the Calico would seem to be an excellent choice. It would make a fine entry weapon for SWAT teams, possibly also a suitable gun for delivering fire as assault teams ma-

neuver into position against a defended crack house or the
like. . . . Although sales to civilians may be restricted in some localities (like our own California) the Calicos remain marketable in others.[59]

The Calicos were not available in California because they had by
then been banned by the state, and pressure was mounting in Washington to ban them nationwide.

The bloom wore off the rose of assault weapons during the 1980s
first because police complained increasingly that the guns were
showing up in the hands of criminals, especially drug gangs. "We've
seen a proliferation because of the drug trade," ATF spokesman
Tom Hill said in 1988. "More and more people want to have increased firepower and the status of having the semiautomatic assault
type weapon. It looks dangerous."[60] The guns not only looked dangerous, they *were* dangerous for law enforcement officials. In 1986,
for example, two FBI agents were killed with a Ruger Mini-14 in a
wild Miami shootout. In 1987, three police officers trying to serve a
$286.40 bad-check warrant in Inkster, Michigan, were killed with
an H&K assault rifle. In 1988, a Manassas, Virginia, police officer
was slain with a Colt AR-15 by a man disgruntled because his wife
had left him. Alarmed police organizations and law enforcement
agencies began to demand a legislative ban as the toll of injury and
death among their members, of which these few examples are representative, mounted. "The real issue is the safety of our officers,"
one police chief said of assault weapons in 1988. "In my opinion,
they should not be sold in the United States."[61]

If police were alarmed, the general public was outraged as mass
shooting incidents with assault weapons became a frightening national phenomenon. In July 1984 James Huberty—armed with an
Uzi, a handgun and a shotgun—went "hunting for humans" at a San
Ysidro, California, McDonald's. He killed twenty-one and injured
ninteen. In April 1987, William B. Cruse killed six and injured ten
with a Ruger Mini-14 at a Palm Bay, Florida shopping center. But
even these horrors were eclipsed on January 17, 1989, when Patrick
Purdy walked onto a Stockton, California, schoolyard with an
AK-47 assault rifle and opened fire on nearly four hundred students
who were outside for recess. Purdy emptied a hundred-round and

thirty-round magazine, and then took his own life. Five children were left dead and thirty others wounded.

The aftermath was a sustained effort to regulate civilian assault weapons and the high-capacity magazines that feed them, and an equally sustained effort by the gun industry and its friends to neutralize any such ban. California enacted what was hoped to be a comprehensive ban in 1989. The Bush administration used its administrative powers in the same year to ban the import of most foreign-made assault weapons on the grounds that they did not meet the sporting-purpose test, but took no action against domestic production.[62] "There are a lot of policemen and chiefs out there who are saying . . . the main purpose of these weapons is carnage and mayhem," national drug czar William J. Bennett said in announcing the ban on imports.[63]

Foreign manufacturers immediately searched out loopholes in the import ban, got them blessed by a compliant ATF, and were soon again shipping slightly modified assault weapons to the United States.[64] Among them were the Norinco NDM-86 rifle and the Century FAL sporter rifle, which *American Rifleman* described respectively as featuring "rule-beating modifications like thumbhole stocks and solid flash hiders,"[65] and "pure and simple a rule-beater . . . altered just enough to make it over the border."[66]

By the early 1990s, polls showed that seventy percent of Americans favored banning the military-style weapons from civilian use.[66a] Some within the industry—including hunters, writers, and even some dealers—found assault weapons so difficult to defend that they argued the industry should "drain the swamp" of assault weapons (i.e, quit defending them) in order to head off broader attacks on the industry at large.[67] Colt took several steps to insulate itself from the issue, including limiting sales of the AR-15 to police and export markets, and slightly redesigning the gun as a "Sporter" model for the civilian market by eliminating some of the features common to assault weapons (such as bayonet lug), limiting the magazines supplied with the gun to five-round capacity, and pinning a solid block of metal into the receiver to prevent converting the gun to automatic fire.[68]

But the industry as a whole dug in its heels, and locked into a fight with gun control advocates. That struggle culminated in a federal quasiban included in the Violent Crime Control and Law Enforcement Act of 1994, enacted on September 13, 1994. Legislators in favor of gun control and many gun control groups hailed the ban as a landmark victory, but the taste of champagne soon turned to ashes as it became clear that the victory was illusory. By August 1997 a stinging five-part series on assault weapons in the *Los Angeles Times* declared that state and federal regulatory efforts "are in tatters . . . thousands of assault weapons are changing hands because of gaping holes in the laws—the result of industry guile, spotty oversight and political neglect."[69]

Key members of Congress knew at the time the federal ban was passed that it had serious structural defects, most of them the result of concessions to the NRA and its supporters in Congress. But they pushed ahead on the theory that something was better than nothing, and in the hope that the ban would be vigorously enforced by the ATF.[70] They were to be disappointed on both counts. Because the new law "grandfathered," or kept legal, all assault weapons and high-capacity magazines that were legally possessed under federal law prior to its going into effect, manufacturers doubled and tripled production as the law's passage began to look likely. This new production dramatically added to the existing stock of weapons. As a result, a huge number of assault guns and magazines remain in civilian hands. They are freely and legally traded in all but a few states. In addition, even after the law went into effect, gun manufacturers have evaded the ban by cosmetic redesign of firearms covered by the letter of the law so that they became "legal."[71] The ATF's passive stance on these redesigns gave the industry a standing green light, and the agency stood quietly by as importers and domestic manufacturers alike continued to reap the whirlwind of assault guns.

Occasionally, the public becomes aware of the more egregious abuses and a flurry of congressional and presidential activity gives the illusion of action on the question. For example, in 1997 it became known through aggressive reporting by the *Los Angeles Times* that the ATF had allowed gun importers to slip over 600,000 cosmetically modified assault guns through the import ban since

1994.[71a] The somnolent Clinton White House aroused itself to indignation when it learned that, even as the President was considering imposing a moratorium on imports and a review of standards, the ATF had barreled ahead and issued permits for another 150,000 guns to enter the country.[71b]

In the end, President Clinton ordered the moratorium and review, and in 1998 the Treasury Department issued a ruling purporting to tighten up on imports. President Clinton announced the new rules amid a phalanx of uniformed police officials. But the echoes had hardly died before it became clear that the Clinton import ban had no more teeth than previous efforts—gun manufacturers and importers announced several ways in which they planned to continue evading the "tightened" rules.

Nearly a decade after the Bush import ban, and almost five years into the 1994 ban on federal assault weapons, it is clear that assault weapons will continue to plague America's streets until Congress passes a major overhaul of the law. Given the fact that in 1995 the House of Representatives under the leadership of Speaker Newt Gingrich passed a bill repealing the existing law (it died in the Senate), such reform seems unlikely for the foreseeable future.

THE RISE OF "POCKET ROCKETS"

Another of the hot gun marketing trends in the United States today is the selling of "pocket rockets"—pistols and revolvers in increasingly high calibers, engineered down to very small palm size for easy concealment. The concealability and firepower of these guns make them among the most lethal weapons America's streets have ever seen. This trend is no accident, nor is it a response to demand. It is a deadly innovation created to revive stagnant gun markets.

The gun industry began serious planning for this generation of "new stuff"—so-called "compact," "pocket," or "mini"-guns—at least as early as 1988. Smith & Wesson, for example, was reported in that year to have hired Wayne Novak, "noted American gunsmith and designer," to produce "chopped," compact versions of two standard-sized pistols in 9-mm and 45 caliber.[72]

This was not Smith & Wesson's first foray into the pocket rocket market. In 1983 it introduced two minigun models which it developed because of its involvement in Pentagon trials for a new standard sidearm.[73] But experts thought these early guns had a "certain chunky character—a "flatter, more concealable pistol" was thought to be "more desirable for some purposes.[74]

The Pentagon's influence on this trend in the civilian market was reported by *International Defense Review* in 1988:

> By choosing the 9mm Parabellum calibre, the US armed forces have given an impetus to pistol manufacturers who anticipate spin-off sales on the police and civilian markets. One design avenue being enthusiastically explored is that of very compact pistols in the calibre. This year, no less than three manufacturers have unveiled or announced pocket-sized 9mm guns suitable for concealed carry by police and security agents.[75]

The U.S. Army gave the industry still more motivation to produce highly concealable handguns when it invited bids to supply a pistol that would be used as a sidearm for such personnel as intelligence agents and generals who were said to prefer a smaller size than the standard issue sidearm. Beretta, Heckler & Koch, Glock, Sigarms, and Smith & Wesson sought the contract.[76] In 1992, Sigarms won the Army contract to produce the compact 9-mm pistol.[77] The award for the Sig Sauer 228 had a halo effect: Because of the contract, the company won "many converts" including civilian law enforcement agencies.[78]

The Sigarms incident—by no mean unique—illustrates another factor often at work in the U.S. firearms market, the introduction into the civilian market of guns originally developed for military use. As *American Firearms Industry* put it:

> Anything in small arms manufacturing that is developed and adopted by the military, always ends up in one form or another at the civilian consumer level. You, as a dealer, have to know what the government contract R&D departments are producing, because it's just a matter of time before sporting arms manufacturers incorporate new methods, ideas and materials into the products they produce and an even shorter period of time before your customers start asking about them.[79]

This seepage into the civilian market applies to lethality-enhancing accessories as well as firearms. The history of laser sighting devices illustrates the issue. These devices project a visible "dot" onto the target, showing where the round will strike and thus ensuring greater accuracy. They were originally developed for law enforcement and military use, and a 1981 article in *American Rifleman* on firearms equipped with lasers by Laser Products Corporation noted that "these laser-equipped firearms may be sold only to police, military and government agencies."[80] The company's ads at the time stressed that its laser sights were "ideal for special forces or elite combat teams."[81]

That restraint quickly evaporated, however, after 1982, when federal health officials permitted sale of the lasers to civilians.[82] Once the general concerns of health officials about lasers were resolved, the gates were wide open for specific firearms applications, because federal gun laws simply do not regulate such accessory devices. Even though proposals have been offered to restrict the sale of laser-aiming devices to civilians, none has ever been enacted by Congress.

Freed of minimal general health restraints, the industry acted according to its usual pattern. By 1987, ads and product reviews in *Guns & Ammo* touted the laser sights' availability and their utility in the civilian "defense" market.[83] By 1991, *Guns & Ammo* reported "a tremendous boom in both laser technology and the laser sight market.[84]

The transfer into civilian markets of guns especially developed for military use continues. Most recently, for example, Heckler & Koch announced that it would begin selling in the civilian market a .45 pistol it originally developed at the request of the U.S. Special Operations Command for use in urban terrorist situations.[85]

Miniguns, spawned in part by industry innovation seeking new markets and in part by military needs, are now fully developed and increasingly hot products in the civilian markets. "If the 1980s was the decade of the high capacity auto, then the nineties look to be the era of compact, full-power handguns," says *Guns & Ammo* magazine.[86] The "current trend [is] toward reduced-size pistols firing full-power cartridges."[87]

As usual, the gun industry network has pumped up demand for the smaller guns through advertising and a plethora of gun magazine articles.[88] The industry initially faced a special problem in marketing this new innovation: Carrying concealed weapons like pocket rockets was illegal in most states. But the industry capitalized on—if it did not directly inspire–a fortuitous wave of new state laws and amendments to state laws permitting concealed carrying of firearms. "If you don't know by now that legal concealed carry is becoming a major factor in the current handgun market, you haven't been reading *Guns & Ammo*," the magazine said in April, 1997.[89] And *Shooting Industry* magazine put the matter this way in January, 1996:

> Two bright rays of sunshine gleam through the dark clouds of the slump in the firearms market. One is the landslide of "shall issue" concealed carry reform legislation around the country. The other is the emergence of a new generation of compact handguns.[90]

The same publication noted that "there are many new concealment guns on the market as manufacturers rush to meet the demand of those who have benefitted from the concealed carry law reform sweeping the nation."[91] The small firearms being offered on the market today are similar to their older cousins, the Saturday night specials. But they are much more lethal. The new guns are more concealable and more powerful, being produced in higher, "full power" calibers (like the .45 and .40 S&W) and, in the case of revolvers, with higher cylinder capacity. The replacement of "snubby" revolvers by semiautomatic pistols also means that pocket guns now carry more ammunition and have faster rates of fire.

A country of people walking around with concealed guns may not strike most of us as a good idea, especially in light of the following disarmingly candid observation by a *Guns & Ammo* writer who thought he was praising small caliber "pocket autos":

> Because such firearms are so portable and lightweight, it's extremely easy to wave them around indiscriminately—unintentionally placing yourself and others in possible danger. Remember, the smaller the handgun, the easier it is to point it in the wrong direction or place yourself in a potentially dangerous position.[92]

The admission that it is too easy to wave guns around "indiscriminately" mirrors precisely the point that critics of concealed carry laws make over and over. The gun press and gun industry spokespersons have tried to deflect such criticisms by characterizing the emergence of mini guns as a reaction to the September, 1994, enactment of the assault weapons ban, which limited the capacity of newly manufactured pistol magazines to no more than ten rounds.[93] For example, the co-founder of Canada's Para-Ordnance Manufacturing said the new law "in and of itself caused all the manufacturers to downsize."[94] And Jack Adkins, director of operations of the ASSC, in effect cast blame on consumers searching for more killing power:

> "Now these [high capacity pistols] are no longer made, people are stepping up to a more lethal calibre that packs a greater power. Instead of having 15 rounds of 9mm, you will have 10 rounds of .45 calibre or five to seven rounds of .357 Magnum, which is a very powerful round as well."[95]

But the evidence flatly contradicts these kinds of arguments, "the-market-made-us-do-it" made in reaction to the 1994 law. Industry leaders were well into minigun development projects as early as 1988—six years before the assault weapons ban became law.[95a] Industry magazines anticipated the introduction of new "super concealable" guns for a "new place in the market" at least as early as 1992—also well before the assault weapons ban law was passed.[96] *American Rifleman* noted in 1991 a trend at the 1990 industry SHOT Show "toward concealment guns."[97]

Moreover, gun manufacturers had actually made and marketed minimodels well before the ban. *American Firearms Industry* reported, for example, that the "hottest selling firearms of 1992 were compact handguns."[98] Para-Ordnance—whose co-founder was quoted above complaining about the effect of the 1994 assault weapons ban—had already moved to small, concealable compacts by 1992.[99] Intratec, a manufacturer of one of the most notorious assault weapons, scheduled production for its "super small" category 9-mm pistols in mid-1993 and introduced its "Category 45" as early as January, 1994—well before the assault weapons law was enacted.[100] Ironically, a *Guns & Ammo* article attributing the emergence of "ultrasmall" 9-mm pistols on the 1994 ban led off its review of pistols with the Kahr K9, which according to the article itself "was first shown at the 1994 SHOT Show in Dallas."[101] That show was held January 13–16, 1994—eight months before the ban was passed by Congress. The article does not explain how a gun introduced before a law was passed could have been caused by the law, especially since the gun lobby had succeeded in bottling up the assault weapon ban for at least three Congresses. In any case, the time from initial design work to production for new pistols takes from two to eight years,[102] so even if fear that the ban would become law had inspired the new models, it is unlikely that so many would have been on the market as quickly as they actually appeared.

In short, production of more concealable and more powerful miniguns represents another deliberate injection of lethal stimulus to a lethargic gun market, not a reaction to the 1994 assault weapons law.

Domestic and foreign gun manufacturers alike have scrambled to exploit this "new place in the market." For example, Smith & Wesson came out with the Sigma, a compact pistol in 380 caliber. "There's a tremendous market out there for it," a Smith and Wesson spokesman said of the gun, adding, "[If] you want to carry concealed, this remains concealed. Flashing a gun in public isn't well received."[103]

Ken Jorgenson, public relations manager for Smith & Wesson, summed up his company's attitude as follows: "Do you want a big gun that holds 10 rounds and a lot of air?"[104]

Austria's Glock quickly set the pace for the upscale market with two versions of a palm-sized pistol it announced as a pocket rocket, and which quickly became known as the "mini-Glock."[105] The Glock models 26 (9-mm) and 27 (40 caliber) were described in a major gun magazine as "so compact and concealable that they fit in the palm of your hand."[106] "Demand is hot as hell," said a Glock spokesman. "We can't keep up."[107] Glock followed up with two more models in 1997, the Model 29 in 10-mm and the Model 30 in 45 ACP caliber.[108]

Others aggressively pursued the new market. Colt introduced a new Colt Pony in .380 ACP, and Brazil's Taurus marketed the PT-111 in 9-mm, 40 and 45 caliber.[109] As noted above, Sig Sauer pushed a new compact 9-mm semiautomatic pistol originally developed for the military onto the civilian market.[110] Kahr Arms produced its palm-sized K9 ultracompact.[111] And Para-Ordnance's P10, the smallest .45 auto ever, "kicked up its heels like a chorus girl" at the 1997 SHOT Show, according to gun writer Ayoob.[112]

Shooting Industry noted a trend within the trend at the 1996 SHOT show, reporting great interest in new "mini-Magnum" or "baby magnum" revolvers, such as Smith & Wesson's small .357 Magnum revolver, as well as the semi-automatic pistols.[113] Brazil's Rossi is pushing a line of imported pistols and revolvers with two-inch barrels, the small size of which raises serious questions about evading the intent and perhaps the letter of the 1968 law that restricts imports of Saturday night specials.

Interestingly, dealers in at least one state where concealed carry remains against the law reported "flat" demand for the new compact pistols, demonstrating the nexus between laws allowing concealed carry and the market for more deadly miniguns. One dealer believed that any new demand for the mini-guns was being fed by heavy advertising by Glock and Smith & Wesson in sports magazines and police journals.[114] Moreover, according to Richard Feldman, executive director of the ASSC, only two to three percent of residents in so-called "shall carry" states are indeed "packing."[115] This tiny minority is putting the other ninty-seven to ninty-eight percent of unarmed residents at ever-greater risk.

9—Exploiting Ties to Law Enforcement

As horrendous as assault weapons and "pocket rockets" have been for public safety, their increasing presence has been noted in the media and some efforts have been made to keep them in check. But far less well-known is another seamy side of the gun industry: the degree to which firearms manufacturers continually cultivate a close, solicitous, and self-serving relationship with law enforcement agencies throughout the country. These ties often lead to great waste and unnecessary taxpayer expense—and, worse still, they may pose serious additional threats to public safety.

The gun industry's attention to police agencies is partly because the law enforcement community is a considerable market in itself. There are more than seventeen thousand state, local, and federal police agencies in the United States. They employ nearly seven-hundred thousand full-time and more than forty thousand part-time sworn officers.[1] On average, each officer represents more than one potential gun purchase, since some officers carry extra back up guns on duty to be used in case something happens to their service gun, and some officers also own separate off-duty guns.

But more important, supplying police departments or federal law enforcement agencies with a given gun enhances the image of both the manufacturer and the gun, which in turn boosts sales in the far bigger and more lucrative civilian market. One industry analyst noted, for example, that the Beretta M9's top selling points include "being the military's choice" and that "it has proved highly popular among the nation's police."[2] Gun manufacturers go out of their way, therefore, to create and maintain special ties with law enforcement agencies.

Ruger, for example, has tried to cultivate connections to the police. In 1990 the company gave twenty-two P85 9-mm pistols to the Newport, Connecticut, police and nine to the Sullivan County (Connecticut) sheriff's departments, enough to rearm the agencies in one of the company's two manufacturing hometowns. In a related ceremony at the Newport Opera House, then New Hampshire Governor Judd Gregg gave his monthly Business Excellence Award and a public plug to Ruger: "They have a national reputation as being one of the finest gun manufacturers in the world."[3] When company chief William Ruger said in 1993 that the company was "doing much more" in the police market, increasing its sales as departments converted from revolver to pistols, he noted that selling to police "enhances the standing of the company and its products."[4]

But Ruger fired all of its law enforcement sales representatives in 1995, a move the industry saw as Ruger's throwing in the towel in the law enforcement market. "Everything they made was sold, so they blew it off," said one of the fired representatives. "And who can blame them? When you sell everything you're making to the home defense and sporting market, do you need to mess around with law enforcement?"[5]

Other companies have been much more aggressive, and apparently more successful, than Ruger in the law enforcement market. Their efforts to curry favor with and exploit police agencies take a number of forms.

Manufacturers often hire former police officials to work in law enforcement sales positions—in effect, to lobby former colleagues to buy the manufacturers's guns and other products. For example, Beretta appointed a twenty-five-year FBI veteran, Ron Kirkland, to be its law enforcement sales manager in 1994. Kirkland had served as a supervisory agent at the FBI's National Academy at Quantico, Virginia, managing domestic and international police training. At Beretta, his responsibilities included "supervising Beretta's law enforcement sales."[6] The company also announced the appointment of Tom Flanagan, former chief of the Ottawa police, as special advisor for Canadian law enforcement.[7]

Kirkland's work at the FBI National Academy gave him a convenient abundance of sales contacts with top officials at domestic and international police agencies. Not to be confused with the FBI's own training program, or with the other federal law enforcement basic training programs conducted at the same site, the FBI National Academy conducts an eleven week leadership and management training program for selected state, local, and foreign police officials. Over thirty thousand students have graduated from the academy since its founding in 1935, including seventeen hundred from one-hundred twenty foreign countries. One out of four of the graduates still on active duty holds the top executive position at his or her police agency.[8]

In 1992, Smith & Wesson appointed Gerry Smith, a twelve-year veteran of the St. Louis County Police Department, as National Law Enforcement Sales Support Manager.[9] It was reported in the same year that Bank Miller, a former Drug Envorcement Administration agent, was director of training for the Sig Arms Academy."[10]

In keeping with its strategy to boost commercial market "after sales" by first winning police contracts, Glock USA has been one of the more aggressive firms in pursuing law enforcement officers to help sell its guns.[11] In 1993 the company did away with outside sales agents, and shortly thereafter introduced "six national sales and service managers, all of whom are former law-enforcement officials or police department armorers."[12]

A recent scandal in New York involving Glock's absurdly excessive sale of upgrades to a single agency illustrates how the increasingly close ties between the gun industry and police agencies can result in waste, favoritism, and violation of the law.

The Department of Environmental Conservation (DEC) is responsible for protecting New York's environment and natural resources. Its responsibilities include protecting forests, wetlands, and waterways; regulating use of pesticides and disposal of hazardous waste; and enforcing the state's environmental conservation law. The Department's Law Enforcement Division (LED) traces its origins to 1880, when the state appointed its first game protectors, and has existed as a separate division within DEC since 1976. The three hundred officers of LED patrol for hunting, fishing, and pollution violations, sometimes make arrests; and occasionally are called upon to kill wounded or diseased animals. From 1981 to 1990, LED officers were equipped with standard-issue Smith & Wesson .357 Magnum revolvers. But in 1988 LED director George Firth decided to explore replacing the revolvers with pistols. Glock loaned LED more than a dozen 9-mm pistols to evaluate. Several

LED officials questioned the idea of converting to pistols; a lieutenant who attended a 1988 seminar conducted by the FBI and the DEA suggested that until the FBI completed its ongoing ammunition evaluation a decision would be premature, and an LED regional director criticized the idea of switching to pistols as "more like *Miami Vice* than Environmental Enforcement."[13]

In spite of this advice, LED went ahead with the upgrade and bought 326 Glock 9-mm pistols in 1990. According to an LED colonel, the pistols were intended to last "a good twenty years."[14] But in 1993, scarcely three years later, LED agreed to another upgrade, and the barely used Glock 9-mms were replaced with more powerful Glock 40 caliber pistols.[15] Glock's aggressive tactics and poor management decisions by the LED were strongly questioned by the state's Inspector General, who issued a scathing 1996 report that detailed the "illegal and unethical conduct" underlying the scandal.[16]

The need for either of these upgrades, and certainly the second, was strongly questioned by the Inspector General, who noted among other things the difference between LED's deals and the guns other police agencies were using at the same time. Environmental conservation officers in the neighboring states of Massachusetts, Pennsylvania, and Vermont, for example, still carried 38-caliber or .357-Magnum revolvers in 1996 and had no plans to convert to pistols. The New York State Police were still using the 9-mm pistols to which they had converted in 1990.[17] In short, the LED's decision to upgrade its sidearms twice within three years was, according to the Inspector General, "premature," "dubious," and "highly questionable"—in a word, wasteful—particularly "at a time when the state's fiscal resources were seriously constrained."[18]

How could two such wasteful deals have occurred within three years, when it was doubtful that even one upgrade made sense? The answer lies in the offensive way in which, as the Inspector General put it, "one hand washed the other" in the "symbiotic" relationship between Glock and senior LED officials.[19]

The nature of this collusive relationship is illustrated by the favors that Glock's sales representative at the time, Milton Walsh (a former Massachusetts state trooper), did for LED director Firth.[20]

Those favors included arranging for Firth to buy at dealer cost a Glock gun that had value as a collector's item, finding and arranging for Firth to buy below retail price a scarce limited edition Desert Storm gun,[21] and allowing Firth to buy at a discount two Glock pistols "loaned" to LED and never paid for. In addition to these favors for the director, Glock went along with unusual contractual arrangements that allowed LED officers to buy back from Glock hundreds of their supposedly traded-in handguns, which many officers then illegally resold in the private market (a matter discussed in more detail below),[22] and arranged bargain prices for selected LED officers to buy night sights.[23]

The Inspector General's report drily relates that "Glock did whatever it could to curry favor with LED, and particularly, its director."[24]

Perhaps the most disturbing aspect of the New York LED story is the outrageously flippant attitude both sides brought to the deadly serious business of outfitting police officers with the lethal force of handguns. Thus, during negotiations with senior LED officials on the second trade, salesman Walsh described the 40-caliber pistols as "the new toy."[25] The remarks echo gun writer Jim Glover's description of the conduct of the gun press as like "kids pawing at a candy jar" when Glock unveiled a new line of pistols. Transforming guns into benign objects like toys and candy removes them from their real world consequences. The New York officials involved in the Glock sweetheart deals not only betrayed their public trust to spend tax dollars wisely, they bought into an infantile view of guns as playthings that permeates much of the gun culture in the United States.

Gun manufacturers entwine themselves in law enforcement in other less dramatic ways, as well.

Smith & Wesson, for example, has operated an "academy" offering "specialized firearms training" for law enforcement and security personnel since 1969, an important link with the more than thirty thousand law enforcement officers who have taken the company's courses, which include instructor and armorer training.[26] Police firearms instructors and armorers are often key personnel in making decisions about which brand of guns a department might buy.[27] The Swiss-owned Sig Arms, Inc. operates a similar academy for law enforcement personnel.

Another means by which gun manufacturers' personnel stay wired into law enforcement circles is active participation in professional law enforcement associations. For example, the vice president of Law Enforcement Sales & International Training for Heckler & Koch, Inc., was at the same time vice president of the International Association of Law Enforcement Firearms Instructors, and the Virginia state director for the American Society of Law Enforcement Trainers.[28]

Specialized industry publications are another tie between the industry and law enforcement. In 1994, Beretta introduced Leadership Bulletin, a law enforcement newsletter. Authors for the first two issues were former FBI official Edward J. Tully and Richard M. Ayres, who served on the faculty of the FBI academy.[29]

The Glock New York scandal typifies how the gun industry has helped sell hundreds of thousands more lethal firearms to police who probably don't need them. Many public officials know little about firearms and are happy to leave the details to the professionals. But when the professionals are trading favors as part of a self-serving network, the dangers of wasteful and even corrupt deals rise.

As bad as waste may be, police rearmament sales have had much more dire consequences. They have pushed many more guns onto the streets and into the hands of criminals, as hundreds of thousands of police guns have been recycled into commercial markets when police "trade up" to higher firepower. In some cases, the old guns simply were given away to the police officers or, as in the New York LED deal, sold directly to them at bargain rates.

Dealers and distributors who take police guns as trade-ins often pay minimal prices for them because the guns have been depreciated, or "costed out," on police accounting ledgers.[30] Aiming to squeeze the most out of both ends of the police market, one gun writer urged retail dealers to aggressively market the "tons of well-maintained" police revolvers being traded in for pistols and resold by distributors at "giveaway prices": "These inexpensive guns will sell at a hot clip to new handgun buyers."[31]

The irony is that many traded-in police guns have ended up in the hands of criminals. A Walther pistol, from the New York state police, for example, ended up being sold in California after trade-in and was used to commit two separate murders.[32] Large quantities of Sig-Sauer pistols taken on trade from law enforcement agencies and then reconditioned were reported to have flooded a 1996 Houston gun show, selling at "well below their normal wholesale numbers." One dealer estimated that "it would take two large trucks just to carry the guns available from one large Dallas-based marketer" at the show.[33]

The Glock trade-in deal with New York's LED even turned the police agency into a "veritable 'supermarket' for guns," according to the Inspector General.[34] The officers were allowed to directly buy back their traded in guns at steep discounts. A number then illegally resold the guns, becoming in effect unlicensed gun dealers.[35] There is no way to know how many of these bootleg guns ended up in the hands of criminals, but a New York State Assemblyman tracked down three that were confiscated in connection with criminal activity.[36] The scandal prompted Connecticut state officials to stop a proposed exchange between Beretta and the Connecticut state police until the terms of the deal could be more closely examined.[37]

A California state lobbyist for the NRA claimed that the handgun market was so saturated that he had "difficulty with the notion that adding what's here [police trade guns] adds to crime."[38] But many police-trade guns were used in crimes; indeed, the fact that police trade-in guns are typically well-maintained, quality firearms that appear in large quantities on the civilian market at low prices makes them instant competitors for the more cheaply made Saturday night special.[39]

There is no complete count of the number of secondhand police guns used in crimes. But a cursory survey by the ATF of police revolvers made by only one manufacturer—Smith & Wesson—revealed 166 instances in *one year alone* in which former police guns were involved in a crime.[40] It is reasonable to infer that many more police-trade guns than those 166 have been used in crimes.

Century Arms, the largest importer of Chinese weapons in the early 1990s, also got into the police trade market. In 1992, for example, it bought 8,400 revolvers from the Detroit Police Department. A company official described the transaction as follows: "It was a good deal for Detroit. . . . The do-gooder liberals would probably say they should have melted them down. But why should they? They got almost $1 million for them."[41]

The possibility that police trades could end up in the hands of criminals has caused considerable debate about trade-in policies.[42] Some jurisdictions destroy their old guns; others require wholesalers to promise to sell the used guns only to law enforcement buyers, but most simply trade the guns in like so many used cars.[43]

Wasteful gun buys, corruption, and the flow of police guns into criminal hands are public concerns. But they aren't reflected on the bottom line of the gun industry's accounting statements, where police sales are first just business as usual and second a marketing device aimed at the civilian market.

The wave of police conversions to 9-mm pistols had barely crested when the gun industry again began to exploit its special relationship with law enforcement agencies to profit from another twist upward in the spiral of police firepower escalation.

In the wake of the FBI conversion decision in 1989, Beretta, Smith & Wesson, Sig Arms, and Glock all began to aggressively market new 40-caliber pistols to law enforcement, in many cases to replace 9-mm pistols to which police departments only recently converted (like the DEC-LED deal described above).[44] In 1990, the Charlotte, North Carolina, police department became the first major agency in the nation to switch to the new .40 S&W.[45] By 1993, *American Rifleman* reported that the .40 Smith & Wesson "already has grabbed a huge portion of the red-hot police market that has been fueled in many localities by asset forfeiture laws that allow agencies to use confiscated funds to buy equipment."[46]

The impetus for the change has *not* been that the often nearly new 9-mm pistols have worn out. Experts say the guns can last a lifetime with normal maintenance, and even under extreme use can be refurbished with replaceable parts such as barrels.[47] On the contrary, once again, many law enforcement officers and public officials are simply being persuaded that police are "outgunned" and need more lethal weapons. When pressed to explain, police officials — including those who admit their officers seldom, if ever, have had occasion to fire a gun, any gun, on duty — give a variety of rote explanations for the need to switch to a higher level of firepower.[48]

It is ironic that law enforcement officials are now concerned that higher caliber pistols like the 40 caliber are showing up in the hands of criminals, because the 40-caliber pistol was developed and marketed directly out of competition to supply the FBI with a more powerful handgun. The firearms industry responded to the FBI's request for more reliable stopping power by developing several new designs, which inevitably ended up as new products on the civilian market.[49] Smith & Wesson developed a 10-mm gun for the FBI but soon eliminated it from its catalog in favor of the more powerful and hotter selling 40 caliber.[50]

Manufacturers continue to press the firepower margins in pursuit of police sales. For example, in early 1994 Ruger introduced a new submachine gun, the MP9,[51] and in 1996, a Glock spokesman reported rumors that competitors are developing yet another round in the lethality spiral, a 400-caliber round that will be based on a 45-caliber casing but with a smaller bullet.[52]

In the meantime, the February, 1997, shootout between two bank robbers clad in body armor and armed with automatic assault weapons and Los Angeles police armed with 9-mm pistols and shotguns "ratcheted up the debate" in that city "over whether it is time to arm police with more powerful [45-caliber] weapons to close the gap with increasingly well-armed crooks."[53]

It appears obvious that the industry will continue to use rearming police for as long as it is able. Since the higher firepower that police are concerned about comes from industry innovation in the first place, the image of a dog chasing its own tail comes to mind. The gun industry, of course, transfers the benefit of its police activity into the more lucrative civilian market and thus the spiral continues.

A number of factors make it possible for the gun industry to offer and police departments to accept such questionable trade-in deals. One is that most local government officials, like the vast majority of Americans, don't know enough about guns to question the local police department's request for what the Glock salesman in the New York scandal called "the new toys." It would take a smart, well-informed, and courageous local official to tell a police department it needn't have the same toys as the "bad guys." Another factor is the increasing availability of millions upon millions in cash and other assets seized from criminals under asset forfeiture programs, mostly under the drug laws. These funds, often shared between federal and state agencies, are essentially off the books money that police agencies can use without having to get the approval of their local legislative body. Finally, sweetheart trade-in deals from gun manufacturers prove hard to resist for even the most responsible agency.

Gun companies do not offer such sweetheart deals out of the goodness of their hearts or a sense of civic duty. Hard, cold dollars lie behind even the best deal. For example, some gun companies — like Beretta, Smith & Wesson, and Sig Arms — and dealers are making "even trades," swapping new 40-caliber pistols to police departments in exchange for their "old" nine millimeters.[54] This might on the surface seem a selfless act of corporate good citizenship. But it is in fact self-serving business interests that put more lethality into the civilian market. The companies and dealers not only get the benefit of the enhanced image that comes from being suppliers to law enforcement. They also get the more tangible benefit of getting their hands on the valuable "grandfathered" high capacity magazines that come back along with the traded-in guns.

Here is how this scheme works.

The 1994 assault weapons ban forbade *new* production of magazines that can hold more than ten rounds, except those made only for government or for use only by law enforcement, which now must be stamped "for law enforcement use only." However, all *existing* magazines were grandfathered, or kept legal, when the new law went into effect. These grandfathered magazines are legal for resale and carry a premium price as pre-ban stocks dwindle from a theoretically fixed number of grandfathered magazines.[55] As prices soared for the old magazines between enactment and effective date of the ban, manufacturers schemed for ways to profit from price inflation, prompting howls of "gouging" even within the industry itself.[56]

One such way was to ship one, instead of the usual two or three, magazines with new guns (thereby making the extra magazines available for separate resale in the fevered market).[57] Another was to increase production. Glock was reported to have been working its production lines round the clock to get as many high-capacity magazines into the United States as possible—and thus grand-fathered—before the ban went into effect.[58] Wholesalers were also reported to have been lifting spare magazines out of shipments and then selling the replacement magazines separately.[59]

But the key here is that the grandfathered magazine pool includes any in police use *before* the ban became effective. By accepting old, grandfathered magazines back in a trade for new guns and magazines, the gun manufacturers obtained magazines that they could then resell at a premium in the civilian market—"forbidden fruit," in the words of one state official.[60] As Joe Constance, erstwhile gun writer and then-Chief of Detectives for the Trenton, New Jersey, police department explained:

> The magazines that are in our possession were naturally made before the cut-off date. This then makes them valuable to the civilian market because the manufacturer can legally sell these magazines, which are now rapidly rising in value due to the ban. As a result of this, Glock is able to offer us new .40-caliber weapons for our old 9 mms in an even swap.[61]

Glock, for example, engineered a deal with the Washington, D.C., police department, through which it got back from the department nearly 5,600 guns and 17,000 pre-ban, grandfathered high-capacity magazines, in exchange for new guns and high-capacity magazines for "law enforcement use only".[62] Glock was thus able to continue shipping grandfathered high-capacity magazines with its new guns in the civilian market, even after the ban went into effect. A Glock spokesman curtly dismissed criticism of its police trade-in schemes: "Is it legal? Yes it is."[63]

And so the little money-making machine hums along.

Criminals ride the escalator of the gun industry's increasing lethality, quickly taking advantage of every new level of firepower — caliber, capacity, and concealability — that the industry has sold to the United States. When the industry pushed small, concealable revolvers in the 1960s and 1970s, Saturday night specials flowed onto the streets in waves and became the criminal gun of choice. When the wondernines came into vogue, criminals quickly took advantage of their increased firepower, and today are snapping up the newest generations of larger caliber pistols, like the .40 S&W, mini-magnums, and pocket rockets. Today, these pistols remain the dominant crime guns on the streets of most U.S. cities, including those used by youth. "For every revolver we see, I would say we see nine or 10 nine-millimeters," said a police officer who works with gangs in Boston.[64] Likewise, semiautomatic assault weapons moved quickly into the arsenals of criminal gangs — not to mention into the hands of mass murderers — when the industry pushed these guns into the dealers' racks and onto America's streets.

The plain fact is that every firearm innovation the industry can imagine will end up in the hands of criminals, children, and other less responsible persons. Yet this flow of lethality continues with only the slightest of regulation. When things get bad enough to start affecting the safety of law enforcement officers, the industry has an easy answer — just crank up the firepower, and sell, sell, sell.

Part Three

Nurturing a
Culture of Fear

10—The Self-Defense Mirage

Firearms have long been seen as tools for self-defense in the United States. Guns were essential to the European settlers who colonized and expanded the nation's frontiers in more or less constant armed conflict with the land's original residents, who did not take kindly to having it wrested from them:

> Such men *had* to rely on firearms. They mightn't have been able to live without them. Especially in the backwoods, the long gun was the instrument that put meat on their tables and defended them against the attacks of hostile native tribes.[1]

The invention and successful marketing of Samuel Colt's mass produced revolver in the mid-nineteenth century brought new potential for the firearm as a means for self-defense at a time when law and order often was roughly administered, especially in the West. The Colt revolver could be more conveniently carried on the person than the long gun and it packed more available and reliable firepower than its awkward predecessors. "A frontier saying had it that God had created men of varying powers and abilities but Sam Colt had made them equal."[2] Smith & Wesson and other manufacturers soon followed suit, developing and marketing their own designs of mass production revolvers.

The frontier, under any credible definition, has been settled since early in this century. But the United States has suffered two noteworthy epidemics of self-defense fever since the end of the Second World War. The gun industry capitalized upon those fevers—indeed largely redefined itself—by designing and marketing firearms, especially handguns, that it sells as particularly suited for self-defense.

The first wave of self-defense marketing came in the mid-1960s, when the country experienced an extraordinary series of violent events: President John F. Kennedy was assassinated in Dallas, Texas, on November 22, 1963; Malcolm X was shot to death as he spoke at the Audubon Ballroom in New York on February 21, 1965; Dr. Martin Luther King was assassinated in Memphis, Tennessee, on April 4, 1968; and Robert F. Kennedy was assassinated in Los Angeles two months later, on June 4, 1968.

Meanwhile, racial tensions rose as the civil rights movement challenged segregation and other discriminatory practices, not only in the Deep South but throughout the country. Dr. King, a staunch advocate of nonviolence who was jailed several times for peaceful protest activities, led a series of mass demonstrations that culminated in the 1963 March on Washington. Dr. King's peaceful intentions notwithstanding, civil rights activists were harassed, beaten, and even murdered by racist mobs and sometimes by recalcitrant law enforcement officials. Other civil rights advocates turned from peaceful protest to more militant activities, and organizations like the Black Panthers sprang up. Large-scale race-related riots, sparked by a variety of causes, broke out in predominantly black sections of major U.S. cities — Harlem and Rochester, New York, in 1964; the Watts section of Los Angeles in 1965; Detroit, Michigan, in 1967; and in numerous cities, including the nation's capital, following Dr. King's assassination in 1968.

The country had certainly experienced racial and political violence and assassinations before. But these extraordinary events, along with a sea change in popular culture, created the widespread perception that violence was out of control and, more specifically, that ordinary people were at growing risk of bodily harm. In part this was due to the nation's military involvement in Vietnam, especially after President Johnson sent over the first substantial contingent of troops in 1965, sparking mass antiwar demonstrations and flamboyant acts of civil disobedience. Moreover, the basic nature of race-related riots had changed. Before the 1960s, almost all race riots in America were initiated by whites and focused primarily on physically assaulting blacks or in some cases other minorities. But the riots of the 1960s were often initiated by blacks and focused on widespread destruction of property.[3] Finally, the rates of violent crime actually did rise significantly during the 1960s: between 1960 and 1967, the rate of violent crime (as calculated by the FBI) rose fifty-seven percent, and the rate of robbery, which by its very nature involves at least the threat of violence, rose seventy percent.[4]

By 1968, polls found that eighty-one percent of the people believed that law and order had broken down; politicians on all sides lamented the situation and promised to "get tough on crime."[5] The cumulative impact of all these disparate events raised in more conservative minds the fear that the country was on the very edge of revolution.

The gun industry found fertile ground in this turmoil, as David Ecker, president of Charter Arms, noted in a 1981 interview. Ecker commented on the fortuity of the upstart company's timing in entering the market in the 1960s:

> You had a terrific civil rights problem, with riots all across the country. There was a terrific boom in firearms sales. So any firearm that was being manufactured or imported was being sold.[6]

Ecker and the gun industry clearly saw the civil rights "problem"—inferentially a matter heavily laden with race-based fears—and especially the disorders associated with racial conflict and the pursuit of civil rights, as a boon for Charter Arms and for the gun industry in general. Domestic production of handguns during the 1960s was twice the domestic production of the 1950s, and with growing foreign imports added in, the number of handguns that poured into the U.S. civilian market during the 1960s was almost three times that of the preceding decade.[7]

Charter Arms is an object lesson in how the gun industry profited from the growing national climate of fear. The company was formed in the early 1960s and immediately went after the small, inexpensive handgun market. Its 1964 introduction of the Undercover, a snub-nosed 38-caliber revolver, set off a full-scale war for market share with old-line Smith & Wesson, which until then had dominated the snub-nosed market with its Chiefs Special. In contrast to the image of law enforcement service the names of the two lines of "snubbies" evoke, notorious criminal uses of the two manufacturers's marks included the murder of ex-Beatle John Lennon and the wounding of Alabama Gov. George Wallace (both with Undercovers) and the fatal shootings of San Francisco Mayor George Moscone and supervisor Harvey Milk, and attempted assassination of President Gerald Ford (with Chiefs Specials). Charter Arms also produced a pocket-sized 44-caliber Bulldog, which was used by

New York's David Berkowitz, the so-called Son of Sam serial killer.[8] The company apparently had at least some difficulty deciding from which side of the law to draw the names of its models: It marketed a matched set of revolvers engagingly called "the Bonnie and Clyde," the Clyde being a 38-caliber revolver and the Bonnie a .32.[9]

Since then, the gun industry has exploited similar fears of violent crime, often with a subtly inferred racial overtone linked to periodic civil disorders and gun play associated with inner-city drug wars.

This exploitation swelled again to a near-frenzy in the mid-1980s and continues today. Gun manufacturers, desperate to reinvigorate saturated handgun markets, designed and produced increasingly lethal "self-defense" handguns and ammunition in this second wave of self-defense marketing. The NRA helped with a series of sensational fear-mongering newspaper ads aimed, according to the *National Rifleman*, at taking "gun owners' rights down to gut level." The ads featured graphically staged photographs that portrayed scary criminals (e.g., a stocking-masked rapist, a drug-glazed all-purpose bearded villain), terrified victims, and violent crimes in progress, using inflammatory copy and headlines to argue for the use of firearms for self-defense. Typical captions included: "Should you shoot a rapist before he cuts your throat?" and "If you're attacked on your porch, do you want your neighbors to be opposed to gun ownership or members of the NRA?"[10]

In addition to inflating the bugaboo of random criminal violence, the gun industry has also capitalized on occasional civil disorders and temporary civic breakdowns following major natural disasters, citing them as evidence of the need to own guns for self-defense. But in the 1990s the industry has moved more aggressively than ever and stepped up its fear-mongering to an unprecedented degree.

Shooting Industry, for example, has directly advised exploiting the fears of the "unquantifiable" number of Americans who feel that they will need a gun to defend their families because of disorders following such events. "Subconsciously or consciously, they will become one of us," the magazine's columnist Massad Ayoob wrote. "We need to reach out to this market."[11] According to Ayoob, the people in this potential new market include all those who watched television footage of such natural disasters as Hurricane Andrew and civil disorders like the 1992 riots in Los Angeles.

Patterns of gun-buying in California after the 1992 riots illustrate how successful the gun industry's program to profit from such surges of public fear can be. The California State Justice Department noted a nearly forty-six percent increase in the number of applications statewide for guns in the four weeks after the riots in Los Angeles in 1992, compared with the same period in 1991. This run on guns tapered off after May, 1992.[12] Even so, the NRA's *American Rifleman* magazine continued to exploit the Los Angeles riots, saying that they provided "thousands and thousands of grim lessons . . . on the meaning of the Second Amendment."[13]

As memory of the riots faded and the immediate fear subsided, California handgun sales decreased fourteen percent from 1993 to 1994. There was a twenty-six percent decline in Riverside County, 25 percent in Los Angeles County, and twenty-four percent in Orange County.[14]

> "It's just like every time there's an earthquake, everybody runs out and buys earthquake supplies," [Westminster Police Chief Jim] Cook said. "I think they're just responding to events that occur. The riots are fading."[15]

California's chief law enforcement officer, Attorney General Dan Lungren decried the idea that more guns made the people safer. "I cannot believe that we will end the plague of crime by buying more guns and living in fear," he said.[16]

In fact, at least one person may have lost his life during the riots precisely because he *was* carrying a firearm:

> Northern California businessman Howard Epstein flew to Los Angeles on the second day of violence to check on his machine shop near 7th and Slauson avenues. Driving in from the airport, he was shot to death and his car looted. Police discovered a holster on Epstein's belt, leading to speculation among detectives that he may have driven into trouble, drawn a gun to scare away would be assailants and was shot.[17]

Epstein's murder remains unsolved. Several months later, unidentified persons said to be witnesses to the event told reporters that Epstein was shot in the head from a passing vehicle and that looters stole his gun from his belt holster after his car careened off the road.[18] Under either scenario, it is clear that Howard Epstein's gun did not save his life and may have helped cause his death by giving him enough false confidence to go into the riot-torn area, even if he did not actually draw the gun.

Contrary to gun industry hype, such unfortunate and wholly unintended consequences happen often when people buy guns for self defense. Scholarly studies by doctors and public health professionals have repeatedly found that having a gun around for any reason increases the likelihood that a family member—as opposed to a criminal—will be injured or killed with the gun. One study showed that members of families that had a history of buying a gun from a licensed dealer were twice as likely to die in a suicide or homicide as were persons similarly situated who had no such family history of gun purchase. This increased risk persisted for more than five years after the gun was purchased.[19]

Other studies have looked specifically at the narrower question of keeping guns in the home for self-defense. One, published in *The New England Journal of Medicine*, found that having a gun in the home makes it nearly three times more likely that someone in the family will be killed:

> Despite the widely held belief that guns are effective for protection, our results suggest that they actually pose a substantial threat to members of the household. People who keep guns in their homes appear to be at greater risk of homicide in the home than people who do not. Most of this risk is due to a substantially greater risk of homicide at the hands of a family member or intimate acquaintance. We did not find evidence of a protective effect of keeping a gun in the home, even in the small subgroup of cases that involved forced entry.[20]

Another study found that for every case in which an individual used a firearm kept in the home in a self-defense homicide, there were 1.3 unintentional deaths, 4.6 criminal homicides, and 37 suicides involving firearms.[21]

These and other studies have documented repeatedly the enhanced risk that comes from bringing a gun into the home. Even the gun press admits the risk in unguarded moments. Describing the demise of so-called "lintel guns," firearms hung over the door ready for immediate action in frontier times, *Shooting Sports Retailer* noted:

> Today, guns in a home used for self protection are not hung over the door but are more likely in a desk drawer or beside the bed in a night stand. When a child is hurt in a firearm accident it is often the self defense gun that was found, played with, and ultimately fired by the youngster.[22]

But how often do people use guns successfully to protect themselves from criminal acts? Does it justify the damage that comes with guns? Apparently not. Most studies have found that guns play a relatively minor role in preventing crime but a major role in committing it. For example, a U.S. Justice Department study found that, on the average, between 1987 and 1992 only one percent of actual or attempted victims of violent crime, or about 62,000 people, attempted to defend themselves with a firearm. On the other hand, criminals armed with handguns committed a record 931,000 violent crimes in 1992 alone.[23]

One advocate of the value of handguns for self-defense is Gary Kleck, a professor of criminology at Florida State University in Tallahassee. Kleck and his colleague Mark Gertz claim their survey research indicates that civilians use guns in self-defense up to a whopping 2.5 million times a year. Naturally enough, the NRA and the gun industry have widely cited Kleck's work as proof of the value of owning a gun. But Dr. David Hemenway, a professor at Harvard's School of Public Health, dissected the work of Kleck and Gertz in *The Journal of Criminal Law & Criminology*, concluding that their survey design contained "a huge overestimation bias" and that their estimate is "highly exaggerated." Hemenway applied Kleck and Gertz's methodology to a 1994 *ABC News/Washington Post* survey in which people were asked if they had ever seen an alien space craft or come into direct contact with a space alien. He demonstrated that, by the application of Kleck and Gertz's methodology, one would conclude that almost twenty million Americans have actually seen a space craft from another planet and more than a million have actually met a space alien.[24]

Be that as it may, the argument over "defensive gun use," or DGU as it is known in the literature of debate, has a more practical implication than whether one's neighbors have chatted with a space alien. The public's view of the merits of gun control is likely to vary depending on whether it believes that guns have an essential and "virtuous" purpose in a civil society. If good people really do use guns to protect themselves from bad people, people of good will may be less inclined to take this tool of virtue away. But the Police Foundation notes three flaws in the "virtuous use" line of argument:

- *Gun use may take the place of others means of avoiding trouble.* Access to a firearm may encourage some people to be less prudent about avoiding confrontations and may enable or embolden others to escalate confrontations.
- *Readiness to use guns in self-defense may lead to fatal mistakes.* Someone who keeps a gun handy for dealing with intruders and other predators may end up shooting the wrong person.
- *The number of DGUs tells us little about the most important effects on crime of widespread gun ownership.* When a large percentage of households and even people on the street are armed, some may change their tactics, acquiring a gun themselves or in some other way seeking to pre-empt gun use by the intended victim.[25]

Not bothering with the niceties of whether their products end up causing more deaths and injuries than they prevent, gun manufacturers have churned out handguns full speed ahead, seizing the personal-defense market as a lifeline out of flat handgun sales. Then-president and CEO of Smith & Wesson L. E. (Ed) Schultz said in 1992 that he expected to see growth in this personal protection market. "For a lot of people, the handgun is the last line of defense."[26] And indeed, by 1997, *Shooting Industry* would say, "Concealment handguns and other defensive firearms are the bright spots in gun retailing," and advise retailers "It's time to jump in on the defensive handgun market if you haven't already."[27]

The extent to which this second wave of personal-defense marketing has changed the U.S. gun market was summed up recently by writer Ayoob in *Shooting Industry:*

I recently was leafing through an issue of *Shooting Industry* from 1971. Talk about a blast from the past! A quarter century later, things have changed dramatically.

In *SI* back then, it appeared that shotguns and .22s were the mainstay of the firearms business. A firearms retailer today knows that . . . that type of shooting market is stagnant at best. The guns that are selling during the sales trough in the industry are defensive firearms, particularly handguns thanks to reformed "shall issue" concealed-carry rules in several states. . . . Defensive firearms, sold with knowledgeable advice and the right accessories, offer the best chance of commercial survival for today's retail firearms dealer.[28]

In another article, entitled " 'Trend Crimes' and the Gun Dealer," the same writer bluntly advised that the industry use fear to sell more guns on impulse:

Customers come to you every day out of fear. Fear of what they read in the newspaper. Fear of what they watch on the 11 o'clock news. Fear of the terrible acts of violence they see on the street. Your job, in no uncertain terms, is to sell them confidence in the form of steel and lead. . . . An impulse of fear has sent that customer to your shop, so you want a quality product in stock to satisfy the customer's needs and complete the impulse purchase.[29]

The steady growth in handgun sales to first place in the U.S. market, described in Chapter Six, reflects the effects of the self-defense boom. Three-quarters of long-gun owners report that they own their long guns primarily for sporting purposes such as hunting or target shooting. But sixty-three percent of handgun owners report that they own their guns for protection against crime.[30]

In 1995, seventy-five percent of Smith & Wesson's pistol sales were reported to have been to people who bought them mainly for personal protection,[31] and a Beretta executive said twenty percent of the company's $120 million 1994 sales came from the personal-defense market, the fastest-growing segment of the company's business.[32] To help push continued sales in the defensive firearms market, Smith & Wesson opened its "academy" to civilians in 1994, and sent instructors on the road to conduct courses in self-defense, including special classes for women taught by female instructors.[33] The company recently invested $2.7 million to expand the facility to include "new classrooms, tactical shooting ranges and a 20-lane commercial range."[34] A Smith & Wesson spokesman said the company may open similar training centers in other locations.[35]

The industry gets plenty of help from the gun press in marketing self-defense. Gun writers push the theme in a repetitive and seemingly endless stream of articles.[36] Selling two guns instead of one to the same customer is better, and three or four, better yet, according to the gun press. Industry writers regularly suggest selling customers several *different* self-defense handguns, supposedly to fit the changing particulars of the situation the customer might find himself or herself in. The customer "needs to know that owning multiple, compatible defensive handguns isn't some BS that a 'gunshop commando' came up with as an excuse to take his money."[37]

GunGames publisher Wally Arida put a slightly different spin on how retailers should follow up to sell more guns to the same customer after a first sale based on scare tactics:

> We scare them to buy one gun. Now let's get these people shooting their guns and educate them to buy more guns. We should tell them, "Now you have your defense gun, now you need to buy a gun to shoot this sport and another one to shoot this other sport."[38]

The industry's efforts to push more lethality goes beyond guns themselves to increasingly lethal "defensive" ammunition, distinguished by its so-called "stopping power." A 1996 *Shooting Industry* survey summed up the genesis of this market:

> Not too long ago, there was only one type of handgun ammo—the brand name. Then Federal introduced Hydra-Shok. This created a new marketplace for "premium" ammunition that usually performs a little better as a defensive round.[39]

"Stopping power" was defined by *Guns & Ammo* writer Jan Libourel as "a load that will drop an attacker in his tracks with almost any reasonably placed hit."[40] By definition, of course, such an ammunition load will have the same effect if used in a criminal aggressor's gun, a suicide, or the unintentional shooting of a relative or innocent bystander.

The mainstay among so-called "defensive," "premium," or "high performance" rounds designed to produce "stopping power" is the expanding "hollow point" (known also in the past as the "dum-dum"). Hollow point bullets are so constructed that the point of the bullet, hollowed out and made of soft lead, will "mushroom" (expand) to a larger diameter on impact with flesh.[41] The expanded point causes larger, more serious wounds than "ball" ammunition, which has a hard jacket and does not so expand. As one gun writer put it in 1995, "Each of the major manufacturers has its own proprietary jacketed hollowpoint bullet painstakingly designed to expand reliably to a certain point to create a large wound channel, while still holding together for deep penetration."[42] In order to help sell such expanding hollow point ammunition, "Most ammo manufacturers produce expanded bullets that can be used as powerful sales aids."[43]

Ammunition manufacturers continually tinker with new ideas to enhance the lethality and stopping power of defensive ammunition. But just as some experts questioned the need for the added firepower of high-capacity pistols, many also question the need for increasingly lethal bullets. A 1993 FBI seminar in wound ballistics, for example, reportedly signaled a "trend away from 'wonder bullets'." Experts who attended the seminar were said to have agreed that "shot placement accounts for 90 percent of effective police shooting, regardless of the round."[44] An NRA writer reached a similar conclusion in 1989: "It would appear that the solution to the problem of ammunition lies not with the ammunition at all, but with the marksmanship of those using it."[45]

These voices of restraint have not slowed down the defensive ammunition train, however. "The search for the ultimate in 'stopping power' has generated seemingly endless hype," according to *Guns & Ammo* magazine, which is itself not an inconsiderable source of hype.[46]

For example, KLA Enterprises, a Florida firm, introduced a "Safeguard" round that consisted of "three bullets in one, sold in stackable sections that telescope onto the next." Firequest, Inc., of Colorado, offered its "Eliminator-X" round, which contained a special "Detano expanding compound," a dense and highly compressed metal that "massively expands the round" upon contact with flesh.[47] Quik-Shok offered a variant of the multiple bullet concept, marketing rounds that stayed in one piece until the target was struck, at which point the round broke into three pieces so that "the bullet's energy might be better employed to make multiple wounds."[48] The Korean ammunition manufacturer PMC developed a completely hollow "Ultra-Mag" round, the effect of which writer Libourel described as follows:

> Being essentially a tube traveling at high velocity, it works like a cookie cutter, and when it hits flesh, it slices a tubular section completely out of the center of the wound channel. There is no expansion, but it creates a very destructive permanent wound channel—one, I imagine, that would be extremely difficult for a surgeon to repair.[49]

In 1993, gun expert Ayoob advised gun shop dealers to push "general purpose and defensive handgun ammunition . . . products that are reliable and priced to give the dealer a healthy margin." Ayoob regularly advises gun dealers on how to push self defense marketing, suggesting packages of accessories from "man-stopping" ammunition to night sights that can pump up the sale—and the dealer's profits.[50] He particularly recommended the "Black Talon," a Winchester brand that was subsequently withdrawn on account of bad publicity,[51] and whose fortune presents a remarkable case study both in defensive ammunition and gun industry cynicism.

Winchester developed the Black Talon, a highly refined variation of the hollow point, in response to the FBI's exacting ammunition tests in search of an effective duty round. In a 1992 article, *American Rifleman* quoted Winchester Senior Product Engineer Alan Corzine on the bullet's genesis: "The Black Talon project began as a challenge to build a bullet that would perform better in the FBI tests than any other hollow-point on the market."[52]

The Black Talon round featured a series of crisscross cuts across the top and down the side of the copper jacket that encased the lead bullet. These notches caused the copper casing to split and peel back when the bullet struck flesh, creating sharp prongs, or "talons." Trauma surgeons said the "talons" create enormous internal damage. "Those prongs just tear up anything inside," Dr. Kildare Clark, associate medical director of Kings County Medical Center in Brooklyn said in 1993. "When you go in, the patient is bleeding from every major thing you can think of. . . . There is no way somebody hit like that is going to live."[53]

The bullet was also hazardous to surgeons and pathologists themselves, who called it the "flying scalpel" because its razorlike talons could tear protective gloves, exposing the doctors to infectious diseases.[54] Winchester advertisements reportedly claimed that the Black Talon cut through flesh "like a throwing star—very nasty."[55]

Although the Black Talon was supposedly originally developed for police use, it also sold well in the civilian market and was soon selling in quantity. After the ammunition came to public attention, moves were mounted in Congress either to ban such rounds or to tax them at prohibitively high rates. Members of Congress vied with each other to issue the most condemnatory press release attacking the bullet, and the Clinton administration announced it was reviewing ways to stop their sale. Stating that "the controversy threatens the good name of Winchester," the company withdrew the handgun version of the ammunition from public sale in November 1993, restricting it to law enforcement purchasers only.[56] Prices of Black Talon handgun ammunition more than doubled as "the public went on a buying frenzy" to snap up ammunition already on store shelves.[57]

With Winchester having absorbed the heat, congressional and presidential enthusiasm for regulating ammunition of the Black Talon type fizzled out. Manufacturers of other similarly designed rounds simply continued selling their less widely known but equally lethal lines of ammunition. PMC, for example, continued selling its Starfire ammunition, which its ads call "the deadliest handgun cartridge ever developed for home or personal defense," and tout the "massive wound channel" and "fast knockdown" that the "controlled expansion" of its "patented rib and flute design" causes.

Industry executives reportedly felt that the Black Talon name was "great from a marketing point of view but bad from a general public relations perspective." The gun industry's final answer was to ditch the name but save the technology. Thus, to preserve its market and finesse the bad public relations, Winchester quietly announced plans to reintroduce the ammunition under a new name,

Supreme Fail-Safe.[58] And in 1994, the company did indeed introduce a new ammunition line, the SXT, which a company spokesman said "utilizes 90 percent of the same technology as Black Talon."[59] *Guns & Ammo* noted that the Black Talon also had an SXT designation in the company's catalog and said the new ammunition "produced penetration and terminal effects that were basically identical to the Black Talon."[60]

A writer for *Shooting Industry* called Winchester's replacement of the Black Talon an act done "for public consumption" and wrote, "I feel no need to mourn the Black Talon with the SXT available."[61] The history of the "flying scalpel" thus illustrates the gun industry's pattern of moving highly lethal products developed for specialized police and military applications into general civilian markets. The story also demonstrates an equally disturbing pattern of federal politicians quickly losing interest in gun issues as soon as a superficial "reform" is made.

Manufacturers of small handguns, sometimes called "pocket pistols," have never hesitated to promote their concealability. But a recent rash of ill-advised "concealed carry" laws has opened up a new market for such guns. The wave of new or amended state laws continues into the 1990s and allows millions of Americans to legally carry firearms hidden on their persons. The laws were strongly pushed by the NRA. And although the NRA claims that it represents the gun consumer and not the gun industry, its chief lobbyist, Tanya Metaksa, claimed credit in a 1996 interview with *The Wall Street Journal* for generating new gun industry sales by means of these laws: "The gun industry should send me a basket of fruit— our efforts have created a new market."[62]

Concealed-carry laws—promoted by the NRA and strongly backed by the interlocked gun industry complex—have helped sell handguns[63] and gun dealer services, "turning into an economic windfall in both guns sales and in classes required to obtain CCW-permits."[64] The marketing vice president for Interarms, the premier gun importer, called concealed-carry laws "the most important star on the horizon."[65] A recent gun industry magazine headline put the matter somewhat more bluntly: "More Gun Permits Equal More Gun Sales."[66]

But not all voices within the industry have been as enthusiastic about concealed carry as Ms. Metaksa. *Guns & Ammo's* "personal security" writer opined in the July, 1992 issue: "If someone carries weapons concealed, he must really be *looking for* or *expecting* trouble instead of *avoiding* it (whether they were carried legally or not)".[67]

Nevertheless, gun dealers correctly "anticipated and planned for increased handgun and accessory sales" when concealed-carry laws passed.[68] They also branched out into firing ranges in order to sell training to new permit holders, such classes often being a condition of obtaining the concealed-carry permit.[69]

In addition to boosting lagging sales by opening up a whole new market for small, powerful "concealable" guns, concealed-carry laws have also spurred sales of accessories, such as holsters, purses, "fanny packs" designed to facilitate concealment, and even ammunition "specifically developed for short-barrel, concealable weapons . . . concealed-carry scenarios as opposed to police-type scenarios."[70] Accessories are the profit "bread and butter" for many if not most retailers. According to an industry survey by *SHOT Business* the most profitable accessories are cleaning products, holsters, and gun cases.[71]

A fundamental premise of the concealed-carry-law movement is that the laws give "good" law-abiding citizens the chance to use guns "virtuously" to protect themselves from "bad" criminals illegally carrying guns. Indispensable corollaries are that people carrying concealed weapons actually will be both competent and able to defend themselves or others safely; criminals will not be able to get concealed carry permits, and that the proliferation of permits will not contribute to crimes of violence.

There are strong reasons to doubt the fundamental premise and all three corollaries. Whether or not Howard Epstein had a concealed-carry permit under California's relatively tough law, his gun did him no good and, having been stolen, became a strong candidate for criminal use. Moreover, people with concealed weapons "looking for trouble," as *Guns & Ammo's* personal security expert described them, hardly fit the profile of virtuous gun users that concealed-carry laws suppose. But such potential hotheads are not the only danger. In an article assessing specialty holsters for carrying concealed weapons, a writer for *American Rifleman* described how an improperly concealed handgun actually *creates* a lethal risk for the permit holder:

> One of the prerequisites of concealed carry is that people don't know you have a gun. Failure to conceal it properly can be a fatal mistake. I was in a restaurant recently and noticed a man sitting at a nearby table. He was wearing jeans and a jean jacket, and every time he reached for a piece of pizza, I could plainly see his SIG P226 in a pancake holster.
>
> I don't know whether he was a cop, had a concealed-carry permit or was a bad guy. I'd bet a cop, but the point was that if I was able to see his pistol, so was everyone else. If there was someone in there planning to rob the place, he would have been identified as a threat and, therefore, he was at risk of being neutralized first by any serious bandit.[72]

In other words, wholly aside from whether the person legally carrying a concealed weapon has a chance to use it competently, the gun's very presence may well put him or her in mortal danger. Indeed, in-depth studies of actual experience under concealed-carry laws discredit the other two corollaries. They show that criminals do get concealed-carry permits, and that permit holders often commit crimes, including gun crimes.[73]

For example, Florida's experience under its concealed-carry law often is held up as a model by the NRA and others. Prior to the enactment of this law, Florida, like most states, had a discretionary system for issuing concealed-carry licenses. Discretionary permit systems give local authorities—usually a county sheriff, judge, or police official—some leeway on whether to grant a permit. As a result of a campaign by the NRA and its Florida affiliate, the United Sportsmen of Florida, Florida enacted a nondiscretionary system under which state authorities *must* issue a concealed-carry permit to any person who meets specific criteria, which in Florida's case were minimal. Such systems, known as "shall-issue" licensing, invariably increase the number of persons with licenses to carry firearms.

Despite assurances from the law's proponents that criminals would never dare even seek a permit, the evidence shows that criminals regularly applied for licenses. Moreover, convicted felons actually obtained concealed-carry permits. Some did it by lying on their applications, in which cases it took as long as two years for the state to catch up with them and revoke the permit. Other convicted felons—including five convicted of varying degrees of homicide—got permits legally by using a state administrative procedure to win clemency and thus restore their firearms privileges. Finally, the evidence shows that persons with concealed-carry permits went out to commit serious crimes with their guns.[74]

A 1996 study revisited the Florida experience with updated data and found that "since the inception of Florida's law hundreds of license holders had committed a wide variety of crimes," including assault with intent to commit murder, kidnapping, and shooting with intent to wound either before or after they got their concealed-carry permits.[75]

And in 1998, a study on the experience of Texas under its shall-issue law found that holders of concealed handgun licenses were arrested for weapons related offenses at a rate twenty-two percent higher than the general Texas population aged twenty-one and over. From January 1, 1996 to October 9, 1997, Texas holders of concealed handgun permits were arrested for 946 crimes, including murder, kidnapping, sexual assault and various weapons-related offenses.[76]

These studies document in much greater detail than summarized here the basic point, which is that—contrary to the pollyannaish fantasies of "virtuous" use the advocates of more guns in the United States promote—concealed-carry laws can and do put guns into the hands of criminals, and permit holders use their concealed guns to commit violent crimes. On balance, it is doubtful that Florida, Texas, or any other place in the United States is safer because more people are carrying concealed firearms.

None of this slows down the gun industry's marketing machinery. If one concealed gun is good, two must be better—at least according to the bizarre logic of handgun manufacturers and gun writers.

The concept of the "backup" gun—a second concealed gun carried at all times and hidden for use in case the "primary" gun fails or is taken away—has taken off in recent years as yet another marketing rationale to sell more than one "defensive" gun to the same person:

> While you may not have an overwhelming number of customers who would carry two firearms, it does open a new market. . . . Each backup gun you sell brings with it ancillary sales of ankle holsters, pocket holsters or belly bands, perhaps some Speed Strips for spare ammo, and of course, ammo itself.[77]

Discussing how to sell guns to a customer worried about car hijacking, one writer suggested, "Maybe that customer is a candidate for a whole second system: a *backup* system."[79] Manufacturers' ads, from main line and Ring of Fire companies alike, tout the utility of small, concealable firearms as backup guns for the civilian market.

As is true of so many gun industry marketing concepts, however, the idea of a backup gun has a dark side. *Guns & Ammo's* personal security expert Jim Grover (a pen name) strayed in his inaugural column from the party line, saying people who carry backup guns are probably "looking for trouble." Grover, said to be a former military person experienced in counterterror and counternarcotic operations, mocked another, unnamed gun writer as follows:

> This . . . writer also suggests carrying not one, not two, but *three* guns! C'mon, we know better . . . we *better* know better. . . . How do you think this thought process or these types of articles make lawmakers, police and concerned citizens feel about gun owners? Irresponsible? Immature? Insecure? Unprofessional? And more, I assure you.[79]

Responding to *Guns & Ammo* readers who were disgruntled by his heretical candor, Grover toned his judgment down slightly in a later column, but stuck to his main point calling the idea of backup guns a "bogus concept":

> . . . if you are a *non-duty* person (not in authority) and feel the need to carry two or more guns, it is my opinion that you have not realistically assessed the threat or are looking (hoping for) trouble. . . . Street shootings routinely take place at distances less than 7 feet, in under 4 seconds, with less than four rounds *total* fired. A citizen's response is to get away unharmed. A citizen's resolution is not arrest. It is to remain alive. (Italics and parenthetical expressions in original.)[80]

Grover's lapse into a hard-nosed check with reality, however, appears to have done nothing to dampen the enthusiasm of gun manufacturers, the gun press, and some consumers for the idea of toting concealed backup guns.

Gun manufacturers recently have also revisited revolver design. They are marketing new models that increase the revolver's lethality in several ways, by increasing the capacity of the cylinder from the old six-shooter to as many as ten rounds (limits on capacity being set only by the minimum thickness of metal necessary to keep the gun from blowing up); making smaller and more concealable revolvers in higher calibers; or by combining both changes.

This increased-capacity revolver market features what *Firearms Business* called in 1996 "a little battle of capacity" between Smith & Wesson and Brazil-based Taurus International. Both companies introduced several revolver models with higher cylinder capacities in a running fight over market share.[81]

The competition between the two companies began in 1995 when Taurus introduced its Model 607, a seven-shot .357-Magnum revolver, described by *Guns & Ammo* writer Libourel as a break with tradition especially suited for the "tactical missions" of "home, shop or vehicle defense."[82] Smith & Wesson "soon followed suit" with its own seven-shot Model 686 .357-Magnum revolver, and "the race was on."[83] Since then, Taurus has added an eight-shot .357-Magnum revolver, and Smith & Wesson has introduced a ten-shot .22 caliber revolver—equal to pistol magazine capacity limits under current law—and a smaller, concealable eight-shot 22-caliber revolver.[84]

The high-capacity revolver competition is reminiscent of the fight between Smith & Wesson and Charter Arms in the early 1980s to secure market share of small, "snub-nosed" revolvers. Like that battle, it illustrates the point that there is little difference between the "blue bloods" of the industry and everyone else when it comes to making a profit through enhanced killing power. One may be sure that other manufacturers will pile on their own versions of higher-capacity revolvers.

Putting sales and profits above all, the gun industry has enthusiastically plunged further into the self-defense thicket. It is making handguns smaller and smaller, and the calibers they come in bigger and bigger. Meanwhile the NRA and its allies continue to press state legislatures to enact "shall-issue" concealed-carry permit laws. And while the gun industry's little money-making machine whirs along, America's gun violence body count continues to pile up.

11—Playing Soldier

The gun industry's little money-making machine has a voracious appetite for customers. To satisfy it, the industry not only develops new products for old customers, but also seeks innovative ways to get new customers involved in the so-called "shooting sports."

Gun manufacturers and the NRA are "sponsoring new kinds of target sports that they hope will draw more people into the world of guns, and create an endless market for new designs," The *New York Times* reported in a 1992 survey of the industry's marketing problems.[1] Some industry hopefuls liken the market potential of these gun sports to golf, tennis, and other mass market, upscale recreational sports.

GunGames magazine, started in 1995, seeks both to capitalize on and promote the idea of more varied shooting sports. It features articles and advertisements about shooting games such as "sporting clays," and various "fast draw" and practical marksmanship competitions.[2] The publisher, Wally Arida, is reported to believe "that shooting sports can make firearms 'politically correct' again," and he sees a magazine that "glorifies the games instead of the gore in the gun business as the route to take the industry forward."[3]

"Cowboy action shooting," one of the ways the industry both sells guns and attracts new customers, is often featured in *Gun-Games* and other gun press publications. The sport started in Southern California in 1982,[4] and has since risen high on the gun industry's marketing hopes. Participants demonstrate their fast draw target shooting ability, sometimes from horseback, using original or authentic reproductions of period firearms—single action revolvers, rifles, or shotguns "of the type used in the Old West."[5] Cowboy action competitions play strongly to the fantasies of the child within grown men and women. Contestants dress up in the frontier costumes of gunslingers and "floozies" to engage in the play-act shoot outs. "Since dressing up to play cowboy is just a tad ridiculous," advised an NSSF newsletter, "a sense of humor is a requirement."[6]

One branch of "cowboy action" enthusiasts compete on horseback, in "cowboy mounted shooting," using "period-type saddlery and tack . . . [that] adds greatly to the wild west show atmosphere" of the events.[7]

In its early days the event offered prizes from a few manufacturers and was sponsored by companies such as Coors beer.[8] The gun industry, however, quickly recognized the sport's potential for marketing and soon went from offering prizes to full-scale selling campaigns. Industry experts describe the new sport as important because of the possibility that the market for defensive guns is now saturated.[9]

Trail's End Magazine (published by Gunslinger Publications, Inc.) publishes *Retailers Guide to Cowboy Action Shooting*, replete with suggestions for cashing in on the trend. In addition to guns, the guide advises, "Shooters and spectators alike spend literally thousands of dollars on clothing and accessories."[10] Current sponsors of events include companies such as Colt's Manufacturing, Starline (brass cartridges), Cimarron Arms, Goex, Inc. (black powder), Red River Frontier Outfitters, Rand's Hats, *Guns & Ammo* magazine, and others.[11] Gun manufacturers and "western goods dealers" often set up booths along "Sutlers Row" at events.[12]

Articles in the broader industry press also urge those in the gun business to "reap the profits as shooters relive the old west."[13] One company that has done this is Sturm, Ruger. Aiming squarely at the new sport, Ruger introduced its single-action Vaquero pistol "in the hopes of capturing the attention of the rapidly growing number of customers who are shooting in 'old west' and end-of-the trail competitions, as well as those who participate in costumed cowboy re-enactment events."[14] A *Shooting Industry* expert advised readers, "If you want to know where the market is going, look at Bill Ruger."[15] The writer of a glowing *Guns & Ammo* review of the Vaquero enthused that the gun "fulfills all of my Wild West fantasies."[16]

Colt's single-action revolver is also favored because of its lineage, which goes back to the so-called "Peacemaker." The company sponsors the "end of trail" shooting event billed as "The world championship of cowboy action shooting," and is reported to be ready to introduce several new products aimed at the sport, which it sees as a positive "for an industry truly lacking in good news."[17] Various Italian gun manufacturers are prominent among the other smaller manufacturers who produce a variety of specialized guns for the market.[18] Ammunition makers also are rushing to meet the demands of the new market by producing special "Cowboy Loads" that permit "rapid shooting at a comfortable level."[19]

The cowboy shooting market fits well into the gun culture because it capitalizes to a great extent on nostalgia for the putatively better days of the frontier:

> . . . it seems that the closer we get to the year 2000, the more people need the image of the past when justice was dealt out swiftly, good usually won out in the end, women were treated in an [sic] chivalric manner, and a man's word and his honor meant something real and were worth fighting for.[20]

That image of the past inevitably gets entangled with another totemic image: the late John Wayne, a virtual saint in the gun culture. In describing how dealers should use cowboy action events to "increase their sales," one gun writer could not resist mimicking the monotonously clipped "tough guy" accent that anyone who has ever seen a John Wayne movie easily recalls:

> Ya can't just show up in your regular duds. And ya got to have the right shootin' irons . . . Ya also got to learn ta squint inta the distance as if you're right thoughtful . . .[21]

The allusion to the sainted Wayne, born Marion Morrison, is neither isolated nor accidental. The "Duke's" death of cancer in 1979 spawned a spasm of "commemorative" gun marketing gimmicks that continues to this day. Winchester unveiled its John Wayne Winchester Model 94 Memorial Carbine at the 1981 NRA convention, even though NRA experts opined that the long gun with a big bow lever that Wayne favored in movies like the 1953 *Hondo* probably never existed in the real frontier, and would have been unsafe and impractical if it had.[22] Colt Firearms introduced its Colt John Wayne Commemorative Single-Action Revolver at the 1982 NRA annual meeting, complete with eagle clutching a John

Wayne banner and an engraved facsimile of the Red River D brand from the 1949 movie *Red River.*[23] In 1989, Dixie Gun Works dedicated its thirty-fifth anniversary catalog "to the memory of this great American," who "remains a symbol of the American Frontier Spirit."[24] The 1997 end of trail event advertised as part of the entertainment a "John Wayne Film Festival."[25]

Wayne's movie performances are the source of the adulation accorded him from within the gun culture. The characters Wayne played in over 150 feature films — men like Ringo Kid in *Stagecoach* (1939), Sgt. John M. Stryker in *Sands of Iwo Jima* (1949), Col. Mike Kirby in *The Green Berets* (1968), and Rooster Cogburn in *True Grit* (1969) — were almost always plain-speaking, flag-waving, pistol-toting tough guys. As Richard Slotkin pointed out in his book, *Gunfighter Nation,* "the linkage of his screen persona and his role as a public figure, made him a public icon. . . . As the public perceived him, he was not only the actor who has played all those Western and Marine Corps heroes; he was somehow, in his own person, a breathing incarnation of the personalities and consciousness" of the persons he portrayed on the screen.[26]

Or, as the John Wayne Birthplace Society puts it on its Web site, "The mere mention of his name produces images of courage and patriotism." One should not underestimate the power of the mythic Wayne to influence real public policy:

> Wayne never served a day in the military . . . but the movie-myth that developed around Wayne became a more than adequate substitute for his lack of real military experience. . . . This confounding of myth and reality would reach its culmination in Congress's authorization of a John Wayne medal, identifying the lifelong civilian as the embodiment of American military virtue.[27]

Those who wonder what fuels the gun culture, and why Congress acts so slowly and ineffectively on gun control issues, would do well to ponder the emotional power that won career civilian Duke Wayne his Congressional medal.

"Sporting clays," a variant of old-fashioned trap and skeet shooting at flying clay targets, also appears regularly in gun industry writings about important new sport-shooting markets. The British sport came to the United States in the late 1980s, after trap and skeet shooting had "reached something of an evolutionary dead end" and were losing thousands of shooters, according to *American Rifleman*.[28] The National Rifle Association created a Department of Sporting Clays Development" in 1992 to "help promote the sport and also increase NRA membership."[29] *Guns & Ammo* noted that sporting clays "is an excellent venue in which to start young shotgunners."[30]

Gun manufacturers have also sought to boost sales by linking their products to the American love affair with the automobile. For example, Smith & Wesson has sponsored the Buddy Baker's NASCAR Report on a sports radio network, "continuing a trend of gun companies establishing ties with auto racing."[31] The company is also a co-sponsor, along with Chevrolet, of the Chevy Truck Sportsman's Team Challenge National Championship, a national shooting competition hosted by NSSF.[32] Remington is heavily involved in NASCAR racing—sponsoring a car and driver with the Remington logo and providing "an opportunity for qualified consumers to get involved with racing personnel." [33] Ruger teamed with Indy Car driver Johnny Unser in the 1993 Champion Spark Plug Los Angeles IndyCar Grand Prix.[34]

"The kids in this country think we're Bubba with a fly rod," rock musician Ted Nugent, an outspoken pro-gunner and shooting industry poster boy, said at the Second Strategic Conference on Hunting and Shooting Sports in June, 1997.[35] "The status quo system of the shooting sports is a noose around your neck," Nugent opined, arguing that the industry needs to make dramatic change to survive.[36]

One of the major changes the industry is pursuing is building more shooting ranges. Ranges were identified as "critical partners" in "developing the potential of the shooting sports market" in a recent report by the Strategic Planning Institute of Boston for the NSSF.[37] The first of six "action points" the study recommended was "a comprehensive program to improve the awareness, customer friendliness and operational efficiency of shooting facilities."[38]

The theory is to introduce new shooters to guns at ranges, thereby winning new lifelong gun buyers. "In studying today's shooters, compared with the U.S. population growth, the trends show the industry is losing ground every day. . . . To increase the number of shooters, there must be improved opportunities for hunting and target shooting."[39] Working closely with the industry, the NRA has mounted a major effort to get people to "fun events" at local ranges,[40] and publishes a pamphlet advising prospective shooting range developers how to get federal funds.[41]

"Ranges are increasingly the only viable means of supporting shooting sports activities, outside of legal hunting," the NRA's executive director for general operations said in 1990, speaking at the first of three national shooting range symposiums that have been underwritten almost entirely by federal tax dollars. "If the shooting sports are to survive, ranges are absolutely essential to their survival."[42] The industry also sees shooting ranges as a political tool: "Getting more people to the range is considered one of the best ways to build not only customer bases but also grassroots support for legislative matters," according to *Firearms Business* magazine.[43]

The federal government's U.S. Fish & Wildlife Service helps underwrite the construction and maintenance of firing ranges,[44] and co-sponsors and pays almost entirely for the national shooting range symposiums, at which range developers and operators discuss ways to promote their business.[45]

In keeping with the industry's strategic plan, a number of manufacturers have announced programs to encourage or subsidize the growth of shooting ranges. For example, Brazilian-owned Taurus USA, "looking to increase consumer awareness of its handguns," has started a program that gives shooting range operators as much as forty-five percent off the retail price of its handguns.[46] Smith & Wesson offers a similar discount program for guns to be used exclusively for range rentals, to "get these guns out onto the ranges where people can try them and buy them," according to a Smith & Wesson spokesperson.[47] The country's best known importer, Interarms, Inc., has also started a subsidy program for retailers who have "on-site" shooting ranges, as has the German firm Heckler & Koch.[48]

Glock also established a special sales policy for public shooting ranges,[49] and the Glock Sport Shooting Association sponsors dozens of events across the United States aimed at selling interest in shooting. A company spokesman compared the program to "an industry survival kit" and said, "We don't sell fear, we sell fun."[50]

The idea of shooting range franchises also enjoys an occasional faddish status, although its commercial feasibility apparently has yet to be proven. A California range announced plans to sell shooting range franchises in 1994, echoing a 1989 franchising plan floated by a major supplier of range equipment supplier.[51]

The owners of a number of ranges in Washington state offered special discounts to adults who brought children to the ranges for "gun safety education."[52]

But shooting ranges also bring the industry headaches—including potential liabilities—it doesn't want. For one thing, ranges are notoriously unsafe. Here, for example, is *Shooting Industry* writer Ross Thurman's expert observation on the issue: "Unfortunately, I've found most safety standards at shooting ranges to be extremely casual. On a number of occasions, I've cut short a range visit because of how carelessly other shooters handled firearms."[53]

Thurman's account is not an isolated example. A reader of *Guns & Ammo* magazine wrote in 1986 to describe "a situation that was unbelievable" at a shooting range as follows:

> . . . a person entered the shooting stall next to mine. He proceeded to take a brand-new handgun from its box and make a very futile attempt to load it. He started loading his ammo in the magazine backward. I offered my assistance, for which he was very grateful. He informed me that he had just purchased the gun (an S&W 639) and did not know anything about it or handguns in general.
>
> I was so concerned by this situation that I took a small, informal survey over a month or so when I visited the range and found that 80 percent of the shooters that came to the range were there for the first time, had just recently purchased a firearm and did not know anything about the firearm or firearm safety.[54]

American Rifleman carried a detailed account in 1992 of how "gross abuse of a public shooting area by slobs with firearms forced

its closing."[55] Although the gun industry likes to portray gun owners as uniformly responsible citizens with only a few "bad apples,"
the author, a federal Bureau of Land Management official wrote,
"we estimated that somewhere between 30% and 40% of the apples
were bad."

Because the agency could not afford to station an employee at the
range, wrote the official, "We trusted the good sense and ethical
standards of the shooting public. We were very disappointed by the
result." Among the problems were the following:

> It very quickly became apparent that not all shooters understood the safe
> handling of firearms and were not true believers in law and order. As
> examples, I personally observed two young men set down their beers as
> they passed a loaded and cocked pistol back and forth to take turns
> shooting. Automatic weapons fire has been reported regularly. . . .
> Fires have been started by people using illegal tracer bullets. . . . It
> was also apparent that there was not much sensitivity to the environment.
> Citizens concerned about our environment do not shoot car batteries so
> that acid runs into stream beds.[56]

"Slob shooters" (as they are known even within the industry) are
not the only cause of these range problems. Range management itself is a serious problem. The Strategic Planning Institute found in
its report that "a large majority of shooting facilities in the country
are not professionally managed, commercial operations." Similarly,
a major supplier of shooting range equipment, Caswell International Corporation, was reported in 1989 by *American Rifleman* to
have looked at the shooting range market and found that "a lot of
people trying to get in on a shoestring" were "cutting corners on
costs that resulted in substandard ranges in terms of safety, environmental concerns and cleanliness."[57]

Even shooting ranges that are "professionally managed, commercial operations" bring with them other problems, such as fre-
quent accidents, suicides, and even occasional murders using
rented guns.[58]

Other problems include whether fully automatic weapons
should be allowed at public ranges, and neighbors who object to
noise and hazards. Missouri found itself at odds with the NRA when

a proposal was floated to ban machine guns from ranges on the grounds that they destroyed target stands and unnerved other shooters.[59] (The NRA opposes restrictions on private ownership of machine guns.[60]) Some ranges have been closed because neighbors objected to noise, especially during early morning or late hours.[61]

The gun industry stands on the threshold of the new century a tired but dangerous beast, trapped in a tightening circle of trouble. Its markets are saturated and stagnant. The greater society around it increasingly rejects its products and finds its culture repulsive. Like a beast with its back to the wall, the gun industry has reacted by making the world around it a more dangerous place to be. It has ruthlessly injected its products with lethality and fomented civil anger, distrust and division to sell more guns. It has invented new "games" to give its shrinking pool of customers things to do with their deadly toys and reasons to buy more guns. It has even cast aside the libertarian philosophy it extols in its advertising, and greedily bellied up to the federal tax nipple to subsidize its shooting programs and its technology development.

But none of this has been enough. So now the industry is turning to women, ethnic minorities, and even children in a desperate attempt to find entirely new pools of customers.

12—Targeting New Markets

The gun industry has recently turned its sights on women and children, trying to boost sales in the same way that the tobacco industry has done. In 1992, for example, the NSSF reported that "bringing women and youngsters to the shooting sports is the goal of fully half of" the NSSF's new programs.[1]

The industry is aggressively pursuing women as a market in its own right. A 1989 article in *American Rifleman* described in detail the reasoning behind Smith & Wesson's development and marketing of its LadySmith revolvers:

> There simply are too many manufacturers for a shrinking or stagnant market—the industry needs to find new markets to survive and prosper.
>
> With that in mind, S&W studied patterns of gun ownership. It found that about 29% of men were interested in owning a gun, but that 28% already owned one. Obviously, gun owners can and do buy more guns. But it was apparent that there was no potential Eldorado of new customers among men.
>
> Among women, however, the story was entirely different. While 19% of women were interested in owning a gun, only 9% had already acquired one. This meant a huge untapped market open to a manufacturer smart enough to pursue it.[2]

Glock's general counsel explained to the *Financial Times* in 1996 how the female market's potential is enhanced by the increased number of women who are also heads of household: "There are more single mothers now than there ever were, and they are now the ones primarily responsible for home defence. It's probably one of the biggest open markets right now."[3]

In pursuit of that market, manufacturers have shaped the design of handguns to make them easier for women (and others with smaller hands) to handle. These design changes also make the guns easier to conceal, so that such guns thus serve two branches of the industry's marketing aims at once.[4] Glock, for example, has described its ultra-compact pistols as "the perfect choice for women."[5]

Gun industry magazines regularly feature articles advising retailers on how to exploit the women's market. Many of the popular gun magazines feature columns devoted exclusively to women, and hardly an issue in the industry press appears without at least one article suggesting ways to sell guns to women, from sponsoring "educational and fun events" to making gun stores more "friendly" to potential female patrons.[6]

The firearms industry typically presents female handgun ownership as one more male bastion falling to women's equality. Arguments against ownership are portrayed as a patriarchal attempt to deny women their freedom. The primary marketing tactic, however, is not equality, but fear. The pitch to women is simple: *You're a woman. Some stranger is going to try to rape you. You'd better buy a handgun.* People buy handguns out of fear, and stranger rape—it is theorized—is what women fear most. As a result, the gun lobby has been relentless in its use of fear of rape to promote handguns as self-defense weapons.[7]

There is great cynical pretense in the gun-industry marketing campaigns. The industry promotes itself as concerned for women's safety in its advertising aimed at women in popular magazines; for example, an ad for the "All-American" 9-mm pistol manufactured by Colt features a mother tucking her child into bed, a Raggedy Ann doll in the little girl's hands. The headline reads, "Self-protection is more than your right... it's your responsibility." But the industry abandons this altruistic pretense in its more hard-boiled industry publications. One Colt ad in *SHOT Business* (March/April 1993)features the same image, but this time additional text aimed at the business world is added. Above the warm cozy ad aimed at women is the revealing headline: "You Might Think This Ad is About Handguns. It's Really About Doubling Your Business." The text reads:

> Women represent 53% of America's population. And here at Colt, we believe that addressing women's security needs is not only a responsible and necessary objective, it's also smart business. When this ad ran in a national women's magazine, it seized nationwide media attention. More important, it gave Colt and its products top-of-mind awareness in a huge and largely untapped market. Today, Colt is making every effort to seek out and capture new markets for our products, and we welcome the fact

that women are now a growing and entitled segment of the firearms market. As potential customers, they must not be ignored.

It should be noted that, although there is no doubt that the industry is pursuing the women's market, it also routinely exaggerates the extent to which it has actually made progress in selling more women on the idea of buying guns. Thus, although industry spokespersons often claim women are buying more guns in significant numbers, professional and disinterested surveys indicate that gun ownership by women has remained virtually unchanged in the United States since 1980.[8]

Although the industry sees women as a lucrative market in themselves, it also sees women as an important means to develop the market for children. As *Shooting Sports Retailer* explained in 1993: "The women's market has no way to go but up. Women are important to the future of the shooting and hunting sports because they can influence law makers and public perceptions as well as the young."[9]

Industry strategists see women in their special role as mothers—and especially as single parents—as the key to this strategy. They are not only themselves part of the women's market, but they can encourage their children also to become interested in firearms: ". . . women bring another aspect with them—the family."[10]

Children who are introduced to the "shooting sports" early often grow up to become lifelong gun buyers. "Almost everyone who currently owns a gun had some experience with guns as a youth, either in military service or (more commonly) from growing up with guns in the home," the Police Foundation study *Guns in America* found.[11]

But the country and its traditions are changing, and the industry is losing its automatic connection with young people. In 1959, for example, the NRA was able to rhapsodize in an editorial in *American Rifleman* that "a gun can be for a boy a most longed-for Christmas gift which carries with it a great wealth of American tradition, all wrapped up in the process of a youngster becoming a man."[12] But in 1997, the NRA's First Vice President Charlton Heston was fretting in the same magazine that "I see a nation of children, a couple of

entire generations, that have been brainwashed into believing that
the Second Amendment is criminal in origin."[13]

The need for new ways to snag children for the gun trade was
discussed at a 1996 NSSF Strategic Conference:

> One important area addressed at the summit was youth involvement.
> Each year scouting, 4-H, FFA and other programs introduce 3 million
> young people to recreational shooting. However, after the initial ses-
> sions, the teens are not introduced to other shooting programs.[14]

The NSSF boasted of reaching five to eight million young
people as "potential customers" by purchasing inserts aimed at
children in scouting magazines like *Boys Life* and *Scouting,* and
the Future Farmers of America publication *New Horizons.*[15]
"The objective" of its youth program, according to the NSSF, "is
to create a fun-filled pathway to the top of the shooting sports similar to those available to young football, baseball, and basketball
players. . . ."[16]

Industry magazines also frequently discuss the need to promote
guns among children. For example, one suggested Kim Rhodes, a
17-year-old Olympic gold medalist in trap-shooting, as "a role
model who can attract young people to the shooting sports. . . .
Without young people, we'll continue to shrink as an industry."[17]
Another noted the success of the fishing tackle industry's "Take a
Kid Fishing Promotion," and suggested "Perhaps it's time for this
industry to counter with a 'Take a Kid Hunting (or Shooting)' program of its own."[18] Gun shop operators were recently urged to emu-
late an annual essay contest for secondary school students
sponsored by the NRA as "a way of stirring the interest of youngsters."[19]

The manager of the NRA's range development department also
urged shooting ranges in 1993 to develop "education and training"
programs, according to the NRA's official journal, arguing that
such programs "would get youth involved in shooting and would
help rebuild the nation's population of recreational shooters."[20]
The NSSF's newsletter for gun ranges noted, "Today's youngsters
can be tomorrow's gun club members and shooting range customers."[21]

Manufacturers also directly market smaller-sized firearms for use by children. (Federal law forbids sale of firearms to children under 18, and handguns to anyone under 21. But broad exceptions permit parents and others to make guns available to children for recreational and other use.) "The Superlight Handi-Rifle Youth was designed for one purpose," a 1998 New England Firearms ad informs. "To give today's young shooters and hunters the affordable, safe and easy to use first centerfire rifle the market has always needed but somehow never offered. . . . [the barrel is] fitted to a special youth-sized synthetic stock and forend." Interestingly, the ad also promotes the industry's commercial strategy, elevating the introduction of one's children to firearms to the familiar level of civic duty. "The future of the hunting and shooting sports require [sic] that we introduce young shooters today. . . . We can win this battle if we all try."[22] Harrington & Richardson placed an ad in the NRA's youth magazine, *InSights*, promoting its 929 Sidekick Revolver as "a quality "First Time" 22 lr. revolver" and "the right way to get started in handgunning."[23]

In addition to developing and marketing smaller or lighter weight guns suitable for use by women and children, the gun industry has been using public and private schools to introduce youth to firearms via NSSF educational materials for grades four through twelve focusing on hunting and "wildlife management." The September/October 1993 issue of NSSF's magazine *SHOT Business* gave the gun business frank advice on how to develop schoolchildren's interest in firearms:

> There's a way to help ensure that new faces and pocketbooks will continue to patronize your business: Use the schools . . . they can be a huge asset. Think about it. Schools collect, at one point, a large number of minds and bodies that are important to your future well-being. How else would you get these potential customers and future leaders together, to receive your message about guns and hunting, without the help of the schools. . . . Schools are an opportunity. Grasp it.[23a]

NSSF did grasp the opportunity, at taxpayer expense. In 1993 the NSSF received a grant totaling more than $229,000 from the U.S. Fish and Wildlife Service, Department of the Interior for its Wildlife Management Education in Schools program. The money was awarded to NSSF (in conjunction with the Wildlife Management Institute) to update and expand materials for its school programs. A second $101,000 grant was awarded to the organization that year for a series of video news releases, taped radio news releases, and a print ad campaign aimed at the general public outlining the success of wildlife management.[24]

The gun industry is also developing ancillary products aimed at sparking kids' interest, such as a CD-ROM hunting game—"a fast-moving, reasonably realistic and challenging game that should be interesting to kids."[25] The United States Practical Shooting Association, which promotes shooting matches simulating pistol combat, has a "junior program," and co-sponsors "Camp Shoot-out" for introducing children to the sport. *GunGames* publisher Wally Arida bragged in a Web site article, "Our Children Can Play With Guns," that his ten-year-old son "won the world speed shooting title for competitors 12 years old and younger." Arida advised that, "We must involve our children into [sic] our gun games. As an industry, we must build the structure for various youth shooting programs."[26]

The question of selling guns to be used by children raises the question, how old is old enough to handle firearms? An NSSF pamphlet, *When Your Youngster Wants a Gun*, provides the gun industry's answer :

> Age is not the major yardstick. Some youngsters are ready to start at 10, others at 14. The only real measures are those of maturity and individual responsibility. Does your youngster follow directions well? Is he conscientious and reliable? Would you leave him alone in the house for two or three hours? Would you send him to the grocery store with a list and a $20 bill? If the answer to these questions and similar ones are "yes," then the answer can also be "yes" when your child asks for his first gun.[27]

Most recently, gun industry analysts have openly conceded that the traditional white, Anglo-Saxon market is saturated and have pushed for aggressive marketing of guns to ethnic and racial minorities.

In a January, 1997, article for *Shooting Sports Retailer* titled, "Gun Industry Must Become Less Racist to Survive in the 21st Century," analyst Bob Hausman wrote:

. . . all of the usual customers the industry reaches (people of Northern European descent) who wanted a gun, now have one. . . .

The numbers of hunters, the mainstay of the industry, is not growing. Reliance on the time-honored method of indoctrination of father-to-son in the hunting tradition can no longer be counted on with the growing urbanization of America.

It is time for a pro-active approach to include those who have not traditionally participated in the shooting sports. . . . A major effort needs to be made to include those groups who are presently referred to as America's racial and ethnic minorities, but who are rapidly becoming the majority. And there is tremendous potential within this largely untapped market.[28]

Analyst Carollee Boyles-Sprenkel penned a similar sentiment in a 1997 article for *Shooting Industry* magazine:

Increasing the percentage of minorities participating in hunting and fishing would help keep these activities alive. . . . "Minorities are very much an untapped market. . . . We need numbers. . . . We need to investigate how other industries, like golf, do it."[29]

The full dimension of this latest gun-industry marketing thrust is yet to be realized, and difficult to measure. Nevertheless, the Police Foundation study on gun ownership suggests that these analysts may be on to something. Among those surveyed, twenty-seven percent of the whites owned a gun, but only sixteen percent of the blacks, and eleven percent of the Hispanics.[30]

Given this potential, and the gun industry's track record, one can easily envision what twisted fruit will grow from the seeds of this thought. Advertisements for the tobacco and alcohol industries have targeted minority communities, so no one should be surprised to see the gun merchants zeroing in on the same communities. The industry may, however, have to sanitize some of its leading spokespersons, whose records for accommodating the sensibilities of minority groups leave something to be desired.

For example, NRA board member Jeff Cooper authors the monthly column Cooper's Corner for *Guns & Ammo* and also writes the newsletter *Jeff Cooper's Commentaries.* Cooper regularly refers to Japanese as "Nips,"[31] and has suggested calling black South Africans from the Gauteng province "Orang-gautengs."[32] Cooper's racist views are not limited to just foreign nations. In 1994, he wrote, "Los Angeles and Ho Chi Min City have declared themselves sister cities. It makes sense—they are both Third World metropolises formerly occupied by Americans."[33] And commenting on the murder rate in Los Angeles, Cooper noted in 1991 that "the consensus is that no more than five to ten people in a hundred who die by gunfire in Los Angeles are any loss to society. These people fight small wars amongst themselves. It would seem a valid social service to keep them well-supplied with ammunition."[34]

In commenting on the Senate debate over the confirmation of Supreme Court Justice Clarence Thomas, Cooper offered his views on sexual harassment, "[W]e find ourselves most harassed by people who get the accent on the wrong syllable. The word is *ha-r*ass, not har*ass*."[35]

Like his fellow board member Cooper, rock musician Ted Nugent laments a changing South Africa. In 1990 he told the *Detroit Free Press* magazine that "apartheid isn't that cut and dry. All men are not created equal. The preponderance of South Africa is a different breed of man. I mean that with no disrespect. I say that with great respect. I love them because I'm one of them. They are still people of the earth, but they are different. They still put bones in their noses, they still walk around naked, they wipe their butts with their hands. . . . These are different people. You give 'em toothpaste, they f---ing eat it . . . I hope they don't become civilized. They're way ahead of the game."[36] In the same interview Nugent expounded on his racial views, "I use the word n----r a lot because I hang around with a lot of n----rs, and they use the word n----r, and I tend to use words that communicate . . ."[37]

When faced with criticism over such comments, Nugent promises, "I don't mean to offend. I'm a fun guy, not a sexist or a racist."[38] Yet in a July 1994 interview in *Westworld Newspaper*, Nugent called Hillary Clinton a "toxic c--t," adding, "This bitch is nothing but a two-bit whore for Fidel Castro."[39] Nugent also offers advice for men whose wives and girlfriends discourage their hunting: "I met a couple guys in line yesterday who go, 'Write something to my girlfriend, she won't let me go hunting.' I wrote her something and I said, 'Drop dead, bitch.' What good is she, trade her in, get a Dalmatian. Who needs the wench?"[40]

The NRA does not appear to be cleaning its act up. Most recently, Charlton Heston promoted the volatile concept of "white pride" in a speech before the right-wing Free Congress Foundation, in which he suggested that the nation is locked in a "cultural war" (echoing a phrase coined in Bismarck's Germany). Heston drew the battle lines between white males and virtually everyone else as follows:

> Heaven help the God-fearing, law-abiding, Caucasian, middle class, Protestant, or — even worse — Evangelical Christian, Midwest, or Southern, or — even worse — rural, apparently straight, or — even worse — admittedly heterosexual, gun-owning or — even worse — NRA-card-carrying, average working stiff, or — even worse — male working stiff, because not only don't you count, you're a downright obstacle to social progress. Your tax dollars may be just as delightfully green as you hand them over, but your voice requires a lower decibel level, your opinion is less enlightened, your media access is insignificant, and frankly mister, you need to wake up, wise up and learn a little something about your new America . . . in fact, why don't you just sit down and shut up?
>
> . . . .
>
> The Constitution was handed down to guide us by a bunch of those wise old dead white guys who invented this country. Now, some flinch when I say that. Why? It's true . . . they were white guys. So were most of the guys who died in Lincoln's name opposing slavery in the 1860s. So why should I be ashamed of white guys? Why is "Hispanic pride" or "black pride" a good thing, while "white pride" conjures up shaved heads and white hoods? Why was the Million Man March on Washington celebrated in the media as progress, while the Promise Keepers March on Washington was greeted with suspicion and ridicule? I'll tell you why: Cultural warfare.[41]

It remains to be seen whether the kind of stew that NRA officials like Cooper, Nugent, and Heston cook up will help the industry sell guns to minorities and women. But one thing is clear: even at its highest levels, the guardians of the gun culture in the United States are fast losing touch with reality. And talk of war, cultural or otherwise, cannot be good for a civil society awash in guns.

—Conclusion
Cleaning Up the Mess

Guns—like prescription drugs, insecticides, household chemicals, and many other products commonly found in American homes—are inherently dangerous. Guns cannot do what they are designed to do without risking injury to the user or someone else. The difference between guns and other dangerous products is that firearms, no matter how lethal manufacturers make them, are unregulated.

The Consumer Product Safety Commission (CPSC) regulates the safety of consumer products. The Food and Drug Administration (FDA) monitors the food supply and evaluates drugs and medical devices before they are permitted on the market. The Environmental Protection Agency (EPA) ensures that unreasonably dangerous chemicals that threaten our health or the environment are not sold.

But no federal agency has the power to ensure that firearms are safe for their intended use. This void results in countless consumers being exposed to unreasonably dangerous, defective firearms. The most infamous example is the Old Model single-action revolver manufactured by Sturm, Ruger & Co. Ruger knew in 1968 that the design of the gun made it prone to accidental discharge. Although the gun had failed ATF "drop" tests, showing that the gun could fire if accidentally dropped, the company did nothing to improve the Old Model's safety. Ruger also had received reports since 1962 of serious injuries and deaths caused by accidental discharges. Only in 1973, after hundreds of lawsuits and complaints, did Ruger incorporate a simple and inexpensive safety device in the gun.

ATF also was powerless to recall the semiautomatic Intratec Scorpion after discovering a part failure that caused the gun to unexpectedly fire repeatedly with one pull of the trigger. Even though it was ATF's opinion that the defect endangered the firearm's users, the agency had no power to recall the pistol. Its only recourse was to work with the manufacturer to stop further distribution and have guns already in the hands of owners repaired.

It is foolish to expect the firearms industry to regulate itself. The gun industry does not see its little money-making machine as responsible for the grim record of its products. On the contrary, like their peers in the tobacco industry, gun industry executives often blame the victims of gun violence. One journalist who examined the trail of a murder gun concluded that a "none-of-my-business attitude permeates the firearms distribution chain from production to final sale, allowing gunmakers and gun marketers to promote the killing power of their weapons while disavowing any responsibility for their use in crime."[1]

That conclusion captures a cavalier attitude often displayed by gun industry executives. When William Ruger, Sr. was asked in 1994 (on his company's forty-fifth anniversary) about the gun industry's responsibility for firearms violence, he said, "It's not my fault. It really isn't."[2] He offered a somewhat muddled elaboration of the defense in the interview:

> But the truth is, there is a huge socially redeeming value to firearms. If you consider them as something on the offense on the street, or that they cause street killing — which they don't [sic]. Guns have the ability to inspire the wrong thinking. The big thing about firearms is that they do give the weak a way to defend themselves against the strong.[3]

Other executives express the same thought in different and more lucid ways, but their variations always boil down to the same evasion of moral, ethical, and practical responsibility. For example, asked in 1981 why Smith & Wesson was selling small, concealable short-barreled handguns, even though ATF data had shown them to be inordinately used in crimes, then-company president James L. Oberg replied, "I sell the guns that the market is demanding."[4]

If this simple-minded "the market made me do it" excuse were valid, it would also justify selling alcohol, cigarettes, or drugs to children. It would justify trafficking in everything from prostitutes to crack cocaine, heroin, and methamphetamine. Markets exist or could easily be developed for scores of products that society bans or heavily regulates. Magnum Research president John Risdall articulated an extreme version of this market rationale by comparing the morality of making and selling guns to the morality of making nuclear weapons. "The morality question for me is that if I thought guns, guns like the ones we manufacture and distribute, are only being used to kill people and stopping this would save lives, I'd stop in a second," he said. "But don't tell me I'm immoral for selling this product. Did the people at Honeywell who were making components for nuclear weapons feel they could be doing something immoral? I don't think so. It was a business."[5]

The condition that Risdall proposed is absurd. He would find making guns immoral only if they are being used "*only*" to kill people. In other words, so long as guns have some other use, no matter how much carnage they wreak, making firearms is just another business. Moreover, the history of the nuclear weapons "business" in the United States is full of examples of people within the industry who publicly questioned the morality of what they were doing, some at great personal cost.

Some gun industry executives blame gun violence on a few "irresponsible" companies. "It's interesting to notice," William Ruger, Sr. told the *New York Times* in 1992, "that some guns are naturally more convenient or cheap for some sort of sick head to get into trouble with."[6] But less than two years after this smug observation, a gun designed and marketed by Ruger—a fifteen-shot P-89 high-capacity semiautomatic pistol—turned out to be "convenient" for a "sick head" named Colin Ferguson to "get into trouble with." Ferguson shot up a Long Island Railroad commuter train, killing six and wounding seventeen.

Asked about that slaughter in a 1994 interview, Ruger said he didn't want "to sound crass or oversimplify things," but he again denied any responsibility. Gun making, he said, "has been an honorable and important business in this country for a long, long time." Warming to his theme, he noted that Sturm, Ruger has always used the talismanic word "responsible" in its catalogues and advertisements. "We're one of the manufacturers that have gone out of the way to make a point of this and to live up to it," he said. "We don't stamp out Saturday night specials in some back room."[7]

In fact, the difference between Saturday night specials and the guns that Ruger and other old-line companies are producing is rapidly becoming academic. Both appear regularly in top ten crime gun lists, in suicides, and in mass shootings. But that aside, when Ruger was asked specifically about the responsibility of manufacturers that *do* "stamp out Saturday night specials in some back room," he declined to assign moral blame even to them. "America is a place of great diversity, and the gun industry is especially diverse and individualistic," he said. "People do their own thing. In any case, in this country you have the constitutional right to make a gun and to buy a gun, however it's made. That's not debatable."[8]

Ruger's arch dismissal of the question as "not debatable" aptly demonstrates that if patriotism is the refuge of scoundrels, the Second Amendment is the refuge of an industry built on instruments of death and injury. But it is not the last refuge of the gun industry. That place is reserved for the old saw to which everyone in the gun industry eventually resorts when all else fails, that "Guns are a matter of individual responsibility. You keep coming back to the fact that people kill people, not guns."[9] No one in the industry seems able or willing to grasp or accept the simple, common-sense concept of *shared* responsibility, or the idea that civilized societies control access to inherently lethal products. This point is underscored when one considers that the risk of death rises dramatically when a gun is involved in an assault. For example, in domestic assaults, the risk of death when a firearm is used is three times greater than in an assault with a knife, and twenty-three times greater than in the case of all other assaults combined, including bodily force (fists, etc.).[10] In short, the ready availability of firearms in the United States escalates the outcome of violent encounters. People attack people, but people *with guns* kill people.

Another industry excuse is to scoff at the U.S. gun problem as overblown news-media hype. In a 1994 interview, for example, Ruger dismissed as "greatly exaggerated" the problem of guns in schools. "I just have to wonder how many schoolchildren go to school and worry about getting shot. If there are some rotten kids who are carrying a gun, that can't happen very often [sic]. But it gets a lot of play with the press."[11]

The 1997 and 1998 rash of children killing other children in schools in towns like Jonesboro, Arkansas, gave the lie to that rationale. That lethal outbreak was predictable, even inevitable. In 1990, the federal Centers for Disease Control (CDC) reported the results of a survey which asked a nationally representative sample of students in grades nine to twelve how many times they had carried a weapon during the past thirty days. One in twenty said they had carried a firearm, usually a handgun.[12] Another survey of eleventh-grade public-school students in Seattle during 1990–1991 found that nearly half of the males (forty-seven percent) reported that they had "easy access" to handguns, and six percent of male students reported having carried a handgun to school at some time.[13]

Blaming the victims is another evasion of responsibility regularly practiced by members of the gun industry. For example, Smith & Wesson chief executive Ed Shultz said in a 1995 interview, "The problem is not the guns. . . . These people that they call children, in my mind, are little criminals and ought to be held accountable."[14]

But newspapers so regularly report shootings of children in cities across the country that we have become numbed to the vulnerability of our own kids to gun violence.[15] In fact, the United States leads the industrialized world in rates of firearm-related deaths among children. A February, 1997 study by the CDC analyzed firearm-related deaths for children under age fifteen in twenty-six industrialized countries and found that *eighty-six percent of the deaths occurred in the United States.* The CDC also found that the overall firearm death rate among U.S. children under age fifteen was nearly twelve times higher than among children in the other twenty-five countries combined.[16] Few of these children were "little criminals" who "ought to be held accountable." On the contrary, children and young adults are the most likely to be victims of unintentional shootings. In the last ten years, more than 2,300 American children fourteen years of age and younger died from unintentional shootings. A recent study by the Violence Policy Center tracked over two hundred incidents of unintentional shooting of children and teenagers, none of whom were "little criminals."[17]

No other consumer industry in the United States—not even the tobacco industry—has been allowed to get away with such evasion of responsibility for the harm it causes.

Why should this be? Is there something about guns that makes them so different from other dangerous products? Common sense and ordinary experience answer "no." In fact, when it suited its purpose, the NRA itself argued that guns are just like other consumer products. In a pamphlet defending semiautomatic firearms, the NRA said, "The development and improvement in firearms are similar to all of the technological progress that Americans have experienced in a wide range of products applicable to any facet of American life."[18]

If one thinks about it, guns are very much like automobiles, one of the most heavily regulated consumer products in the United States. Guns and motor vehicles are the two most lethal consumer products in the United States. The CDC estimates that by the year 2003, firearms will supplant motor vehicles as the leading cause of product-related deaths in the United States. There is no more reason to permit Ruger or Lorcin to manufacture a gun that fires unexpectedly, and therefore kills or wounds users or bystanders, than there is to allow Toyota or General Motors to sell cars that unexpectedly burst into flames or lose steering control.

Although the gun industry has so far successfully avoided being regulated like the automobile industry, the conceptual similarity between guns and motor vehicles is so compelling that even spokespersons for the gun industry cannot help referring to it themselves. They compare guns and their marketing to automobiles and the automobile industry over and over again. Here are just a few examples:

- "We need to teach women that handling a gun is no different than driving a car." Roy Melcher of Interarms, a major gun importer.[19]
- "[You can] buy a Hyundai and it will get you to work, or you can buy a 'Vette or a Porsche Carrera and it will get you there better." Jabie Gray, general manager of Dunn's Discount Gun Mart, referring to semiautomatic assault weapons.[20]
- Manufacturers modify guns the same way carmakers change their designs to keep consumers interested, according to Bob Ricker, the western regional legislative director of the ASSC.[21]
- The Marlin Model 39 22-caliber rifle is the "Chevrolet of the gun industry," according to Marlin executive Frank Kenna, Jr.[22]
- Beretta "is the Rolls-Royce of guns," according to Michael Cornman,

representing Beretta in a trademark infringement suit against General
Motors Corporation.[23]

- A trade-press gun writer tells retailers to learn from the way car dealers
  sell accessories to make their gun stores more profitable. "When shopping for a high-ticket item, like a car or a new handgun, customers go to
  great lengths to make sure they get the lowest possible price. When the
  same customers shop for accessories, however, price is often overlooked
  for quality."[24]

These telling allusions from within the gun industry itself underscore what is obvious to most other people—guns and automobiles
are peas in a pod as consumer products. And in terms of the risks
they present to the public's health and safety, they ought to be regulated and controlled in analogous ways.

The federal government is the only entity in the United States
capable of doing this job. The shortcomings of control measures at
the state level are obvious. Because firearms move in interstate commerce and any measure adopted by a state necessarily stops at the
state line, federal controls setting a regulatory floor are essential (although a given state might implement stronger measures if it
chooses). To be successful, any such product regulation must at a
minimum:

- adequately and effectively regulate firearms as consumer products
- restrict the availability of weapons shown to cause an unreasonable risk
  of injury
- ensure that products developed by the firearms industry do not pose a
  threat to public safety or present an unreasonable risk of injury or death
  to consumers

The first step toward such a rational regimen is to recognize firearms for what they are—inherently dangerous consumer products.
The second is to design a comprehensive, workable regulatory
framework. Let us examine what that framework might look like.

The most extensive body of expertise and knowledge concerning firearms currently resides in the ATF. But the agency has limited
powers and its recent leadership has shown neither the inclination,
the backbone, nor the imagination to use what powers it does have
to take on the gun industry to reduce gun violence. (This is in
marked contrast to the admirable work of ATF agents in investigat-

ing *criminal* trafficking in and use of guns — dangerous, hard work that ATF agents do exceptionally well). This must be changed. Meaningful regulation of the manufacture, distribution, and sale of firearms, firearms-related products, and ammunition will only come about through comprehensive legislation giving ATF regulatory tools like those used every day by other federal health and safety agencies to protect Americans from unreasonably dangerous and defective products.

All of this can be accomplished while still allowing the public to have access to guns with legitimate sporting purposes. There is a national consensus that some firearms should remain available to the civilian population. It is possible to create a regulatory system that acknowledges this consensus and controls firearms just as we currently control other potentially dangerous consumer products. Just as regulation of pesticides did not lead to an outright ban on their use, neither would expanding ATF's authority result in a gun-free United States.

It could, however:

- reduce the availability of specific categories of weapons to criminals, minors, and others currently prohibited from purchasing weapons;
- continue to rein in the abuse of federal firearms dealer licenses;
- place controls on an industry that today is free to manufacture and sell firearms or related products without any consideration of the consequences to the public health and safety; and
- protect purchasers and owners of firearms from products that present a serious risk of injury because of a hazardous design characteristic or manufacturing defect.

The only protection consumers now have against poorly designed firearms is the possibility of a lawsuit after someone has been injured or killed. But the recognition that lawsuits alone are an unsatisfactory product safety approach helped push the Consumer Product Safety Act through Congress. During the debate on the Act in the House of Representatives in 1972, Congressman Edward Roybal of California argued, "The problem . . . is that [a lawsuit] can only aid people after they have suffered injury but it cannot protect them from the initial contact with the improper goods."[24a] In addition, consumers injured by defective firearms may have a harder time recovering for injuries than those hurt by other products because of the highly politicized nature of suits involving guns. Some commentators have argued that courts apply the law differently and far more narrowly to gun cases than to other consumer product suits.[25]

It may make sense to split ATF into two entirely separate agencies, or divide it into two relatively autonomous divisions, one focused on criminal enforcement and the other on product regulation. In any case, existing regulatory models suggest ways to give an enhanced ATF meaningful authority over firearms. Although none of these existing systems are perfect, each offers a far more thorough and thoughtful approach than the current system and each contains components that would vastly improve federal firearms regulation.

The CPSC regulates more than fifteen thousand different consumer products, from baby walkers to coffeemakers to all-terrain vehicles. Virtually every household and product except firearms is within its jurisdiction. It even has jurisdiction over pellet and air guns.

CPSC has the power to ban products, set mandatory safety standards, issue recalls of defective products, monitor industry compliance with standards, and disseminate safety information to the public. In addition, CPSC maintains the National Electronic Injury Surveillance System, a network of about ninety hospital emergency rooms that report product-related injuries. CPSC then conducts in-depth follow-ups on a select number of cases. This system allows CPSC to identify emerging product hazards and to quantify the injury rates associated with the products within its jurisdiction. This information is critical to the agency's ability to respond effectively to specific product hazards.

The National Highway Traffic Safety Administration (NHTSA) oversees the safety of automobiles and automobile equipment. Under the National Traffic and Motor Vehicle Safety Act of 1966, NHTSA has the power to set mandatory safety standards to protect the public from unreasonable risk of accidents resulting from design and manufacturing defects, and from unreasonable risk of injury or death in the event that accidents do occur. The agency may issue recall orders, but the courts have interpreted the Motor Vehicle

Safety Act to prohibit NHTSA from banning a class of vehicles. Nevertheless, the agency probably could issue a safety rule that would in effect ban certain vehicles.

NHTSA has jurisdiction not only over automobiles and trucks but over automobile equipment, such as infant safety seats. This enables the agency to regulate auto safety in a comprehensive and coordinated manner. NHTSA also maintains the Fatal Accident Reporting System, a census of data on all fatal traffic accidents in the United States.

The EPA regulates the manufacture, sale, and use of pesticides pursuant to the Federal Insecticide, Fungicide and Rodenticide Act (FIFRA). No pesticide may be sold in the United States that has not ben registered under the FIFRA. In addition, under the Federal Food, Drug, and Cosmetic Act (FFDCA), EPA establishes acceptable levels of pesticide residues that may be present in food. EPA also may promulgate legally binding labeling requirements under FIFRA.

Congress enacted FIFRA in 1947 in response to the rapid development of new pesticides, their widened use, and their known but not well understood dangers. Although many in the debate supported the continued use of pesticides, a consensus agreed that controls were needed over their manufacture, sale, and use. A central assumption of FIFRA is that pesticides should be available but should be broken down into categories based on the hazards each presents. The most hazardous are singled out for stringent control or prohibition. This logic is applicable in the case of firearms. Where the risks associated with a specific class of firearm are unreasonable when compared to the benefits of use, that use can be controlled without threatening the availability of weapons whose benefits are viewed as exceeding the risk.

If EPA determines that a new pesticide presents an unreasonable risk of adverse effects, the agency may deny the registration altogether, restrict use to specific crops or geographic areas, or require that it be applied only under the supervision of specially trained applicators.

In addition to overseeing pesticides under FIFRA, EPA also administers the Toxic Substances Control Act (TSCA), which is designed to protect human health and the environment by imposing testing and use restrictions on certain potentially harmful chemicals. TSCA authorizes EPA to review the safety of existing chemicals, regulate hazardous substances, and receive premanufacture notification of new chemicals. The agency has the burden of proof to find that a chemical presents an unreasonable risk to public health or the environment.

The FDA is responsible for enforcing laws regulating drugs and medical devices. Under the FFDCA, the FDA must review a drug before it may be tested on humans or marketed. Before the FDA approves a drug, clinical trials must be performed. If the FDA determines that there is sufficient evidence of safety and effectiveness, the agency permits sale of the drug and mandates proper dosages and labeling.

After approval, FDA monitors use of the drug through post-market surveillance and reporting by the manufacturer. Drug manufacturers must report serious and unexpected reactions. The FDA can require modifications in labeling or dosages to remedy problems identified by post-marketing surveillance but lacks the authority to independently order drug companies to recall their products. The FDA also regulates medical devices, which it classifies and controls according to the degree of risk they present.

Each of these systems offers approaches useful in constructing a strategy to effectively regulate firearms as potentially hazardous consumer products. Some are exceptionally instructive.

For example, the primary reason for the creation of the CPSC was the acknowledgment that the number of deaths and injuries associated with certain consumer products was unacceptable, combined with the realization that a piecemeal approach to product regulation was ineffective. The parallels to the gun violence problem are striking.

Congress deals with gun issues in a piecemeal manner, and the ATF can take no action on its own to deal with new hazardous products. Congress also tends to only consider gun control legislation in response to tragedy. For example, the assassinations of Robert Kennedy and the Reverend Martin Luther King, Jr., helped ensure passage of the Gun Control Act of 1968. Likewise, the massacre of schoolchildren in Stockton, California in 1989 sparked efforts to restrict semiautomatic assault weapons. As the sponsors of the CPSA recognized more than twenty years ago, this is not an efficient way to conduct public policy making.

The EPA's regulation of pesticides and the FDA's regulation of medical devices also provide valuable analogies to gun control. Each takes into account the fact that different chemicals and devices present varying degrees of risk. Therefore, those presenting a high risk are subjected to more stringent regulation. Firearms are treated this way to a limited extent under existing law. The National Firearms Act (NFA) has tightly controlled machine guns and certain other especially destructive weapons since 1934. Civilians who want to own a machine gun, rocket, or sawed-off shotgun must fill out a special form, submit photographs and fingerprints, undergo a background check, and pay a transfer tax.

The ATF should have the authority to categorize all weapons that fall under the Gun Control Act of 1968 according to the level of risk each presents to public health and safety. It should have the power to restrict weapons that present unreasonable risks to public health and safety.

The common thread throughout all of these regulatory strategies is protection of consumers and the general public from unreasonable risk of injury or death. By adopting the unreasonable risk standard, a workable legislative framework can be developed from aspects of the regulatory approaches applied to other dangerous products, while still recognizing the unique properties of firearms and the firearms industry.

Independent regulatory agencies are generally better insulated from political pressure, have greater prestige, and can more effectively compete for resources and authority than can the competing divisions of a large executive agency. However, budgetary constraints would probably preclude creating an independent firearms safety agency from scratch. Given that political and fiscal reality, and acknowledging that the ATF already has unique expertise and experience, comprehensive regulatory authority should be vested in the ATF with accompanying budget and staff increases where necessary.

Some have suggested that CPSC, rather than the ATF, be given jurisdiction over firearms. But CPSC is ill-suited for such a task. It has suffered extensive budget and staff cuts and lacks the resources to adequately oversee even the products now within its jurisdiction. In light of CPSC's resource deficiencies and ATF's expertise in the area, it would make more sense to transfer nonpowder firearms (air and pellet guns) from CPSC's jurisdiction and place them under a beefed up ATF. Others have suggested folding ATF into the Federal Bureau of Investigation or into the Secret Service, a branch of the Treasury Department. Neither of these is a good idea. Although both agencies have exceptional law enforcement expertise, neither has the depth of expertise in firearms that ATF has. In addition, neither has any experience in the kind of regulatory role that the enhanced ATF should have. Finally, from time to time both agencies change the focus of their efforts, and thus shift their resources, in response to changes in the nature of the criminal threat. This would subject the firearms safety function—which is not exclusively or even primarily a law enforcement matter—to the hazard of being downgraded or even eliminated if the FBI or the Secret Service decided that the staff or budget could better be used in a criminal law enforcement program. A more effective approach would be to improve the coordination of efforts of all various federal agencies with firearm interests.

ATF should be empowered to operate as a health and safety agency with the ability to:

- set safety standards for firearms, monitor compliance with such standards and issue recalls of defective firearms
- restrict the availability of specific firearms, classes of firearms and firearm products when appropriate, i.e., where the products present an unreasonable risk of injury or death and no feasible safety standard would adequately reduce the risk
- take immediate action to stop the sale and distribution of firearms or firearm products found to be imminent hazards.

Included within these new powers should be enhanced ATF authority to regulate manufacturers, importers, distributors, and dealers in firearms, including requiring much greater information about foreign manufacturers. Stricter regulation of dealers in automatic weapons should also be imposed. The agency should have explicit authority over firearm-related products such as laser sights, and weapons such as rocket and grenade launchers. (Curiously, ATF currently can only regulate the actual rocket or grenade, not the launcher.) Its jurisdiction should be expanded to include nonpowder firearms, such as air and pellet guns.

To effectively carry out these new responsibilities, it would be essential that ATF develop complete data on injuries and deaths associated with firearms and firearm products. Even after decades of debate on guns and violence, the available data on guns and gun violence is limited mainly to incidents of murder compiled in the FBI's *Uniform Crime Reports* and some information culled from death certificates. There exists no coordinated data collection on gun injuries and deaths that includes vital information such as the specific type of weapon, caliber and source. This kind of data would be essential for ATF to identify weapons and weapon types that present a particular public hazard and would help it prioritize its compliance and enforcement efforts.

ATF should also have limited power to prevent products from being marketed if they present an unreasonable risk to public safety. Extensive pre-market testing like that utilized by the FDA over drugs and medical devices may not be appropriate in the case of firearms. But ATF should have the power to issue and enforce rules requiring that it be given pre-market notification of new firearms technology and firearm products. It should have the power to identify and the authority to prevent the marketing of new firearms or firearm products that pose a significant threat to public safety, such as caseless ammunition, armor-piercing ammunition, or nondetectable firearms.

The availability of specific classes of firearms where the evidence clearly demonstrates that such weapons present an unreasonable risk of injury and death should be severely restricted.

- Weapons regulated under the NFA, including silencers, "destructive devices" such as missiles used in grenade and rocket launchers, and land mines, should be banned for future sale.
- Weapons that fall within the definition of assault weapons would be banned in the same manner as were machine guns in 1986. No new versions of assault weapons could be made.
- Handguns should be phased out, starting with a ban on future sale.

It will obviously take time and work to build the national will to take on as well organized and as tough a special interest lobby as the gun industry and its friends in the NRA and other radical groups. But the experience of chipping away at the tobacco industry should give everyone hope that reason can prevail over greed and mass paranoia.

In the meantime, other mechanisms for controlling the gun industry's recklessness should be aggressively explored. They include legal attacks, before the Federal Trade Commission and other state and federal regulatory mechanisms, on the industry's dangerously false and misleading advertising, and on its unconscionable appeals to children. Civil rights and women's groups, ethnic associations, children's advocacy groups, and health care workers should continue to unite in active coalitions to expose the gun industry's cynical marketing efforts and to educate the vast majority of Americans who do not own guns about the risks and cost they bear to indulge the fanatical minority who insist on more and more firepower.

State attorneys general can also apply to the gun industry the lessons they have learned in winning compensation from the tobacco industry for the enormous health care burden it dumped on the United States through its cynical and reckless marketing. If anything, the gun industry's pattern is worse, not only because every single firearm is a lethal weapon, but because the public words of its own senior executives and experts prove that it has deliberately increased lethality solely to sell more guns.

Lawyers and gun control groups must also become smarter about using the growing body of research on the industry to devise and pursue creative new product liability theories.

The bad news in this area is that too many tort lawyers think gun liability law suits are just like "slip and fall" or dangerous power saw cases. They are not. Firearms have been accorded special protection in U.S. law, and simply running again and again into the same wall does more harm than good. The good news, however, is that we are learning more and more about how guns are designed, manufactured, distributed, and sold in the United States. New theories of liability, running from the retail store through the whole-saler to the manufacturer, are being developed.

The prospect of the lawsuits that will inevitably come out of this new knowledge is a growing area of concern for the gun industry. Product liability promises to be the industry's Achilles heel, as vic-tims find new ways to force accountability upon the industry.[26]

Even in 1978, before the current wave of new research and think-ing about gun industry liability began, losses in product liability cases were causing huge premium increases in the gun industry. An industry executive said, "Product liability is the most significantly increasing cost we have."[27] The problem still looms large over the firearms industry: "This issue is real and dangerous," Frank James, *Shooting Industry* gun expert, says. "If we continue with liability, manufacturers will stop manufacturing firearms, and the American gun market will eventually die out."[28]

The heat has seriously affected some manufacturers and threat-ens more. California-based junk-gun manufacturer Lorcin Engi-neering, Inc., filed for bankruptcy protection, citing a large number of product liability suits against it.[29] Hellfire Systems, Inc., the Colorado manufacturer of a device that enhanced the rate of fire of semiautomatic guns, went bankrupt and out of business in the wake of a product liability suit.[30] The Hellfire trigger device was used on a TEC-9 assault pistol by a gunman who murdered eight people and wounded six others in a 1993 shooting at a San Francisco law office.

"Courts always seem to go against the defendant and make it a windfall for the plaintiff," William Ruger, Sr., complained in 1994 about lawsuits by victims of his company's defective products. "Millions! You're lucky when you shoot yourself in the foot in Texas. It's what soldiers used to call the million dollar wound."[31]

Glock has had similar problems. As of December, 1996, at least thirty-five suits had been filed against the company. Although Glock denied liability, it had settled some cases confidentially and refitted a number of guns.[32]

Liability issues even affect the repair of brand new guns. For ex-ample, when a gun manufacturer goes out of business and is bought out, the successor company often refuses to repair guns made by the predecessor, even if they were sold out of dealer stock. "It would create a liability situation for us," said one gun importer. "If we fix a problem gun, then we're liable for it."[33]

Some in the gun industry have realized that there is no inherent reason to limit the risks of liability only to manufacturers. As more studies reveal the pivotal role of dealers and distributors, they also will become fair legal game:

> Is there a problem creeping up on wholesalers and retailers? One they know is out there, lurking in every courtroom . . . ? The answer is "yes" and a lot of wholesalers and retailers don't want to talk about it because the problem is security of firearms and ammunition in the home and the liability associated with that concern.[34]

Thus, dealers who push "defensive packages"—when the truth is that these packages actually increase risks and endanger lives—or who sell guns to incompetent persons will increasingly become the subject of lawsuits. Wholesalers who recklessly distribute firearms to rogue dealers, relying on minimal paperwork, may also soon find themselves hauled to account.

These and other new strategies are of serious concern to the industry, and rightly so.[35] Victims, policy analysts, lawyers, and judges alike will all reconsider ancient legal doctrines as we learn more about the industry's modern record of intentional marketing of lethality.

Finally, the industry should be opened up to the light of day. Congress, state legislatures, and other governing bodies should hold comprehensive hearings and conduct thorough investigations to pierce the veil of the gun industry's secrecy, and bring to light the full story of these merchants of killing power. Americans have the same right to know what drives the gun industry as they do to know what drives the tobacco industry.

Is this a fool's mission? I think not. Most Americans don't own a gun. Most Americans want a safe, and a civil, society. Just as the tide finally turned against the tobacco industry, I believe it will turn against the gun industry when the vast silent majority of Americans learns what it is paying, in lives destroyed and health dollars wasted, to feed the gun industry's little money-making machine.

—Notes

INTRODUCTION: THE MESS

1. U.S. Department of Justice, National Institute of Justice, *Guns in America: National Survey on Private Ownership and Use of Firearms* (May 1997), pp. 6–7.

2. This description does not include well-organized channels of illegal gun trafficking that operate interstate and intrastate in most areas of the United States. Criminals, including juvenile street gangs, use these underground channels, as well as direct transactions in the secondary markets described above, to get guns denied them in the primary market through licensed dealers. Although the operation of these criminal channels per se are beyond the scope of this book, they do serve as important conduits through which the increasingly lethal guns described in later chapters pass into criminal hands.

3. See, "No. 1 With a Bullet; Sales Are Booming, but U.S. Gunmakers Fear Legal Curbs and Foreign Rivals," *The Washington Post* (Jan. 16, 1994), p. H1.

4. Congress has examined the operations of military armaments and munitions manufacturers, usually after a war and in the context of whether the manufacturers gouged the country while supplying its arsenal. Congress also has looked into discrete gun-related problems, such as criminal trafficking in guns, the danger of specific classes of guns like assault weapons, and ways to regulate gun sales. But it has never examined the civilian firearms industry and its practices as a whole to document its structure and workings.

5. The Census of Manufacturers, for example, collects information from appropriate manufacturers about their production of "small arms" and "small arms ammunition." This data includes the number of companies, number of establishments, costs of raw materials, value added in production, and so forth.

   However, the Census Bureau defines "small arms" as weapons with a bore (internal barrel diameter) of 30 mm (or 1.18 inch) or less, and "small arms ammunition" as ammunition for such weapons. This range of barrel bores includes a wide range of military armament, weapons that for the most part are not available to civilians. In fact, the National Firearms Act—the basic federal law that restricts civilian access to military weapons such as grenades, rockets, machine guns, and bombs—classifies any weapon with a barrel bore of more than one-half inch as a "destructive device," subject to strict controls, including federal registration.

   Since the Census Bureau does not reduce the data it collects to finer detail, it is virtually impossible to draw meaningful conclusions about the manufacture of civilian firearms and ammunition from data collected in the Census of Manufacturers.

6. The Census of Retail Trade does provide somewhat more refined detail for "sporting goods" that are sold through "specialty-line sporting goods stores" (as opposed, for example, to "general line sporting goods stores," "discount or mass merchandising," and "department stores"). The Bureau breaks out "firearms, hunting equipment, and supplies" as a separate category of sales through such specialty stores. Again, however, the data is too vague to be of use in defining the firearms industry in particular, since "hunting equipment and supplies" cover a wide range of merchandise

other than guns and ammunition, such as clothing, camping supplies, decoys, and so forth. Moreover, a substantial number of firearms are sold through the other kinds of stores (e.g., mass merchandising) for which the Bureau does not report even this level of detail for sporting goods.

7. "No. 1 With a Bullet; Sales Are Booming, but U.S. Gunmakers Fear Legal Curbs and Foreign Rivals," The Washington Post (Jan. 16, 1994), p. H1; "Gun Industry Has Hidden Economic Impact," USA Today (Dec. 29, 1993), p. 3B; Violence Policy Center, *Who Dies* (August, 1997) (chart).

8. Sporting Arms and Ammunition Manufacturers' Institute, Inc., "Market Size and Economic Impact of the Sporting Firearms and Ammunition Industry in America," undated Background Paper #2, obtained from SAAMI exhibitor's booth at 1998 industry trade show; National Shooting Sports Foundation, *Profile of the Shooting Sports: 1996* (October 1997), p. 10.

9. "Turning Against Guns in Wake of Slaughter," *The Washington Post* (Nov. 7, 1997), "Britain Votes to Ban Handguns," *The Washington Post* (June 12, 1997), p. A1.

10. The president of a major U.S. gun control advocacy group observed pessimistically that "because of long-standing attitudes about guns in America . . . it's unrealistic to expect we"d adopt the laws Britain and Japan have." "Britain Votes to Ban Handguns," *The Washington Post* (June 12, 1997), p. A1.

11. Violence Policy Center, *Who Dies?* (August 1997), and sources cited therein.

12. Ibid.

13. Ted R. Miller and Mark A. Cohen, "Costs," Chapter Five in Rao R. Ivatury, M.D. and C. Gene Cayten, M.D., *The Textbook of Penetrating Trauma* (Williams & Wilkins, Baltimore, 1996), pp. 49–59.

14. The earlier studies cited in and distinguished by Miller and Cohen were Wendy Max and Dorothy P. Rice, "Shooting in the Dark: Estimating the Cost of Firearms Injuries," *Health Affairs*, Winter 1993, pp. 171–185; and Dorothy P. Rice, et al., *Cost of Injury in the US: A report to Congress* (San Francisco, Institute for Health and Aging, University of California and the Johns Hopkins University, 1989).

15. Miller and Cohen arrived at their sobering figures using medical databases containing national gunshot injury and death figures. They applied to that data means of estimation that they found documented in relevant analytical literature. The pair identified six categories of cost incurred when a person is shot with a firearm:

- *Emergency transport and services*, which includes emergency medical transport, police response, and coroner transport in the case of fatalities.
- *Medical care*, which includes the entire range of medical care from emergency treatment at the scene to, in the most severe survival cases, lifetime care. Autopsy and burial costs are included here for fatalities.
- *Administrative costs*, which includes such costs as investigating and processing insurance and other compensation claims, and the costs of administering public welfare payments, for example, to permanently disabled survivors.
- *Productivity losses*, which includes loss of paid and unpaid work for the victim and others immediately affected by the incident. It includes a wide variety of effects from lost wages to replacement costs and schedule dislocations.
- *Costs of pain, suffering, and lost quality of life, which includes the intangible,*

nonmonetary, but nonetheless real costs that are incurred in any injury and that are well recognized by economists and the legal system.

Miller and Cohen analyzed the rates of incidence of shootings and computed the resulting costs for each of these categories. Excluding gunshot deaths due to legal intervention, they found that the total cost *per victim* of gunshot wounds was slightly more than $2.3 million for fatal wounds, $318,000 for nonfatal hospitalizations, and $82,000 for nonfatal victims receiving only emergency department care. The substantially greater cost of fatal wounds is accounted for by the much greater productivity loss in the case of a fatality and by the higher amounts attributed to pain, suffering, and lost quality of life.

16. See, "Guns, Money & Medicine," *U.S. News & World Report* (July 1, 1996), p. 31, 37.
17. Violence Policy Center, *Who Dies?* (August, 1997), and sources cited therein.
18. Ibid.
19. Erik Larson, "The Story of a Gun," *The Atlantic* (January, 1993), p. 48.
20. This discussion of the history of the exclusion of firearms and ammunition from the federal product safety laws is based largely on the statement of Rep. John D. Dingell in Hearings before the Senate Subcommittee on Consumers of the Committee on Commerce, Senate Report 94–12, 1st Session (Feb. 27, 1975). The Senate oversight hearings explored, among other things, the power of CPSC to regulate ammunition. Rep. Dingell, formerly a long-time NRA board member, was among the principal authors of the consumer product safety legislation. He testified in detail about how guns and ammunition came to be excluded from the commission's reach.
21. Remarks of Rep. John Moss quoted in the statement of Rep. John Dingell in Hearings before the Senate Subcommittee on Consumers of the Committee on Commerce, Senate Report 94–12, 1st Session (Feb. 27, 1975), p.135.

PART I. THE GUN BUSINESS

CHAPTER 1: THE MANUFACTURERS

1. For a brief summary of the economic history of the gun industry in the Connecticut River valley, see Christopher Geehern, "Arms and the Man," *New England Business* (August 1990).
2. A private company located in Geneseo, Illinois, now makes and imports firearms under the name Springfield Armory.
3. Various Colt's Manufacturing Company catalogs in files of Violence Policy Center and Colt's Web site; "Glory days gone, Colt shops for investor," *USA Today* (Dec. 29, 1993), p. 3B.
4. "Historical Timeline," from Smith&Wesson company Web site (February 1998).
5. "Winchester History" from company Web site (February, 1998).
6. "A Brief History of Sturm, Ruger & Company, Inc.," from company Web site (February 1998).
7. ATF summarizes the license process as follows: "A license application must include a photograph and fingerprints of the applicant. An application will be approved if the applicant " (1) is 21 years of age or over; (2) is not prohibited from transporting, shipping, or receiving firearms or ammunition in or affecting interstate or foreign commerce; (3) has not willfully violated any provision of the [1968 gun control

law];(4) has not willfully failed to disclose any material information or made any false statement; (5) has in a State premises from which to engage in business; and (6) certifies that the business will comply with State and local law and that local law enforcement officials have been notified of the application." "Licensing," at ATF Web site (March 3, 1998).

8. Wintemute, GJ, Ring of Fire:The Handgun Makers of Southern California (Sacramento, Violence Prevention Research Program), 1994.

9. "The assault gun that won't die," *The Miami Herald* (Nov. 17, 1997), p. 1A.

10. Information about gun manufacturing volume comes from reports manufacturers are required to file with ATF. However, next to nothing is publicly available about the finances of the gun industry. For greater detail about the production of individual manufacturers, see Violence Policy Center, *Firearms Production in America* (annual editions), a compendium of tables from ATF production data.

11. This is the number of licensees. Because a few manufacturers have multiple licenses, the actual number of manufacturing installations may be slightly smaller.

12. In general, individuals are free to manufacture their own guns without obtaining a federal license, provided they aren't legally barred from possessing firearms, and don't sell them. This dispensation does not apply, however, to certain classes of banned firearms, such as semiautomatic assault weapons, machine guns, and assembling certain imported firearms from kits. "Frequently Asked Questions: Does the GCA prohibit anyone from making a handgun, shotgun or rifle?" ATF Internet Web site (March 3, 1998).

13. "Tinier, Deadlier Pocket Pistols Are in Vogue," The Wall Street Journal (Sept. 12, 1996), p. B1.

14. Unless otherwise indicated, the source of gun import data used in this book is the Foreign Trade Division of the U.S. Bureau of the Census. Both the Census Bureau and ATF publish import data. But the data sometimes vary widely for a given year in a way that is impossible to reconcile. This is ultimately because of the different way in which the data are reported to and then aggregated by the two agencies. In some years Census data is higher and ATF lower, in others the opposite. For the sake of consistency, we have chosen to use Census Bureau data, except for years before 1978, for which Census Bureau data is not available.

15. Excludes military weapons, black powder and air guns, flare guns, starter pistols, and other guns not capable of firing a fixed cartridge. It should be noted that Census import totals depend on which standard customs classifications one asks the Bureau to tabulate. In short, it would be entirely possible for another analyst to arrive at somewhat different import figures by including or excluding given categories. We believe the customs categories we have included fairly represent most firearms imported for the civilian market.

16. See, generally, Wendy Cukier, "International Perspectives on Gun Control" (Jan. 5, 1997), Ryerson Polytechnic University, Toronto.

17. These long guns were made by the Miroku Firearms Manufacturing Company, the New SKB Arms Company, and Howa Machinery. In addition to the 80 percent sent to the United States, 18.8 percent were sent to the European market and other countries. The guns are sold in the U.S. under American brand names, such as Browning, Weatherby, and Winchester. "US Buys Most Japanese Guns," *Firearms Business*

(Sept. 1, 1994), p. 6; "US Buys Most Japanese Guns," *Gun Tests* (October 1994), Vol. IV, no. 10, p. 30.

18. "Where are Browning guns made?" from Browning's Web site (February 24, 1998).

19. "Taurus Shoots for the Top!" *Guns & Ammo* (May 1986), p. 46, 48.

20. Ibid, p. 46, 49.

21. "IWA 92—Success for U.S.," *American Firearms Industry* (June 1992), p. 41.

22. U.S. Department of the Treasury, Bureau of Alcohol, Tobacco and Firearms, "Federal Firearms Regulations Reference Guide" (October, 1995), "Canadian Firearms Information [From the Canadian Firearms Policy Centre, Minister of the Solicitor General]," 92.

23. Ibid.

24. "The Para-Ordnance Story," *Guns & Ammo* (June, 1996), pp 68–73.

25. For such a criticism of U.S. tobacco exports, see, e.g., "Expanding a Deadly Export Business," The Washington Post (September 11, 1997), p. A15; for a description of U.S. tobacco marketing abroad, see "Two on Top of the World," *The Washington Post* (July 7, 1997), Washington Business, p.10.

26. See, e.g., "Orlando's Newest Tourist Attraction Draws Fire," *Calgary Herald* (Dec. 26, 1993) p. C23.

27. "Japan Clamors for Stricter Gun Laws," *The Washington Post* (March 16, 1997), p. 23.

28. "Japanese Tourists Get a Bang Out of Local Pastime," *GunGames* (February/March, 1997), vol. 3, no. 1, p. 24.

29. Alaska Department of Public Safety, *Crime Reported in Alaska 1995*, p. 221. (North Pole reported four assaults by firearm, one assault with a knife, one aggravated assault by hands, fist, or feet, and thirty-nine "simple assaults" in 1995.)

CHAPTER 2: THE DEALERS

1. See, e.g., NRA Institute for Legislative Action, *Compendium of State Laws Governing Firearms* (1997), back page; Wright, James and Peter H. Rossi, "Weapons and Violent Crime: Executive Summary," in "Handgun Control Legislation," Hearings Before the Subcommittee on Criminal Law of the Senate Committee on the Judiciary, 97th Congress, 2nd Session (March 4 and May 5, 1982), p. 156.

2. For an overview of current and proposed firearms regulation in the United States, see Josh Sugarmann and Kristen Rand, *Cease Fire: A Comprehensive Strategy to Reduce Firearms Violence* (Violence Policy Center 1997), Chapter Two, "Three Tiers of Regulation," p. 9.

3. The Brady five-day waiting period was to expire in November 1998, after which buyers were to be cleared on the spot through a national "instant check" system. The system contemplates a national computerized database through which gun dealers could immediately check the records of would-be buyers to see whether they are criminals or insane. Enormous technical impediments, however, remained at this writing, including serious deficiencies in the national computerized database.

4. The 1968 GCA, as amended, prohibits the following classes of person from possessing or transferring firearms, and transferring firearms to them: persons indicted or convicted of felonies; fugitives from justice; drug addicts and unlawful users; illegal aliens; persons discharged dishonorably from the military; persons who have re-

nounced U.S. citizenship; persons adjudicated mental defectives or committed to mental institutions; persons under court orders restraining them from stalking or harassing intimate partners or their children; and persons convicted of misdemeanor crimes of domestic violence. 18 U.S.C. Section 922(d), (g).

5. In less than a handful of exceptional states and a few cities with uncharacteristically tough laws the would-be purchaser might be frustrated from legally buying a handgun if she cannot show to the satisfaction of a permitting authority the need to own such a gun. But this is rare.

6. "Frequently Asked Questions: Who Can Get a License?"ATF Web site, March 3, 1998.

7. See, e.g., "Variety is the Spice of Interarms — and Your Store," *Shooting Sports Retailer* (July/Aug. 1992), p. 22.

8. "About Century International Arms," Century International Arms Web site (March 10, 1998).

9. Interarms 1998 catalog.

10. "Arms Dealer Samuel Cummings Dies," *The Washington Post* (May 2, 1998), p. D6.

11. Navy Arms Company catalog, distributed at 1998 industry trade show.

12. "Supplying the Next Generation, " *American Firearms Industry* (January 1993), p. 22.

13. "1997 Distributors Guide," *Shooting Industry,* (Feb. 1997), p. 43.

14. Ibid.

15. Interview with ATF officials, Los Angeles field office.

16. In 1993, the Clinton administration tightened administrative procedures to include more detailed background checks and more cooperation between ATF and local law enforcement regarding licensing. The Brady Law raised license fees. The 1994 crime bill codified many of President Clinton's administrative reforms, required licensees to comply with all state and local laws and to report firearms thefts or losses to ATF, and increased further the flow of information between ATF and local authorities.

17. "Licenses and Inspections," ATF Web site (March 3, 1998).

18. "The Retailers" Biggest Mistake," *American Firearms Industry* (May 1992), p. 68.

19. "Survey Reveals Habits of Gun Buyers," *Shooting Industry* (June, 1995), p. 10.

20. "Is My Customer Qualified to Choose and Buy a Handgun?" *Shooting Sports Retailer* (July/August 1994), p. 8.

21. "Possible Widespread Smuggling of AK47s Probed," *The Washington Post* (May 9, 1989), p. A4.

22. Ibid.

23. See, e.g., "Looks Good, Sounds Better," *Shooting Industry* (July 1995), p. 34.

24. "Merchandising Ethics; Question of Judgment," *Shooting Industry* (December 1979), p. 10.

25. National Shooting Sports Foundation, 1997 SHOT Show Conference Video Series, Volume V: "The Image You Project Is The Image You Sell."

26. "A Lesson on Liability," SHOT Business (July/August 1994), pp. 22, 23.

27. Ibid.

28. Erik Larson, "The Story of a Gun," *The Atlantic* (January, 1993), p. 48.

29. U.S. Department of Justice, National Institute of Justice, *Guns in America: National Survey on Private Ownership and Use of Firearms* (May 1997), pp. 6-7.

30. Federal law defines a "dealer" as "any person engaged in the business of selling firearms at wholesale or retail," as well as gunsmiths and pawnbrokers. 18 U.S. Code, Section 921(a)(11). It limits being "engaged in the business" of a dealer to persons who do so "as a regular course of trade or business with the principal objective of livelihood and profit through the repetitive purchase and resale of firearms," and specifically excludes "a person who makes occasional sales, exchanges, or purchases of firearms for the enhancement of a personal collection or for a hobby, or who sells all or part of his personal collection of firearms." 18 U.S. Code, Section 921(a)(21)(c).

31. For a complete discussion of the history and terms of McClure-Volkmer, see Violence Policy Center, *Gun Shows in America: Tupperware® Parties for Criminals* (1996).

32. Quoted in Violence Policy Center, *Gun Shows in America: Tupperware® Parties for Criminals* (1996), pp. 16, 18.

33. The pro-gun organization Jews for the Preservation of Firearms Ownership offers an "Ask the Rabbi" section on its Web site. Asked about this issue, JPFO's respondent, identified as "Rabbi Mermelstein," replied, "Not only have Jewish gun owners every reason to be outraged by this, but all Americans as well." However, he asked regarding the "sympathy with the Nazi movement" evidenced by such memorabilia, "Is it a reaction to white Protestant anger over perceived reverse discrimination, the result of liberal affirmative action programs?" "Ask the Rabbi," JPFO Web site (March 18, 1998).

34. "Gun Show Dealers Spread Thin," *Firearms Business* (Nov. 15, 1995), p. 4.

35. For a complete discussion of private sales in general and gun shows in particular, see Violence Policy Center, *Gun Shows in America: Tupperware® Parties for Criminals* (1996).

CHAPTER 3: THE PROMOTERS

1. All circulation figures cited in this chapter are from *Bacon's MediaSource* (1st quarter, 1998), except that for *Firearms Business,* which comes from its publisher.

2. Erik Larson, "The story of a gun; Cobray M-11/9," *The Atlantic* (January, 1993), vol. 271, no. 1, p. 48.

2a. Dick Williams, "Ruger West: Sturm, Ruger & Co.'s Plant in Prescott, Arizona," *Shooting Industry* (December, 1993), p. 108.

3. "Gun Industry's Role Is Shrinking," The *New York Times* (August 9, 1981), p. 25.

3a. Dick Williams, "Ruger West: Sturm, Ruger & Co.'s Plant in Prescott, Arizona," *Shooting Industry* (December, 1993), p. 108.

4. The 175 "Proof House" reviews were contained in 60 *Guns & Ammo* issues between 1989 and 1997. The Center did not have all issues for those years at the time the survey was made, but all the issues it did have were included in the survey of evaluations.

5. "Pen Pals Beware! Letters I will and won't answer and why," *Guns & Ammo* (December 1992), p. 22, 23.

6. "How to Choose the Best Handgun for Your Needs!" *Guns & Ammo* (December 1992), p. 34, 35.

7. "Colt's 9 mm AR-15," *Guns & Ammo* (July 1985), pp 34, 76.

8. "New Chief for G&A," *Guns & Ammo* (September 1997), p. 18.

9. "Petersen Publishing Signs Partnership with NSSF," *SHOT Business* (August 1997), p. 4.

10. *SHOT Business* (January 1998), p. 4.

11. "GunGames publisher wants change in industry," *Firearms Business* (July 1, 1995), pp. 3, 4.

12. Ibid.

13. "Studies, Advertising Entice Local Agencies to get Bigger Barrels," *The Palm Beach Post* (June 2, 1996), p. 4B.

14. See, e.g., "Beretta's M9 Anniversary Will Help You Sell This Semi-Auto," *Shooting Industry* (October, 1995), p. 24.

15. *Guns & Ammo* (March 1995), p. 45.

16. 1996 Kahr Arms advertisement in *Shooting Industry* magazine.

17. "First Look! The Kahr K9: A Potent Pocket 9mm," *Guns & Ammo* (May 1995), p. 57.

18. Cover and "Jennings Seeks To Escape 'Gang Gun' Image," *Shooting Industry* (Feb. 1993), p. 12. Jennings is one of the Ring of Fire companies that specialize in the "1990s descendants of the Saturday Night Specials of the 1960s and "70s " poorly made, easily concealable handguns that are disproportionately used in crime."Wintemute, Garen J., *Ring of Fire: The Handgun Makers of Southern California*, Violence Prevention Research Program (Sacramento 1994), p. 2.

19. "Para-Ordnance Super Sub Compact P10," *Guns & Ammo* (January, 1997), pp. 32, 34; see also, "The Para-Ordnance Saga," *Guns & Ammo* (June, 1996), pp 68–73.

20. "Para-Ordnance Super Sub Compact P10," *Guns & Ammo* (January, 1997), p. 82.

21. "Taurus Shoots for the Top!" *Guns & Ammo* (May 1986), p. 46, 90.

22. See, e.g., "The Para-Ordnance Saga," *Guns & Ammo* (June, 1996), p. 68; "Rossi Roundup," *Guns & Ammo* (January, 1996), p. 76; "Industry Insights," *American Firearms Industry* (July 1994), p. 68 (trip to Brazil's Rossi hosted by Interarms); "New Sigma," *Guns & Ammo* (June 1994), p. 34 (gun writers visit Smith & Wesson to try new gun);"Taurus Shoots for the Top!" *Guns & Ammo* (May 1986), p. 46 (gun writer's visit to Brazilian gun manufacturer).

23. "Glock's New Pocket Rockets!" *Guns & Ammo* (January 1996), p. 36, 37.

24. "First Look! AMT's Super-Small .45 Auto," *Guns & Ammo* (November 1994), p. 64;see also, "First Look! M11 — U.S. Army's New Sidearm!" *Guns & Ammo* (Nov. 1992), p. 34; "First Look! Taurus' New .357 Seven-Shooter" *Guns & Ammo* (August 1995), p. 41.; "Exclusive First Look! Beretta Model 800 Cougar," *Guns & Ammo* (May 1995), p. 38.; and "Exclusive! S&W's Revolutionary New . . . Airlite," *Guns & Ammo* (March 1997), p. 44., among literally hundreds of other examples.

25. "4-Gun Combat Cartridge Shootout! 9mm Para vs .357 Magnum vs .40 S&W vs .45 ACP — Is There Just One Combat Champ?" *Guns & Ammo* (March 1995), p. 50; see also "Shoot-Out! .357 SIG Versus .357 Magnum," *Guns & Ammo* (April 1995), p. 40, and others in many issues.

26. "Combat Wheelguns — Selecting the Ideal Revolver for Defense," *Guns & Ammo* (January 1994), p. 48; see also, "Home Defense Gun Buyer's Guide," *Guns & Ammo* (July 1992), p. 38; "Combat Revolver Buyer's Guide,"*Guns & Ammo* (June 1995), p. 64; "Nightstand Guns." *Guns & Ammo* (October 1995), p. 56.

27. Shooting magazines are not alone in their fawning reviews. A *Popular Mechanics* writer, for example, wrote a glowing review of the Beretta 9mm after a visit to the

company's Maryland plant, where he "spent some quality time with it [the gun] at the shooting range." Alex Zidock, "Armed force, subjected to rigorous testing and combat in Desert Storm, the Beretta 92 FS passes muster as the official military sidearm," *Popular Mechanics* (Dec, 1993), vol. 170, no. 12, p. 40.

28. Letter from J. Sutton in *Guns & Ammo* (July 1987), p. 8.

29. "Guns of TV and Movies: Behind the Scenes," *Guns & Ammo* (December 1985), pp. 42–43.

30. Alan Farnham, "Inside the U.S. Gun Business," *Fortune* (June 3, 1991), p. 191.

31. Erik Larson, "The story of a gun; Cobray M-11/9," *The Atlantic* (January, 1993), vol. 271, no. 1, p. 48.

32. "Mossberg Model 500 Bullpup," *American Rifleman* (April 1989), p. 58.

33. "Gun Designer Defends 'American Tradition,'" *Los Angeles Times* (September 11, 1994), p. A-18.

34. "Beretta keeps going great guns," *The Baltimore Sun* (May 1, 1995), p. 6C.

35. "Exploded Views: Smith & Wesson Model 29," *American Rifleman* (September 1987), p. 58.

36. "Dirty Harry's Baddest Magnum," *Guns & Ammo* (June 1984), p. 36.

37. "Smith & Wesson Survives New Age," *The Sunday Gazette Mail* (May 28, 1995), p. 13A.

38. "The Retailers' Biggest Mistake," *American Firearms Industry* (May, 1992), p. 68.

39. "Industry Insights," *American Firearms Industry* (August 1992), p. 76.

40. "Fridley firm boasts a gun 'Dirty Harry' would be proud of," *Star Tribune* (Feb. 1, 1994), p. 1A.

41. Violence Policy Center, *Joe Camel with Feathers: How the NRA with Gun and Tobacco Industry Dollars Uses its Eddie Eagle Program to Market Guns to Kids* (1997).

42. "Gun makers have a friend in the NRA," *The Boston Globe* (December 19, 1993), p. 35.

43. See, e.g., "Government Watch," *Shooting Sports Retailer* (Nov./Dec. 1993), p. 16 (describes funding support and attendance by gun industry, publications and organizations at "eighth annual Gun Rights Policy Conference" in Arlington, Va.).

44. Undated brochure, "The National Shooting Sports Foundation;" see also, "SHOT Show, a comprehensive showcase," *Shooting Sports Retailer* (July/August, 1995), p. 50.

45. "SAAMI Joins Political Fray," *Firearms Business* (Aug. 1, 1994), p. 6.

46. "National Rifle Association," *American Firearms Industry* (May, 1992), p. 14.

47. Undated brochure, "ASSC: Representing The Firearm Industry: American Heritage, History and Tradition;" see also, "American Shooting Sports Council: Giving the Firearms Industry Real Muscle," *The New Gun Week* (Jan. 27, 1995 reprint);"ASSC Hires Team for Anti-Gun Battle; NASGW Gives $100,000 to War Chest, Others Pledge Thousands," *Shooting Industry* (July 1994), p. 14; "Firearms Amnesty, Staying in Business and Attacking Lasers," *Shooting Industry* (Sept. 1996), p. 78; membership lists, files of Violence Policy Center; "Heritage Supports ASSC," *Shooting Industry* (Sept. 1996), p. 13; "ASSC Gains Members, Money," *Firearms Business* (June 1, 1994), p. 8; "American Shooting Sports Council," *American Firearms Retailer* (March 1997), p. 16. "ASSC Re-elects Board, Officers," *Firearms Business* (March 1, 1996), p. 6; "ASSC Elects Board Members," *Firearms*

Business (Feb. 1, 1995), p. 5; "HK President Named to ASSC Board," *Shooting Sports Retailer* (July/Aug. 1993), p. 64; "ASSC Opens Washington Office," *Shooting Industry* (March, 1997), p. 10.

CHAPTER 4: THE MARKET

1. The figure is the net of guns manufactured domestically, imported from abroad, and exported abroad.
2. The Secretary of the Treasury may authorize the import of firearms only if they are not controlled under the National Firearms Act (e.g., machine guns, sawed-off shotguns), 26 U.S. Code 5845(b), and are "generally recognized as particularly suitable for or readily adaptable to sporting purposes . . . ." 18 U.S. Code, Section 925(d), ATF has promulgated a set of standards ("factoring criteria") by which firearms proposed to be imported are evaluated, embodied in ATF Form 4590. These factors consider such things as caliber and barrel length. Interestingly, the criteria actually reward higher calibers (more powerful guns)with higher points.
3. "Beretta: A direct investment plan to recapture its U.S. market," *Business Week* (April 24, 1978), p. 96.
3a. "The Industry While Papers: Expert Intelligence on the State of the Industry; the Future of the Gun Industry," *Shooting Industry*, (July 1993), p. 40.
4. "Cheap imports flood weapon market; China source of pistols, semiautomatics, ammo in US; guns aiming for profit," *The Boston Globe* (Dec. 20, 1993), p. 1. See also, "Foreign Affairs," *Shooting Sports Retailer* (March/April 1995), p. 44, 46 ("The imported firearms and inexpensive ammo starts more shooters and collectors down the path of buying firearms . . ."); "Supplying The Next generation," *American Firearms Industry* (January 1993), p. 22 ("you have to remember, the man or woman who buys these [Ukrainian] guns are people [sic] who are developing an interest in firearms and are looking for an inexpensive entry into the sport.")
5. "Just Who Makes & Who Imports What?" *American Rifleman* (March 1986), p. 36.
6. "PMC 10mm Auto Ammo," *Guns & Ammo* (September 1988), p. 118.
7. "H&K"s USP: Key to a Comeback?" *American Rifleman* (October, 1993, pp. 45–46.
8. This can be seen by "netting out" firearms production and imports in the following two tables, covering 1994 and 1995, the latest years for which both domestic production and foreign import data are available.

Source of Handguns, Rifles, and Shotguns on the U.S. Market, 1994 and 1995

1994

	Handguns	*Rifles*	*Shotguns*	*Total Guns*
Domestic Manufacture	2,602,786	1,349,116	1,254,926	5,206,828
Exported from U.S.	-173,971	-82,226	-146,524	-402,721
Net Domestic Guns	2,428,815	1,266,890	1,108,402	4,804,107
Foreign Imports	1,395,320	698,907	145,233	2,239,460
Total Guns	3,824,135	1,965,797	1,253,635	7,043,567
Percent Foreign Guns	36%	36%	12%	32%

1995

	Handguns	Rifles	Shotguns	Total Guns
Domestic Manufacture	1,722,930	1,331,780	1,173,645	4,228,355
Exported from U.S.	-229,603	-89,053	-100,894	-419,550
Net Domestic Guns	1,493,327	1,242,727	1,072,751	3,808,805
Foreign Imports	865,826	276,288	137,221	1,279,335
Total Guns	2,359,153	1,519,015	1,209,972	5,088,140
Percent Foreign Guns	37%	11%	25%	

Source: ATF, U.S. Census Bureau Foreign Trade Division. Imports do not include military imports. Tables *understate* foreign benefit from the U.S. gun market, since they count as domestic production guns made by companies owned by foreign investors (such as Beretta USA and Smith & Wesson).

9. "Cheap imports flood weapon market; China source of pistols, semiautomatics, ammo in US," *The Boston Globe* (Dec. 20, 1993), p. 1; "AK47 rifles flood into U.S. from Chinese sales war," *The Washington Post* (February 2, 1989), p. A1.

10. "AK47 rifles flood into U.S. from Chinese sales war," *The Washington Post* (February 2, 1989), p. A1, A19.

11. Ibid.

12. "Possible widespread smuggling of AK47s probed," *The Washington Post* (May 9, 1989), p. A4, A-5.

13. "Navy Arms EM45B-3 Airgun," *Guns & Ammo* (October 1988), p. 104.

14. "AK47 rifles flood into U.S. from Chinese sales war," *The Washington Post* (February 2, 1989), p. A1.

15. "Possible widespread smuggling of AK47s probed," *The Washington Post* (May 9, 1989), p. A4.

16. "Cheap imports flood weapon market; China source of pistols, semiautomatics, ammo in US," *The Boston Globe* (Dec. 20, 1993), p. 1.

17. Ibid.

18. "BATF Issues Rules On Imported SKS Rifles," *Shooting Industry* (January, 1994), p. 18; "Chinese Guns, Ammunition Banned," *Firearms Business* (June 15, 1994), p. 1.

19. "Chinese Guns, Ammunition Banned," *Firearms Business* (June 15, 1994), p. 1; "Chinese Gun, Ammo Imports Banned," *Shooting Industry* (August, 1994), p. 38.

20. "Importers Sue Over Chinese Ban," *Firearms Business* (July 15, 1994), p. 1.

21. *Shooting Sports Retailer* (Jan. 1995), p. 91.

22. Open letter in *American Firearms Industry* (January, 1996), p. 27.

23. "Market Weighs Import Options," *Firearms Business* (June 15, 1994), p. 3; "Importers Sue Over Chinese Ban," *Firearms Business* (July 15, 1994), p. 1.

24. "Gun Sting Implicates Chinese Firms," *Firearms Business* (June 1, 1996), p. 1.

24a. "No Recession for Firearms Industry," *The New York Times* (January 13, 1992), p. A12.

25. "A Brazilian Tinsmith's Legacy," *American Rifleman* (December 1988), pp. 22, 82.

26. "No Recession for Firearms Industry," *The New York Times* (Jan. 13, 1992), p. 12.

27. "Industry Insights," *American Firearms Industry* (July, 1994), p. 68.

28. "The Evolution of the Glock Revolution," *Glock Autopistols Annual '95*, vol. 1, no. 1,

p. 7; "The Glock Revolution," International Defense Review (Oct. 1, 1988), vol. 21, no. 10, p. 1352.

29. "The Evolution of the Glock Revolution," *Glock Autopistols Annual '95*, vol. 1, no. 1, p. 7.

30. "The Marketing 100; Gaston Glock; Glock," *Advertising Age* (June 26, 1995), p. 830.

31. Ibid.

32. "The Evolution of the Glock Revolution," *Glock Autopistols Annual '95*, vol. 1, no. 1, p. 7.

33. "ATF Update: Imports From Behind the 'Iron Curtain,'" *Shooting Industry* (August, 1992), p. 14; "CZ Pistols and Rifles Now Brought to America by Magnum Research," *Shooting Industry* (August, 1994), p. 20.

34. "Great Guns from the Great Bear," *American Firearms Industry* (August 1993), p. 34.

35. "Foreign Affairs," *Shooting Sports Retailer* (March/April 1995), p. 44, 46.

36. "Supplying the Next Generation," *American Firearms Industry* (January 1993), p. 22.

37. See, e.g., "Magnum Research Imports CZ Firearms," *Shooting Sports Retailer* (Sept./Oct. 1994), p. 36; "Czech Ammo to U.S. Firm," *Firearms Business* (Jan. 15, 1994), p. 5.

38. U.S. Bureau of Alcohol, Tobacco and Firearms, "Imported Firearms by Country and Type: November 1992 through November 1993," and "Imported Firearms by Country and Type: January 1994 through December 1994."

39. "Russia Imports Denied; Study Set," *Firearms Business* (October 15, 1944), p. 3.

40. "U.S.-Russia Import Deal Irks Trade," *Firearms Business* (March 1, 1996), p. 1-2.

41. "Clinton to Expand Gun Import Restrictions," *Shooting Industry* (February, 1997), p. 13.

42. "Why the *Firearms Business* has tired blood," *Business Week* (Nov. 27, 1978), p. 107.

43. "Domestic Handgun Report," *American Firearms Industry* (April, 1992), p. 58.

44. Beretta originally won the competition in January 1985, but the final award was delayed until May 1989 after Congress ordered a new round of tests inspired by losing domestic competitors. "U.S. Selects M1911 Pistol Successor," *American Rifleman* (March 1985), p. 58; Beretta U.S.A. advertisement in *Guns & Ammo* (September 1989), p. 7.

45. "Beretta: A direct investment plan to recapture its U.S. market," *Business Week* (April 24, 1978), p. 96.

46. "SI Profile: Beretta U.S.A.; firearm manufacturer; company profile," *Shooting Industry* (December, 1989), p. 78.

47. "Italian Gun Maker Beretta Hits U.S. Market With a Bang," *The Plain Dealer* (August 18, 1993), p. 6G.

48. "Beretta keeps going great guns," *The Baltimore Sun* (May 1, 1995), p. 6C; "Beretta wins Navy contract; $18.5 million worth of guns ordered," The Baltimore Sun (Sept. 21, 1995), p. 1C.

49. See, e.g., "Local gun sales healthy, cowboy shooting booming and Beretta teams with Winchester," *Shooting Industry* (May 1996), p. 56.

50. "Kahr K9 is a perfect concealment gun for women," *Shooting Industry* (April, 1996), p. 22.

51. "Son of Moonie leader runs arms factory," *Sunday Telegraph* (Nov. 12, 1995), p. 5.

52. International Association of Fish and Wildlife Agencies, *Proceedings of the First National Shooting Range Symposium* (1990), p. 89.

53. Production figures in this section are based on data from U.S. Bureau of Alcohol, Tobacco and Firearms, "Civilian Firearms—Domestic Production, Importation, and Exportation."

CHAPTER 5: "A LITTLE MONEY-MAKING MACHINE"

1. For an exhaustive treatment of the role the frontier myth has played in American cultural history, see Richard Slotkin, *Gunfighter Nation: The Myth of the Frontier in Twentieth Century America* (Atheneum, 1992).

2. "Hunting in the 21st Century," *Shooting Sports Retailer* (May/June, 1995), p. 16.

3. $148.8 million of Ruger's 1996 sales, and $141.8 million of its 1997 sales were from firearms. "Board chairman William Ruger, Sr. found cause for optimism despite the fact that 1997 results did not meet the record levels achieved in 1996. He pointed out that his company's earnings per share during the second half of 1997 were better than those recorded during the comparable period of 1996. Ruger also noted significant improvement on the balance sheet in cash, short term investments and inventories." "Ruger 1997 Earnings Well Below Previous Year," *Firearms Business* March 1, 1998), p. 4.

4. "Two Short Guns Vie for Pocket Space; chiefs special and undercover: weapons coveted by discriminating thugs," article reprinted in series titled "The Snub-Nosed Killers, Handguns in America," by Cox Newspaper Services (Fall, 1981), p. 10.

    Smith & Wesson has continued "focusing on dollars" into the 1990s by, e.g., marketing firearms especially targeted at women, and by pushing small, concealable, powerful semiautomatic pistols and revolvers, including so-called "minimagnums." "Smaller Size Big Seller in New Era of Handgun," *The Plain Dealer* (Dec. 14, 1995), p. 16A; "Reading the Handgun Market," *Shooting Industry* (June, 1992) vol. 37, no. 6, p. 29.

5. Joel Millman, "Steady Finger on the Trigger," *Forbes* (Nov. 9, 1992), p. 188.

6. Ibid.

7. "Sturm, Ruger & Co., Inc.; Corporate Facts," *The Hartford Courant* (May 13, 1996), *Business Weekly*, p. 4.

8. "Heiress Gets 60 Days In Polo Player's Slaying," *The Washington Post* (May 14, 1998), p. A1 (reporting voluntary manslaughter conviction and sentencing of Cummings" daughter).

9. "Any handgun cartridge will kill, given the right placement." Handgun "expert" Jan Libourel, "Handgun Stopping Power: The Current Controversy," *Guns & Ammo* (Oct, 1992), p. 40.

10. Violence Policy Center, *Who Dies? A Look At Firearms Death and Injury in America,* (August 1996), p.1

11. "Semi-Auto Firearms: The Citizen's Choice," NRA pamphlet quoted in "Gun Makers Have a Friend in the NRA; Guns Aiming for Profits," *The Boston Globe* (Dec. 19, 1993), p. 35.

PART II. THE SPIRAL OF LETHALITY

CHAPTER 6: THE DEADLY ROLE OF INNOVATION

1. Massad Ayoob, "Presentation Guns Make Ideal Gifts While Increasing Sales," *Shooting Industry* (February, 1996), p. 14. For the most part, Ayoob's "Lethal Force" column advises gun dealers on how to boost sales through emphasizing the "self-defense" market.

2. "Used Firearms Draw Customers," *Firearms Business* (March 15, 1996), p. 5.

3. "Huge Used Gun Market Helps Keep the Cash Flowing," *Shooting Industry*, (August, 1995), p. 22.

4. "Why the *Firearms Business* has tired blood," *Business Week* (Nov. 27, 1978), p. 107.

5. "Gun Industry's Role is Shrinking," *The New York Times* (Aug. 9, 1981), p. 25.

6. "Shot-in-arm Sought for Rifle Biz; Shotguns Bang-up," *Discount Store News* (Jan. 23, 1984), vol. 23, p. 24.

7. "Rambo Fad in Weapons Draws Fire; High Tech Arms and Easy Access Center of Debate," *The San Diego Union Tribune* (January 23, 1989), p. A-1.

8. "Ailing Gun Industry Confronts Outrage Over Glut of Violence," The *New York Times* (March 8, 1992), sec. 1, p. 1, col. 1.

9. "Hunting in the 21st Century," *Shooting Sports Retailer* (May/June, 1995), p. 16.

10. U.S. Department of Justice, National Institute of Justice, *Guns in America: National Survey on Private Ownership and Use of Firearms* (May 1997), p. 2.

11. North American Hunting Club, *National Shooting Range Symposium: Proceedings* (1993), p. 33 (emphasis in original). See also, remarks of U.S. Fish & Wildlife Service deputy director Ken Smith at the same symposium, p. 11. ("Let us put it on the line — hunters are facing a rapidly growing image problem in this country and the number of hunters has declined in recent years. Some recent studies have predicted that by the middle of the next century, hunting in this country will be history.")

12. "The Four-gun Family in Their Sights: US Gunmakers Are on the Offensive," *Financial Times* (March 2, 1996), p. 7.

13. "Hunting, Shooting Remains Static," *Firearms Business* (Dec. 1, 1996), p. 8.

14. "Discount Chains Weigh Gun Sales," *Firearms Business* (Nov. 15, 1993), p. 3.

15. "Wal-Mart to Banish Handgun Sales at All Stores," *Shooting Industry* (February, 1994), p. 12; "Discount Chains Weigh Gun Sales," *Firearms Business* (Nov. 15, 1993), p. 3; "Mall of America Won't Sell Handguns," *Shooting Industry* (October, 1993), p. 21.

16. "Running Scared: The Pressures that Forced America's Largest Discounter to Quit Stocking Handguns," *Shooting Sports Retailer* (July/August 1994), p. 12.

17. "Doing Business in the Golden Age of the Consumer," *Shooting Industry* (February 1997), p. 29.

18. "The industry white papers: expert intelligence on the state of the industry; the future of the gun industry," *Shooting Industry* (July, 1993), vol. 38, no. 7, p. 40.

19. "Sizzling .50 Action Express," *Guns & Ammo* (April, 1996), p. 78.

20. "Ruger P-85 9 mm Pistol," *American Rifleman* (July, 1987), p. 60, 62.

21. "Ailing Gun Industry Confronts Outrage Over Glut of Violence," The *New York Times* (March 8, 1992), sec. 1, p. 1, col. 1.

22. Joel Millman, "Steady finger on the trigger," *Forbes* (Nov. 9, 1992), p. 188.

23. Ray Ordorica, "Industry News," *Handguns '98: 10th Annual Edition* (DBI Books, 1998), p. 7.

24. "A Home Grown Product," *American Firearms Industry* (March 1997), p. 70.

25. "Sure as shootin'—No longer gun shy, Californians discover a new status symbol," *Chicago Tribune*, Tempo section, p. 1.

26. "The defensive handguns your customers will be looking for in 1996," *Shooting Industry* (March, 1996), vol. 41, no. 3, p. 16.

27. "Headache Cure #2000," *Shooting Sports Retailer* (January 1997), p. 6.

28. "Ailing Gun Industry Confronts Outrage Over Glut of Violence," The *New York Times* (March 8, 1992), sec. 1, p. 1, col. 1.

29. "Industry Insights," *American Firearms Industry* (February, 1993), p. 74.

30. "Understanding the Modern Revolver," *Guns & Ammo* (August 1989), p. 86.

31. For a discussion of some of these reasons, see "Is the 9mm Dead?" *Guns & Ammo* (December 1991), p. 30.

32. "Jordan on Handguns: Sixgun vs. Auto," *Guns & Ammo* (December 1980), p. 30–31. See also, "Jordan on Handguns: Wheelgun Fan," *Guns & Ammo* (April 1981), p. 31 (for "serious work" advises reader to "shoot a revolver like the smart cops do.")

33. See, e.g., Sterling Arms Corp. advertisement, *Guns & Ammo* (March 1981), p. 81 (". . . an all American-made .32 double action automatic pistol"); "Jordan on Handguns: Wheelgun Fan," *Guns & Ammo* (April 1981), p. 31 (for certain types of target-shooting advises reader to "shoot an automatic. . . .").

34. See, "Trigger Trickery," *Guns & Ammo* (February 1991), p. 20.

35. See, "Handgun Breakthrough: New Double-Action Only Autos," *Guns & Ammo* (November 1990), p. 49.

36. "The Double-action 9mm Pistol," *American Rifleman* (April 1983), pp.38, 41.

37. Description of a given pistol's ammunition capacity sometimes varies, depending on whether it can be safely carried with a round in the chamber, in addition to those in the magazine proper. Thus, a gun that has a fourteen-round maximum magazine capacity, but can also carry one additional round in the chamber, may be described as having "14," "14+1", or "15" round capacity.

38. Ailing Gun Industry Confronts Outrage Over Glut of Violence," The *New York Times* (March 8, 1992), sec. 1, p. 1, col. 1.

39. "Gun firms spur market; Stronger weapons sales coincide with more violence," *The Boston Globe* (December 19, 1993), p. 1.

40. "Top 10 Gun Trends of the Decade! Handguns," *Guns & Ammo* (September 1989), p. 38.

41. "Ailing Gun Industry Confronts Outrage Over Glut of Violence," The *New York Times* (March 8, 1992), sec. 1, p. 1, col. 1.

42. "High-Tech Handguns: Futuristic Firepower!" *Guns & Ammo* (January, 1994), p. 32, 35.

43. "Astra Model A-80," *Guns & Ammo* (January 1982), p. 66.

44. Beretta U.S.A. advertisement in *American Rifleman* (October 1993), p. 15.

45. U.S. Department of Justice, Office of Justice Programs, *Guns in America: National Survey on Private Ownership and Use of Firearms* (May 1997), p. 6

46. "Magazine Capacity: How Much Is Enough?" *Guns & Ammo* (September 1987), pp 66, 67.

47. "Springfield's New .45 Super V-12 Pistol," *Guns & Ammo* (September, 1997), p. 48.

48. See, e.g., "The 9mm Flood! G&A Reviews 10 Top Choices," *Guns & Ammo* (October 1987), p. 42.

49. "30 Years of Handguns," *Guns & Ammo* (September 1988), p. 74; "Handgun Firepower: How Much Do You Need?" *Guns & Ammo* (November 1991), p. 32, 77; "The Double-action 9mm Pistol," *American Rifleman* (April 1983), pp. 38, 67.

50. "9 mm gun the choice on streets," *Chicago Tribune* (June 13, 1993), p. 1.

51. Quoted in "Gun firms spur market; Stronger weapons, arms sales coincide with more violence," *The Boston Globe* (Dec. 19, 1993), p. 1.

52. "Ruger Divulges Production Figures," *Shooting Industry* (April, 1994), vol. 39, no. 4, p. 14.

53. "Top 18 handguns used by criminals," *USA Today* (June 3, 1992), p. 4A.

54. "9 mm gun the choice on streets," *Chicago Tribune* (June 13, 1993), p. 1.

55. "Gun firms spur market; Stronger weapons sales coincide with more violence," *The Boston Globe* (December 19, 1993), p. 1.

56. "Guns, Money & Medicine," *U.S. News & World Report* (July 1, 1996), p. 31, 34.

57. "9 mm gun the choice on streets," *Chicago Tribune* (June 13, 1993), p. 1.

58. "Gun firms spur market; Stronger weapons, arms sales coincide with more violence," *The Boston Globe* (Dec. 19, 1993), p. 1.

59. "Juvenile Weapons Arrests Double," *Firearms Business* (Dec. 1, 1995), p. 7.

60. William Ecenbarger, "The Allure of Killer Weapons," *The Houston Chronicle* (January 23, 1994), *Texas Magazine*, p. 10.

61. "9 mm gun the choice on streets," *Chicago Tribune* (June 13, 1993), p. 1.

62. Erik Larson, "The story of a gun; Cobray M-11/9," *The Atlantic* (January, 1993), vol. 271, no. 1, p. 48.

CHAPTER 7: A DOMESTIC ARMS RACE

1. "Police and Firearms," *American Rifleman* (March 1981), p. 32.

2. See, e.g., "For Our Police: Auto or Revolver: Which is Best?" *American Rifleman* (December 1983), p. 38; "D.C. Police Consider Upgrading Weapons; Increased Firepower of Criminals Cited," *The Washington Post* (June 19, 1987), p. C1; "Escondido's police force is going for a faster gun," *The San Diego Union-Tribune* (July 18, 1987), p. B-8; "P.G. Police to Boost Firepower," *The Washington Post* (Feb. 21, 1988), p. C1; "Feeling outgunned, police turn to automatic weapons; Revolvers are out, pistols are in with many departments," *The Boston Globe* (Sept. 5, 1988), p. 25; "New pistol scores hit with officers," *St. Petersburg Times* (Dec. 25, 1988), *Citrus Times* section, p. 1; "Cops move firepower toward par with foes," *The San Diego Union-Tribune* (March 4, 1989), p. II-1; "The arming of America; in cars, buses, trains and planes, guns make their way from Southern states with lenient gun control laws to criminals in New York and Massachusetts," *The Boston Globe* (April 23, 1989), p. 16 (Boston, Mass.); "Lodi Police Reach for 9mm Guns," *The Record* (July 16, 1989), p. 5; Gordon Witkin, "Cops Under Fire," *U.S. News & World Report* (Dec. 3, 1990), vol. 109, no. 22, p. 32; "FBI trading its revolvers for more potent firepower," *St. Petersburg Times* (April 6, 1991), p. 12A.

3. Lt. Tommy Merritt, Citrus (Fla.) County Sheriff's office, quoted in "New pistol scores hit with officers," St. Petersburg Times (Dec. 25, 1988), *Citrus Times* section, p. 1.

4. "What's New? A Look at the Latest in Handguns," *Guns & Ammo Annual* (1989), p. 20; "Beretta Draws Bead on Market for Faster Guns," *Washington Business Journal* (March 7, 1988), vol. 6, no 41, p. 1.

5. "Semi-Auto Pistol Schools Scheduled," *American Rifleman* (March, 1988), p. 58; "Selecting the Police Pistol," *American Rifleman* (December, 1987), p. 36; "Seminar Features Semi-Auto Pistols," *American Rifleman* (October, 1987); "Seminar Features Semi-Auto Pistols," *American Rifleman* (August, 1987).

6. "Selecting the Police Pistol," *American Rifleman* (December, 1987), p. 36.

7. "Cops Under Fire," *U.S. News & World Report* (Dec. 3, 1990), p. 32.

8. Kevin Krajick, "Arms Race on Hill Street," *Newsweek* (Nov. 19, 1990), p. 58; "How much firepower do police need? The arguments for semi-automatic pistols are gaining ground, even though the statistics don't back them up," *The Toronto Star* (Dec. 7, 1993), p. A17.

9. U.S. Department of Justice, Bureau of Justice Statistics, "Law Enforcement Statistics," Web site (April 6, 1998).

10. U.S. Department of Justice, Federal Bureau of Investigation, *Law Enforcement Officers Killed and Assaulted 1993*, Section I, Table 4, p. 14; Section II, Table 4, p. 68.

11. "Police and Firearms," *American Rifleman* (March 1981), p. 32.

12. "9 mm gun the choice on streets," *Chicago Tribune* (June 13, 1993), p. 1.

13. "Combat Wheelguns: Selecting the Ideal Revolver for Defense," *Guns & Ammo* (January 1994), p. 48, 53.

14. Kevin Krajick, "Arms Race on Hill Street," *Newsweek* (Nov. 19, 1990), p. 58; see also, "Bigger Guns No Help to Police?", *The Toronto Sun* (Feb. 13, 1994), p. 2 (Canadian study argued firepower increase irrelevant because "in most cases" of police being fatally shot the officers "had no reason or opportunity to even draw their firearms . . . let alone to actually use them.").

15. Kevin Krajick, "Arms Race on Hill Street," *Newsweek* (Nov. 19, 1990), p. 58.

16. "Marc Cobb Wins Police Crown," *American Rifleman* (December 1989), p. 34, 35; see, "Philip Hemphill is 1988's Top-Shooting Lawman," *American Rifleman* (December 1988), p. 30..

17. "Was NYPD Too Quick To Fire? Critics question rush to 9 mms.," *Newsday* (June 8, 1995), p. 19.

18. "Escondido's police force is going for a faster gun," *The San Diego Union-Tribune* (July 18, 1987), p. B-8.

19. "Cops move firepower toward par with foes," *The San Diego Union-Tribune* (March 4, 1989), p. II-1.

20. Kevin Krajick, "Arms Race on Hill Street," *Newsweek* (Nov. 19, 1990), p. 58.

21. "Handgun Firepower: How Much Do You Need?" *Guns & Ammo* (November 1991), p. 32, 78.

22. "Firepower, Cops & 9 mm Guns; Sidearmed and Dangerous; Are NY Cops gun crazy after switch to 9-mms?", *Newsday* (June 4, 1995), p.5.

23. Lars Erik-Nelson, "Glock Pistol May be a Loose Cannon," *Daily News* (New York)(October 16, 1995), p. 29.

24. Ted Gest, "Trying to take gun makers to court," *U.S. News & World Report* (Dec. 2, 1996), p. 38; Lars Erik-Nelson, "Glock Pistol May be a Loose Cannon," *Daily News* (New York)(October 16, 1995), (editorial), p. 29.

25. "Handgun Firepower: How Much Do You Need?" *Guns & Ammo* (November 1991), p. 32, 78.

26. "What about the wheelgunner? Does it always make sense to switch from the re-volver to the auto?" *Guns & Ammo* (September, 1990), P. 90.

27. "10-shot combat shooting tactics," *Guns & Ammo* (February 1995), p. 66, 67.

28. See, e.g., "Mayhem in Miami: What *Really* Happened?" *Guns & Ammo* (June 1988), p. 96; "The FBI Ammo Tests," *American Rifleman* (June 1990), p.35; "Is the 9mm Dead?" *Guns & Ammo* (December 1991), pp. 30, 34.

29. "Mayhem in Miami: What *Really* Happened?" *Guns & Ammo* (June 1988), p. 96.

30. "Mayhem in Miami: What *Really* Happened?" *Guns & Ammo* (June 1988), p. 96; "The FBI Ammo Tests," *American Rifleman* (June 1990), p. 35; "Is the 9mm Dead?" *Guns & Ammo* (December 1991), pp. 30, 34.

31. "The FBI Ammo Tests," *American Rifleman* (June 1990), p.35.

32. Ibid.

33. "A First Look . . . Colt's New 10mm Auto," *Guns & Ammo* (January 1987), p. 34.

34. "Is the 9mm Dead?" *Guns & Ammo* (December 1991), pp. 30, 79.

35. "Colt's Delta Elite: New 10mm Auto," *Guns & Ammo* (February 1988), p. 48; "Bren Ten: The 10mm Powerhouse," *Guns & Ammo* (August 1984), p. 36.

36. "Bren Ten: The 10mm Powerhouse," *Guns & Ammo* (August 1984), p. 36, 41.

37. "Colt's Delta Elite: New 10mm Auto," *Guns & Ammo* (February 1988), p. 48, 49. See also, Letter from David Germanaro to *Guns & Ammo* (July 1985), p. 12.

38. "Colt's Delta Elite: New 10mm Auto," *Guns & Ammo* (February 1988), p. 48.

39. "A First Look . . . Colt's New 10mm Auto," *Guns & Ammo* (January 1987), p. 34.

40. "Today's Tremendous 10mm Guns and Ammo," *Guns & Ammo* (September 1989), p. 58.

41. "Is the 9mm Dead?" *Guns & Ammo* (December 1991), pp. 30, 34.

42. "The FBI Ammo Tests," *American Rifleman* (June 1990), p. 35.

43. "A Pair of Tens," *American Rifleman* (June 1990), p. 33, 35.

44. See, e.g.,"Is the 9mm Dead?" *Guns & Ammo* (December 1991), pp. 30; "9 vs 10: A Matter of Power!" *Guns & Ammo* (June 1990), p. 82.

45. "FBI to Use Semiautomatic Handguns; Sessions Issues Order in Response to Crimi-nals' Increased Firepower," *The Washington Post* (Sept. 12, 1989), p. A28. For a critique of the FBI's decision to go for 10 mm over 9 mm, and an overview of the American move to 9 mm pistols in general, see Don Walsh, "Firefight," *Defense & Foreign Affairs* (April, 1989), p. 20.

46. "The FBI Load: A Restrained 10mm for the Feds," *Guns & Ammo* (January 1990), p. 83.

47. "Smith & Wesson Model 1076 10mm Pistol," *Guns & Ammo* (January 1991), p. 72.

48. ".40 S&W: The end of the 9mm?" *Guns & Ammo* (June 1990), p. 42.

49. "The Fightin" .40 S&W," *Guns & Ammo* (July 1991), pp. 34, 37.

50. "Smith & Wesson's Hot New .40 Auto Cartridge," *Guns & Ammo* (April 1990), pp. 48, 51.

51. "Ruger P90DC Pistol," *American Rifleman* (November 1991), p. 52.

52. ".40 S&W: The end of the 9mm?" *Guns & Ammo* (June 1990), p. 42.

53. ".40 S&W Ammo: Choices Aplenty," *American Rifleman* (September 1991), p.40.

54. "New Ultra-Compact '40': Smallest Mid-Bore Yet!" *Guns & Ammo* (February 1991), p. 32.

55. "Ruger P90DC Pistol," *American Rifleman* (November 1991), p. 52.

56. "Combat Handgun Trends," *Guns & Ammo* (May 1991), pp. 30, 32.

57. See, e.g., "Ruger P90DC Pistol," *American Rifleman* (November 1991)(high capacity .45 auto makers listed); "Glock Model 21 .45 Auto," *Guns & Ammo* (October 1991), p. 83; "Smith & Wesson Model 4516," *American Rifleman* (February 1990), p. 52.

58. "Para-Ordnance Steel-Frame 14-Shot .45 Kit," *Guns & Ammo* (January 1990), p. 70; "Para-Ordnance 13-Shot .45 Kit," *American Rifleman* (July 1989), p. 65. The difference in the two articles" headlines illustrates the ambiguity one often finds in descriptions of pistol capacity. The *Guns & Ammo* headline ("14-Shot") counts thirteen rounds in the magazine proper and one in the pistol chamber (13+1) for a total of fourteen overall.

59. Telephone interview by Violence Policy Center staff with Miami Beach Police Department detective; "Cunanan found dead amid sodas, handguns," *The Miami Herald* (August 6, 1997); "Hunt over, mystery continues," *Amarillo Globe News* (July 25, 1997); "With a last defiant act, he denies us answers," *The Philadelphia Daily News* (July 25, 1997); "Evidence that Cunanan is serial killer mounts," *Sun-Sentinel* (July 22, 1997); "Versace gun matches other killings," *The Miami Herald* (July 22, 1997).

CHAPTER 8: THE RAMBO FACTOR

1. See, e.g., *The Gun Digest Book of Assault Weapons* (3d ed.1993), p. 41 (". . . one could not afford to waste even one round climbing over their heads when you were hosing them down.").

2. See, e.g., J. Flores, *Full Auto Modification Manual* (Desert Publications 1987), which includes narrative instruction and machining diagrams for converting Ingram MAC 10 and MAC 11, Ruger Mini 14, H&K 91 and 93, Colt AR-15, and the M-1 Carbine. The author has videos demonstrating certain conversions.

3. Duncan Long, *Assault Pistols, Rifles and Submachine Guns* (Citadel Press 1986), p. 3.

4. "Partisan Avenger .45 Assault Pistol," *Guns & Ammo Handgun Annual* (1989), p. 26.

5. See, e.g., "Sites Spectre HC Pistol," *American Rifleman* (December 1990), pp. 56, 58 (". . . a gun like the Spectre is primarily intended for hip-firing."); "Steyr Mannlicher SPP Pistol," *American Rifleman* (August 1993), pp. 70, 72 (". . . where the SPP really shines is in firing from the hip.");"Colt's 9mm AR-15," *Guns & Ammo* (July 1985), pp. 34, 76 ("fired from the hip . . . about as natural a pointer as you can get."); "H&K's 9 mm Para Carbine," *Guns & Ammo* (November 1983), p. 42, 44 (hip-shooting "surprisingly easy" with the HK 94 9 mm Carbine). Reviewers also commented on other assault weapon features. For example, a *Guns & Ammo* review of the SPAS 12 shotgun listed "pistol grip design," "oversized fore-end with the ventilated hand-guard," and "skeletonized folding stock" as components of the gun's " 'assault' format." "The Formidable SPAS 12 Shotgun," *Guns & Ammo* (March 1983), p. 60. (". . . built from the ground up to be an 'assault' shotgun.").

6. "Calico M-100 rifle," *American Rifleman* (January 1987), p. 60, 61.

7. "How Effective is Automatic Fire?", *American Rifleman* (May 1980), p. 30.

8. *The AK-47 Assault Rifle* (Desert Publications 1969), p. 1.

9. *The Gun Digest Book of Assault Weapons* (3d ed.1993), p. 41.

10. "Partisan Avenger .45 Assault Pistol," *Guns & Ammo Handgun Annual* (1989), p. 26.

11. *The Gun Digest Book of Assault Weapons* (3d ed.1993), p. 141; *The AK-47 Assault Rifle* (Desert Publications 1969), p. 3. ("In the traveling position, in movement on skis, and in parachute jumps, the metal stock is folded beneath the receiver.")

12. See "FN FNC Rifle," *American Rifleman* (January 1988), p.58.

13. Silencers are regulated under the National Firearms Act. Civilian owners are required to register such devices and pay a special tax. 26 U.S. Code Ch. 53.

14. Some assault weapons apologists have attempted to dismiss flash suppressors or "flash-hiders" as nothing more than muzzle brakes, intended to reduce recoil and "muzzle flip." See, e.g., "Tomorrow's State-of-the-Art Sporting Rifle," *Guns & Ammo* (July 1981), pp. 48, 53. But for a review of such a flash suppressor's actual effectiveness, see "Bushmaster's A-Team," *Guns & Ammo* (August 1983), pp. 42, 84 ("Only a small brief flash was observable with this little wonder"). Also, the NRA regularly described such features as "flash hiders" without qualification in its reviews of assault weapons. See,e.g., "Valmet M78 Rifle," *American Rifleman* (April 1988), p. 64; "Beretta AR.70 Rifle," *American Rifleman* (March 1988), p. 64; "FN FNC Rifle," *American Rifleman* (January 1988), p. 58.

15. *Ruger Carbine Cookbook* (Desert Publications 1995), pp. 46–47.

16. PFM advertisement in *American Rifleman* (June 1981), p. 22

17. Gander Mountain advertisement, *American Rifleman* (October 1984), insert between pp. 24–25.

18. Ram-Line advertisement, *American Rifleman* (August 1986), p. 4.

19. "Ram-Line Magazine Loader," *American Rifleman* (February 1987), p. 41.

20. "Bantam Battle Rifles," *Guns & Ammo* (January 1987), p. 76.

21. *Ruger Carbine Cookbook* (Desert Publications 1995), p. 49.

22. "The Scorpion"Intratec's New TEC-22," *Guns & Ammo Handguns Annual 1989*, p. 52.

23. In addition to other articles cited in this chapter, a sampling from the period 1980 to 1990 includes: "Kimel AP-9 Pistol," *American Rifleman* (January 1990), p. 55; "Intratec Tec-22 Scorpion," *American Rifleman* (September 1989), p. 67; "Sterling Mark 6 Carbine," *American Rifleman* (December 1988), p. 54; "Federal Engineering XC-450," *American Rifleman* (June 1988), p. 58; "Valmet M78 Rifle," *American Rifleman* (April 1988), p. 64; "Beretta AR.70 Rifle," *American Rifleman* (March 1988), p. 64; "Heckler & Koch Model 94 Carbine," *American Rifleman* (February 1988), p. 46; "Feather AT-22 Rifle," *American Rifleman* (November 1987), p. 66; "Chinese AK-47 .223," *Guns & Ammo* (August 1986), p. 84; "Daewoo K1A1 Carbine and K2 Rifle," *American Rifleman* (May 1986), p. 52; "UZI Semi-Automatic .45 Carbine," *American Rifleman* (January 1986), p. 59; "A Sterling Duo," *Guns & Ammo* (February 1984), p. 62; "UZI Semi-Automatic Carbine," *American Rifleman* (August 1981), p. 55; "The Military Look-Alikes," *American Rifleman* (April 1980), p. 30.

24. "Rambo fad in weapons draws fire; high tech arms and easy access center of debate," *The San Diego Union-Tribune* (January 23, 1989), p. A-1.

25. Ailing Gun Industry Confronts Outrage Over Glut of Violence," The *New York Times* (March 8, 1992), p. A1.

26. "UZI Semi-Automatic .45 Carbine," *American Rifleman* (January 1986), p. 59 ("The sole reason for the lengthy development time was so that BATF could . . . allow its importation"); "Sterling Mark 6 Carbine," *American Rifleman* (December 1988), p. 54 ("a gun "primarily designed to meet the demand of U.S. civilian enthusiasts," as the company literature states."); "The Incredible UZI," *Guns & Ammo* (January 1982), p. 33 ("a semi-automatic derivative aimed primarily . . . at the commercial American market.").

27. "Navy Arms EM45B-3 Airgun," *Guns & Ammo* (October 1988), p. 104 ("looks just like a full-sized assault rifle . . .").

28. Ailing Gun Industry Confronts Outrage Over Glut of Violence," The *New York Times* (March 8, 1992), p. A1.

29. "Wooters Chooses the 10 Best Gun Designs . . . [etc.]," *Guns & Ammo* (July 1982), p. 58, 68.

30. "Top 10 Gun Trends of the Decade! Rifles," *Guns & Ammo* (September 1989), pp. 40, 104.

31. See, e.g., Heckler & Koch advertisement for "HK 91 Semi-Automatic Assault Rifle" in *Guns & Ammo* (July 1984), p. 9 ("When you"re determined to survive, you leave nothing to chance . . . In a survival situation, you want the most uncompromising weapon that money can buy."); CA Inc. advertisement for Mark 45 in *Guns & Ammo* (April 1983), p. 101 ("For Sport, For Survival").

32. "Volunteer Enterprises Commando Mark 9," *Guns & Ammo* (December 1981), pp. 67, 96 (". . . would be in the running as a "survival" piece"); see also, e.g., "The SAM 180: The Tommy Gun's 'Twenty Two Twin,'" *Guns & Ammo* (June 1982), pp. 57, 87 ("as a survival tool . . . it is without peer).

33. "A Sterling Duo," *Guns & Ammo* (February 1984), p. 62.

34. See, e.g., Ballard Cutlery advertisement in *Guns & Ammo* (March 1983), p. 52 ("The widest selection of survival knives available . . . ").

35. See, e.g., advertisements for the series of "Mack Bolan" novels in *Guns & Ammo* (April 1983), p. 85 and (March 1983), p. 4. The character Bolan is supposed to have "learned his deadly skills in Vietnam, where he was dubbed "The Executioner,""and has reassembled his "famous Death Squad . . . to battle urban savagery too brutal and volatile for regular law enforcement," and his "Phoenix Force . . . to fight the dirtiest of anti-terrorist wars around the world."

36. See, e.g., Parellex Corporation advertisement featuring "genuine military fatigues" and camouflage, "military gun cases," magazines and pouches, and other equipment in *Guns & Ammo* (Sept. 1983), p. 51; Sherwood International Export Corporation advertisement for assorted military gear, including camouflage uniforms, combat harness assembly, bayonets, gun cases, etc. in *Guns & Ammo* (August 1983), p. 27.

37. See, e.g."Australian Arms .223 Carbine," *Guns & Ammo* (June 1987), p. 68 (". . . finished in your basic assault rifle black matte. . . . a goodly number of .223 assault rifles on the market in the same price range."); "AMT 25/.22 Lightning Carbine," *Guns & Ammo* (March 1985), p. 60 (". . . a rimfire version of many of the centerfire, assault-type semi-autos that are so popular today."); "Federal Engi-

neering XC-220 Rifle," *American Rifleman* (July 1984), p. 62 ("The 'assault rifle' fans can thus enjoy a great deal of shooting . . ."); "Beretta M-70/Sport Rifle," *Guns & Ammo* (December 1983), p. 64 (". . . resembles many other assault rifles in general outline."); "Bushmaster's A-Team," *Guns & Ammo* (August 1983), p. 42 ("Bushmaster's assault rifle is made in two versions," "a longer-barreled, full-stocked assault rifle," "Bushmaster's assault rifle . . ."), and front cover ("Bushmaster Assault Systems"); "Now: A Civilian AKM," *Guns & Ammo* (January 1983), p. 62,74,75 (". . . Egyptian version of the Russian assault rifle," "like most of today's assault-type rifles, the AKM thrives on use," "price . . . in line with some of the other imported assault rifles now being offered in this country," ". . . the trigger pull is uncommonly light for an assault rifle," ". . . quite simply one of the best assault rifles in the world.").

38. "The HK 91 Semi-Automatic Assault Rifle from Heckler & Koch . . . was derived directly from the G3," a military weapon used by the German army and other European countries. Heckler & Koch advertisement in *Guns & Ammo* (July 1984), p. 9. Another ad described the HK 94 Carbine as "a direct offspring of HK's renowned family of MP5 submachine guns." Heckler & Koch advertisement in *Guns & Ammo* (June 1984), back cover.

39. Intratec advertisement, *Guns & Ammo* (January 1989), p. 77.

40. Magnum Research advertisement, *Guns & Ammo* (November 1982), p. 59. See also, e.g., advertisement by Paragon S&S Inc. for AR 10, *Guns & Ammo* (July 1981), p. 90 ("Used world wide by military and LAW ENFORCEMENT officers. This famous assault rifle is now available in a semi-auto form!").

41. See, e.g., Assault Systems advertisements in *Guns & Ammo* (July 1981), pp. 90 ("assault rifle case"), 92 ("lightweight assault bipod"); (November 1983), p. 101 ("assault rifle cases" and "padded Assault Rifle sling"); Beeman advertisement in *Guns & Ammo* (December 1982), p. 14 ("Beeman Short Scopes: New for Assault Rifles to Airguns . . . Use on assault rifles . . ."); Adventurer's Outpost ad for rear and fore end shotgun pistol described as "assault grips" in *Guns & Ammo* magazine (September 1990), p. 11; Ventech Inc. advertisement for "Assault Weapon Accessories" in *Guns & Ammo* (February 1991), p. 96 ("Mini-14 . . . 10/22 . . . AR-7").

42. See, e.g., "Color it Black," *American Rifleman* (October 1992), p. 7; "A rose by any other name," *American Rifleman* (September 1991), p. 33; "What's An Assault Rifle?" *American Rifleman* (May 1989), p. 58.

43. E-mail from Duncan Long to Violence Policy Center (Jan. 23, 1998).

44. Duncan Long, *Assault Pistols, Rifles and Submachine Guns* (Citadel Press 1986), p. 1.

45. For example, *Guns & Ammo* published a book in 1982 entitled *Assault Rifles*, and advertised that the book featured "complete data on the best semi-automatics." Advertisement, *Guns & Ammo* (July 1982), p. 20. *Guns & Ammo* handgun expert Jan Libourel defined an "assault pistol" in 1988 as "A high-capacity semi-automatic firearm styled like a submachine gun but having a pistol-length barrel and lacking a buttstock.""Handgunner's Glossary," *Guns & Ammo* (August 1988), p. 42. The cover of the July 1981 *Guns & Ammo* headlined "The New Breed of Assault Rifle," and the article inside discussed "assault-type rifles."*Guns & Ammo* (July 1981),

front cover and p. 48. The 1989 *Guns & Ammo Handguns Annual* touted an "Experts Review: High Firepower Assault Pistols." Inside, the magazine enthusiastically reviewed the "Partisan Avenger .45 Assault Pistol," matter-of-factly described as "an entirely civilian-legal closed-bolt semi-automatic .45 ACP assault pistol based on an extensive redesign of the original MAC-10" (a fully automatic weapon developed for special military and police use) and as "a formidable assault pistol that can be legally purchased by civilians." "Partisan Avenger .45 Assault Pistol," *Guns & Ammo Handgun Annual (1989), p. 26; See also, Guns & Ammo* (January 1987), front cover and article, "Bantam Battle Rifles," pp.36; "A.A. Arms AP9 Assault Pistol," *Guns & Ammo Handgun Annual* (1989), p. 48.

46. See, e.g., "Color it Black," *American Rifleman* (October 1992), p. 7;

47. "Kimel AP-9 Pistol," *American Rifleman* (January 1990), p. 55.

48. "Colt's 9mm AR-15," *Guns & Ammo* (July 1985), pp. 35, 76.

49. "H&K's 9 mm Para Carbine," *Guns & Ammo* (November 1983), p. 42.

50. CA Inc. advertisement, *Guns & Ammo* (March 1981), p. 92.

51. CA Inc. advertisement, *Guns & Ammo* (April 1980), p. 81.

52. "A.A. Arms AP9 Assault Pistol," *Guns & Ammo Handgun Annual* (1989), p. 48, 51.

53. *Guns & Ammo* (January 1987), front cover and article, "Bantam Battle Rifles," pp. 36, 38.

54. Cover, Feather Industries, Inc. 1991 Product Catalog.

55. Advertisement for Fleming Firearms, *Machine Gun News* (September 1990), back cover.

56. "Calico M-100 rifle," *American Rifleman* (January 1987), p. 60, 61.

57. "H&K's 9 mm Para Carbine," *Guns & Ammo* (November 1983), p. 42.

58. "Competing With Those "Non-Sporting" Rifles," *American Rifleman* (March 1992), p. 42.

59. "Calico 9mm M900 Carbine and M950 Pistol," *Guns & Ammo* (Sept. 1990), p.100, 101.

60. For an early and detailed discussion of assault weapon abuse and criminal use in the 1980s, see generally, Josh Sugarmann, *Assault Weapons and Accessories in America* (Violence Policy Center 1988), upon which much of the discussion in this section is based.

61. "Arms Race Escalates," *The Washington Post* (February 23, 1988), p. B5.

62. "U.S. Bans Imports of Assault Rifles in Shift by Bush," The *New York Times* (March 15, 1989), p. A1; "Bush Widens Ban on Import of Semiautomatic Rifles," *The Washington Post* (April 6, 1989), p. A1.

63. "Administration Bans Assault-Gun Imports," *The Washington Post* (March 15, 1989), p. A1.

64. See, e.g., "Assault Pistols Now Being Imported in Place of Banned Rifles," *The Washington Post* (January 17, 1990), p. A12; "Gun makers take aim at ban," *Chicago Tribune* (October 5, 1989), p. 37.

65. "Norinco NDM-86 Rifle," *American Rifleman* (July 1992), p. 60.

66. "Century FAL Sporter Rifle," *American Rifleman* (July 1993), pp. 53–54.

66a. U.S. Dept. of Justice, Bureau of Justice Statistics, *Sourcebook of Criminal Justice Statistics — 1993*, Table 2.65, p. 208.

67. "Assault Rifles . . . Love 'Em or Leave 'Em?", *Shooting Sports Retailer* (May/June 1995), p. 48.

68. "Colt Sporter HBAR Rifle," *American Rifleman* (December 1990), p. 52.

69. "Crackdown on Assault Weapons Has Missed Mark," *Los Angeles Times* (August 24, 1997), p. 1.

70. As the Democratic counsel on the House Crime Subcommittee responsible for gun issues, the author was present at numerous strategy and technical meetings during consideration of the assault weapons ban.

71. See, "Crackdown on Assault Weapons Has Missed Mark," *Los Angeles Times* (August 24, 1997), p. A1 (first in a four-part series on assault weapons).

71a. "Flood of Assault Guns Aimed at U.S.," *Los Angeles Times* (Nov. 12, 1997), appears in *Los Angeles Times* reprint "Outgunned: The Holes in America's Assault Weapons Laws," p. 53.

71b. "ATF Group Rushed Imports of Assault Guns, Officials Say," *Los Angeles Times* (Nov. 13, 1997), appears in *Los Angeles Times* reprint "Outgunned: The Holes in America's Assault Weapons Laws," p. 57.

72. "Chop without change," International Defense review (Nov. 1, 1988), vol. 21, no. 11, p. 1462. For a description of Novak's work for Smith & Wesson see "Defense Gun Dilemma," *Guns & Ammo* (January 1989), p. 54.

73. "S&W's 9mm "Mini-Gun,"" *Guns & Ammo* (February 1984), p. 36.

74. "Defense Gun Dilemma," *Guns & Ammo* (January 1989), p. 54.

75. "Pocket firepower," *International Defense Review* (Nov. 1, 1988), vol. 21, no. 11, p. 1461.

76. "Concealed sidearm competition," *International Defense Review* (Dec. 1, 1991), vol. 24, no. 12, p. 1369.

77. "SIG Wins Army Contract," *American Firearms Industry* (May 1992), p. 14.

78. Alex Zidock, "Armed force, subjected to rigorous testing and combat in Desert Storm, the Beretta 92 FS passes muster as the official military sidearm," Popular Mechanics (Dec, 1993), vol. 170, no. 12, p. 40.

79. "Ceramic Gun Barrels," *American Firearms Industry* (September, 1992), p. 6.

80. "Laser products for Law Enforcement," *American Rifleman* (April 1981), p. 62.

81. Laser Products Corporation advertisement, *Guns & Ammo* (July 1981), p. 88 ("Combat Laser Aiming is Here . . . incredibly effective for law enforcement . . .").

82. "Laser Sights Today & Tomorrow," *Guns & Ammo* (November 1991), p. 66, 68.

83. "LS45 laser Aiming System," *Guns & Ammo* (August 1987), p. 68; Avin Industries Lasersight advertisement *Guns & Ammo* (November 1987), p. 14.

84. "Laser Sights Today & Tomorrow," *Guns & Ammo* (November 1991), p. 66, 71.

85. "'SOCOM'" Goes Civilian," *Guns & Ammo* (February, 1997), p. 44.

86. "The Stealth C-1000 — A Pocket-Size Auto With a Punch," *Guns & Ammo* (August, 1996), p. 64.

87. "Sneak Preview " New SIG P239," *Guns & Ammo* (January 1996), p. 52,53.

88. "Concealed-Carry Handguns: 10 "Best-Kept" Secrets," *Guns & Ammo* (January 1997), p. 42. See also, "Exclusive! Glock's New "Mini" Big Bores," *Guns & Ammo* (April 1997), p. 46; "The Beretta Tomcat . . . A Feisty Fistful," *Guns & Ammo* (April 1997), p. 66, 67; "New! Para-Ordnance's Super Sub Compact P10," *Guns &*

Ammo (January 1997), p. 32; "S&W's New 9mm Blowback Pocket Pistol," *Guns & Ammo* (November 1996), p. 66;"Glock's New Pocket Rockets!" *Guns & Ammo* (January 1996), p. 36; "Combat Compact Shootout: A Look at Today's New Breed of Ultra-Small 9mm Autoloaders," *Guns & Ammo* (March 1996), p. 32; "Sneak Preview " New SIG P239," *Guns & Ammo* (January 1996), p. 52; "Sigma .380," *Guns & Ammo* (September 1995), p. 52 ("a top contender in the hideout-pistol category).

89. "The Beretta Tomcat . . . A Feisty Fistful," *Guns & Ammo* (April 1997), p. 66, 67.

90. "Building a Big Market With Small Handguns," *Shooting Industry* (Jan. 1996), p. 16.

91. "Kahr K9 is a perfect concealment gun for women," *Shooting Industry* (April, 1996), p. 22. "Kahr K9," *Guns & Ammo* (February 1997), p. 86. With more and more states issuing concealed-carry permits, a definite trend toward producing more pocket-sized handguns has developed in the firearms industry. Massad Ayoob, a regular gun industry writer, predicted success for so-called "baby magnum" revolvers in *Shooting Industry*. "Each will get very heavy advertising. Each will get big play in the gun magazines. And, each will sell like hotcakes." "Selling the Baby Magnums is Easy—With the Right Advice," *Shooting Industry* (July, 1995), p. 26. As a result of this kind of play, "there is a major demand for small handguns," said Bob Lesmeister, managing director for the National Association of Federally Licensed Firearms Dealers. "Smaller Size Big Seller in New Era of Handgun," *The Plain Dealer* (Dec. 14, 1995), p. 16A. "Today, you're talking small packages with large caliber." " 'Pocket rockets' hit target: buyers; Weapons: The market for compact guns has shot off, thanks to relaxed laws and widespread fear of crime," *The Orange County Register* (Dec. 30, 1995), p. A22.

92. "Pocket Autos for Defense and Fun!" *Guns & Ammo* (September, 1993), p. 38,41.

93. John McNabb, "Rethinking pocket pistols," *The Chattanooga Times* (Aug. 1, 1996), p. G5.

94. "Tinier, Deadlier Pocket Pistols Are in Vogue," *The Wall Street Journal* (Sept. 12, 1996), p. B1.

95. The Four-gun Family in Their Sights: US Gunmakers Are on the Offensive," *Financial Times* (March 2, 1996), p. 7.

95a. See, e.g., "Pocket Firepower," *Int'l. Defense Review* (November 1, 1988), p. 1461 ("one design avenue being enthusiastically explored is that of very compact pistols . . . this year, no less than three manufacturers have unveiled or announced pocket-sized 9mm guns suitable for concealed carry . . .")

96. "9mm Mini," *Shooting Industry* (May 1993), p. 54; "Handgun Trends for 1992," *Guns & Ammo* (April, 1992), p. 54 ("I predict that we will see more miniaturization in defensive auto pistols"); "Compact Combat Auto Pistols," *Guns & Ammo* (June 1992) ("an increasing number of handgun manufacturers now offer compact versions of their full-sized auto pistols"); "What Are The Top 10 Handgun Trends?" *Guns & Ammo* (September, 1992) ("New Trends . . . 3. Compacts"); "Taurus' All-New Compact Combat Auto," *Guns & Ammo* (June 1993), p. 48 ("creating this new, compact pistol was a shrewd marketing move on the part of Taurus"); "Compact .45 Autos," *Guns & Ammo* (August 1993), p. 40 ("it looks like there are quite

a few more on the way"); "Pocket Auto Buyer's Guide," *Guns & Ammo* (September, 1993) ("The pistols shown here represent just a few of the pocket autoloaders available on today's market); "New Compact Beretta Pistols," *Guns & Ammo* (May, 1994), p. 22; see also, "A Complete Look at Hideout & Pocket Handguns," *Guns & Ammo* (October, 1994), p. 48 (promoting "final option firepower: pocket pistols & hideout guns"); "First Look! AMT's Super-Small .45 Auto," *Guns & Ammo* (November 1994).

97. "Shot Show 1991," *American Rifleman* (March 1991), p.22.

98. "Big Profits Come In Small Packages," *American Firearms Industry* (February 1993), p. 18.

99. "Para-Ordance P12.45: This .45 auto combines high firepower with ultra- compact size," *Guns & Ammo* (July 1992), p. 68.

100. "Intratec," *American Firearms Industry SHOT Show Issue* (January 1993), p. 52; "Intratec," *American Firearms Industry* (February 1993), p. 18; "Intratec," *American Firearms Industry* SHOT Show Issue (January, 1994), p. 114.

101. "Combat Compact Shootout," *Guns & Ammo* (March 1996), p. 32.

102. See, e.g., "New Sigma: The real story behind the development of Smith & Wesson's 'Top Secret' polymer-frame Combat Pistol," *Guns & Ammo* (June, 1994), p. 34.

103. " 'Pocket rockets' hit target: buyers; Weapons: The market for compact guns has shot off, thanks to relaxed laws and widespread fear of crime," *The Orange County Register* (Dec. 30, 1995), p. A22.

104. "Smaller Size Big Seller in New Era of Handgun," *The Plain Dealer* (Dec. 14, 1995), p. 16A.

105. "Glock Introduces New Compact Pistols," *Shooting Industry* (October 1995), p. 18.

106. "Glock perfection — only smaller," *Shooting Sports Retailer* (January, 1996), p. 86.

107. " 'Pocket rockets' hit target: buyers; Weapons: The market for compact guns has shot off, thanks to relaxed laws and widespread fear of crime," *The Orange County Register* (Dec. 30, 1995), p. A22.

108. Colt Pony Gallops; Taurus Polymers Pistol; Glock Big-bores Sub-Compacts," *Shooting Industry* (April 1997), p. 44.

109. Ibid.

110. "Packaging punch in compacts, this trio of slim nines demand attention," *Shooting Industry* (March, 1995), vol. 40, no. 3, p. 69; "Smaller Size Big Seller in New Era of Handgun," *The Plain Dealer* (Dec. 14, 1995), p. 16A.

111. "Palm-size 9 mm packs power," *Shooting Industry* (March, 995), p. 71; "Kahr K9 is a perfect concealment gun for women," *Shooting Industry* (April, 1996), vol. 41, no. 4, p. 22.

112. "SHOT Show Indicates Defense Guns on the Roll," *Shooting Industry* (April 1997), p. 16.

113. "The defensive handguns your customers will be looking for in 1996," *Shooting Industry* (March, 1996), p. 16.

114. "As laws relax, little guns are big business — Growing market seen for concealed weapons," *Milwaukee Journal Sentinel* (Dec. 24, 1995), p. 1.

115. "'Pocket rockets' hit target: buyers; Weapons: The market for compact guns has shot off, thanks to relaxed laws and widespread fear of crime," *The Orange County Register* (Dec. 30, 1995), p. A22.

CHAPTER 9: EXPLOITING TIES TO LAW ENFORCEMENT

1. U.S. Department of Justice, Bureau of Justice Statistics, *Sourcebook of Criminal Justice Statistics 1996*, Table 1.25; "Law Enforcement Statistics," Web site (April 6, 1998).
2. See, e.g., "Beretta's M9 Anniversary Will Help You Sell This Semi-Auto," *Shooting Industry* (October, 1995), p. 24.
3. "Gun Maker Re-Arms Sullivan Law Enforcers," *The Union Leader* (Jan. 24, 1990), p. 5.
4. "Sturm, Ruger Flourishes As An Independent Firearms Firm," *Investor's Business Daily* (August 24, 1993), p. 36.
5. "Ruger fires all law enforcement reps," *Firearms Business* (Oct. 15, 1995), p. 1.
6. "Beretta Appoints Top Managers," *Shooting Industry* (April, 1994), p. 2; see also, "Smith & Wesson Increases Sales Staff," *Shooting Industry* (March, 1996), p. 12 (former South Dakota state trooper named "director of Law Enforcement Sales"); "Marx Moves to Michaels," *Shooting Sports Retailer* (Nov./Dec. 1992), p. 46 (former Chicago police officer moves from top law enforcement marketing job at Smith & Wesson).
7. "SSR Industry On-Line," *Shooting Sports Retailer* (March/April, 1995) p. 65.
8. "FBI National Academy," at FBI Web site (April 7, 1998).
9. "Smith & Wesson New Manager Appointments," *American Firearms Industry* (Sept. 1992), p. 63.
10. "SIGARMS: Police 'R' Us," *American Firearms Industry* (September 1992), p. 10.
11. "The Marketing 100; Gaston Glock; Glock," *Advertising Age* (June 26, 1995), p. 830.
12. "Glock Drops Rep Groups, Names In-House Sales Force," *Shooting Industry* (October, 1993), p. 15; "Glock Reps Out, Factory Salesmen In," *Firearms Business* (August 15, 1993), p. 1; see also, "Karst Member of Glock sales Team," *Shooting Sports Retailer* (March/April 1993), p. 44 (former member Edmonton Police Department to work Canada for Glock); Lars Erik-Nelson, "Glock Pistol May be a Loose Cannon," *Daily News* (New York), (October 16, 1995), (editorial), p. 29.
13. State of New York, Office of the State Inspector General, "The Best Bang for Their Buck: An Investigation of Firearms Purchases and Management in the New York State Department of Environmental Conservation Division of Law Enforcement" (December, 1996), pp. 21–23.
14. Ibid, p. 24.
15. Ibid.
16. Ibid, p. 1.
17. Ibid, p. 67.
18. Ibid, pp. 65, 67.
19. Ibid, pp. 82, 84.
20. According to the Inspector General's report, Walsh has been a sales representative for various gun manufacturers since the early 1970s, joined Glock in 1988, and has since moved on to Sturm, Ruger.

21. Glock made only 1,000 of the "Desert Storm" guns, the first nineteen of which went to President George Bush and other senior government officials.

22. "DEC Police Accused of Peddling Guns," *The Buffalo News* (Dec. 17, 1996), p. 1A; State of New York, Office of the State Inspector General, "The Best Bang for Their Buck: An Investigation of Firearms Purchases and Management in the New York State Department of Environmental Conservation Division of Law Enforcement" (December, 1996), pp. 82–83.

23. State of New York, Office of the State Inspector General, "The Best Bang for Their Buck: An Investigation of Firearms Purchases and Management in the New York Department of Environmental Conservation Division of Law Enforcement" (December, 1996), pp. 61–63, 83.

24. Ibid, p. 82.

25. Ibid, p. 37.

26. "S&W Invests $2.7 Million in Training Facility," *Shooting Industry* (Shot Show Super Issue 1997), p. 20;"Improvements Expected as Smith & Wesson Invests $2.7 Million in Springfield, Massachusetts Training Facility," *GunGames* (Feb/Mar 1997), p. 25; "Smith & Wesson Academy Begins Personal Protection Training for Citizens," *Shooting Sports Retailer* (July/August 1994), p. 66. The National Rifle Association also has long conducted a variety of training schools for police and security personnel. See. E.g., "NRA Law Enforcement Firearms Instructor Development Schools," *American Rifleman* (April, 1997), p. 24; "NRA Official Journal," *American Rifleman* (February, 1987), p. 62–63.

27. In addition to guns, Smith & Wesson also sells handcuffs, leg irons, and restraint chains for law enforcement use. Smith & Wesson, "Handguns, Handcuffs and Accessories, Suggested Retail Price List," effective January 11, 1996.

28. "Heckler & Koch Promotes Vice President," *Shooting Industry* (November, 1995), p. 17.

29. "SSR Industry On-Line," *Shooting Sports Retailer* (July/August 1994), p. 67.

30. "Bargain Police Revolvers," *American Rifleman* (November 1989), p. 30.

31. "The three levels of self-defense: sell your customer the right gun for their experience and threat level," *Shooting Industry* (December, 1993), vol. 38, no. 12, p. 132.

32. State of New York, Office of the State Inspector General, "The Best Bang for Their Buck: An Investigation of Firearms Purchases and Management in the New York State Department of Environmental Conservation Division of Law Enforcement" (December, 1996), pp. 90.

33. "Sig, Remington Below Wholesale," *Firearms Business* (Sept.1&15, 1996), p. 6.

34. State of New York, Office of the State Inspector General, "The Best Bang for Their Buck: An Investigation of Firearms Purchases and Management in the New York State Department of Environmental Conservation Division of Law Enforcement" (December, 1996), pp. 68.

35. "DEC Police Accused of Peddling Guns," *The Buffalo News* (Dec. 17, 1996), p. 1A.

36. State of New York, Office of the State Inspector General, "The Best Bang for Their Buck: An Investigation of Firearms Purchases and Management in the New York State Department of Environmental Conservation Division of Law Enforcement" (December, 1996), pp. 92.

37. "Gun purchase stalled by fear of street sales," *The Hartford Courant* (Dec. 14, 1995), p. A1.

38. "Sales of Old Police Arsenals Draw Criticism," *Los Angeles Times* (Sept. 5, 1993), p. B-1.

39. "Armed by the police; used weapons find way into criminal hands," *Newsday* (Dec. 12, 1993), p. 6; "DEC Police Accused of Peddling Guns," *The Buffalo News* (Dec. 17, 1996), p. 1A.

40. Ibid.

41. "Cheap imports flood weapon market; China source of pistols, semiautomatics, ammo in US; guns aiming for orofit," *The Boston Globe* (Dec. 20, 1993), p. 1.

42. "City Rejects Gun Trade In," *Oakland Post* (June 14, 1992), p. 1; "Oakland police to sell used revolvers to dealer," *The Houston Chronicle* (June 4, 1992), p. 1; "Sales of Old Police Arsenals Draw Criticism," *Los Angeles Times* (Sept. 5, 1993), p. B-1.

43. "Sales of Old Police Arsenals Draw Criticism," *Los Angeles Times* (Sept. 5, 1993), p. B-1; "Armed by the police; used weapons find way into criminal hands," *Newsday* (Dec. 12, 1993), p. 6 (Out of forty-five departments surveyed: thirty-six either sold or traded in guns, four sold or gave them to their officers, one locked them in a vault, one destroyed them, and one was undecided about what to do with them. The remaining two departments had not upgraded their guns.)

44. See, e.g., "Missouri Troopers To Get Semiautomatic Pistols," *St. Louis Post-Dispatch* (Feb. 5, 1991), p. 4A; "CHP Officers Get New Pistol," *The San Francisco Chronicle* (Sept. 3, 1991), p. A14; "Sheriff's Dept. seeks to upgrade deputies' guns," *The Atlanta Journal and Constitution* (Nov. 7, 1992), J-4; "Knox Deputies Getting More Powerful Pistols," *Knoxville News-Sentinel* (May 19, 1994), p. A1; "Troopers training with bigger guns," *The Commercial Appeal* (July 10, 1994), p. 2B; "Police Get New Attitude; U. Mount Bethel Police Upgrade Training, Guns," *The Morning Call* (Allentown) (Sept. 16, 1994), p. B3; "Cops close to getting 12– shot weapons; Private funds may buy semiautomatics," *The San Francisco Examiner* (Dec. 22, 1994), p. A-25; "County beefs up police firepower; New semiautomatics will help officers fight better-armed criminals," *Pittsburgh Post-Gazette* (Sept. 30, 1995), p. D1; "Kenner Police Better-armed; Department Issues .40–caliber Semiautomatics," *The Times-Picayune* (Nov. 21, 1995), p. A1; "Bethlehem Twp. Weighs Pistol Trade," *The Morning Call* (Allentown) (Feb. 21, 1995), p. B4; "Studies, Advertising Entice Local Agencies to get Bigger Barrels," *The Palm Beach Post* (June 2, 1996), p. 4B; "Police Loading Up With More Firepower," *The Palm Beach Post* (June 2, 1996), p. 1B; "Wetumpka Gets First Black Mayor," *The Montgomery Advertiser* (Aug. 20, 1996), p. 1b; "Conn. police get high-powered gun," *The Patriot Ledger* (Sept. 21, 1996), p. 22; "State police get new pistols; Taneytown officers also to trade 9 mm gun for .40–caliber model," *The Baltimore Sun* (Jan. 8, 1997), p. 1B.

45. "Charlotte PD Picks a Pistol," *American Rifleman* (May 1991), p. 24.

46. "SIG's Shorty Forty," *American Rifleman* (August 1993), pp. 38, 40.

47. "Studies, Advertising Entice Local Agencies to get Bigger Barrels," *The Palm Beach Post* (June 2, 1996), p. 4B.

48. For example, Police Chief Melvin Diggs said Taneytown [Md.] officers seldom fire a weapon in the line of duty, but added, "Any time we can upgrade to the same thing the criminals have on the street, that's fine with me." "State police get new pistols; Taneytown officers also to trade 9 mm gun for .40–caliber model," *The Baltimore Sun* (Jan. 8, 1997), p. 1B. "But no [Village of Lloyd Harbor, New York] police officer

has ever fired a weapon on the job, or been fired upon, in the seven years that [John] Martin has been commissioner, and no one can remember it happening in all the years that anyone remembers." "More firepower for Quietsville," *Newsday* (Nov. 14, 1991), p. 6. The bottom line seems to be the induced perception, expressed by the president of the Connecticut State Police union, that "the 9mm bullets just aren't stopping the bad guys." "Conn. police get high-powered gun," *The Patriot Ledger* (Sept. 21, 1996), p. 22. A Florida newspaper recently gave this account of this logic: "A growing number of South Florida police officers and sheriff's deputies are switching to heavier-caliber pistols that they believe will give them more protection. . . . 'Bigger, wider bullets are better than smaller, narrower bullets,' has become a mantra for some. . . . 'To me, bigger is better.' [Palm Beach County sheriff's deputy Larry Enstrom]." "Police Loading Up With More Firepower," *The Palm Beach Post* (June 2, 1996), p. 1B. In short, "God forbid something would happen and there wasn't enough firepower or stopping power," said Allegheny (Pa.) County police superintendent Bob Kroner. "County beefs up police firepower; New semiautomatics will help officers fight better-armed criminals," *Pittsburgh Post-Gazette* (Sept. 30, 1995), p. D1.

49. "The Man Stopper; It's sleek, powerful, and designed to kill," *Newsday* (April 19, 1992), p. 6.

50. "Smith & Wesson dumps 10 mm," *Richmond Times-Dispatch* (March 18, 1994), B-1.

51. "Ruger Targets Cops," *Shooting Industry* (February, 1994), p. 70; "Peeking at the New 'P'," *Shooting Industry* (January, 1994), p. 70.

52. "Studies, Advertising Entice Local Agencies to get Bigger Barrels," *The Palm Beach Post* (June 2, 1996), p. 4B.

53. "Gunfight Fuels Debate Over Police Weapons," *Los Angeles Times* (March 2, 1997), p. A1.

54. See, e.g., "Conn. police get high-powered gun," *The Patriot Ledger* (Sept. 21, 1996), p. 22; "State police get new pistols; Taneytown officers also to trade 9 mm gun for .40-caliber model," *The Baltimore Sun* (Jan. 8, 1997), p. 1B.

55. See, e.g., "Run On High-Cap Magazines," *Firearms Business* (June 15, 1994), p. 3; "Consumers Still Want Magazines," *Firearms Business* (April 15, 1996), p. 6. There is some question about how finite the grandfathered magazine pool is, however, since ATF has permitted the import of magazines supposedly made before the ban, a question of fact ATF admits is difficult to ascertain. "Crackdown on Assault Weapons Has Missed Mark," *Los Angeles Times* (August 24, 1997), pp. A1, A17.

56. "Makers Decry Magazine Gouging," *Firearms Business* (Sept. 1, 1994), p. 5.

57. "Magazine Prices Keep Soaring," *Firearms Business* (Nov. 15, 1994), p. 4.

58. "Glock Beefs Up Magazine Imports," *Shooting Industry* (Feb., 1994), p. 70.

59. "Where's my Spare? Editor's Note," *Guns & Ammo* (June 1995), p. 95.

60. See. e.g., "Dealing through loophole; Sale of used THP pistols legal but still questionable," *The Nashville Banner* (Nov. 24, 1995), p. A18; "Gun purchase stalled by fear of street sales," *The Hartford Courant* (Dec. 14, 1995), p. A1.

61. "Unintended Consequences of the Gun Ban," *Guns & Ammo* (August 1995), p. 10.

62. "Glock magazines Get ATF Okay," *Firearms Business* (Nov. 1, 1994), p. 3.

63. "As laws relax, little guns are big business — growing market seen for concealed weapons," *Milwaukee Journal Sentinel* (Dec. 24, 1995), p. 1.

64. "Regulators fire blanks at gun manufacturers," *The Boston Globe* (August 22, 1993), p. 1; see also, e.g., "More teens turning to 9mm guns — Semi-automatics replace revolvers as weapons of choice, police say," *Milwaukee Journal Sentinel* (July, 1996), p. 1.

PART III. NURTURING A CULTURE OF FEAR
CHAPTER 10: THE SELF-DEFENSE MIRAGE

1. Jervis Anderson, *Guns in American Life* (Random House, New York, 1984), p. 20.
2. Jervis Anderson, *Guns in American Life* (Random House, New York, 1984), p. 55.
3. Hugh Davis Graham and Ted Robert Gurr, *Violence in America: Historical and Comparative Perspectives* (Bantam Books 1969), p. 55.
4. Hugh Davis Graham and Ted Robert Gurr, *Violence in America: Historical and Comparative Perspectives* (Bantam Books 1969), figure 13–4, p. 503.
5. Hugh Davis Graham and Ted Robert Gurr, *Violence in America: Historical and Comparative Perspectives* (Bantam Books 1969), p. 486.
6. "Two short guns vie for pocket space; chiefs special and undercover: weapons coveted by discriminating thugs," article reprinted in series titled "The Snub-Nosed Killers, Handguns in America," by Cox Newspaper Services (Fall, 1981), p. 10.
7. Production figures in this section are based on data from U.S. Bureau of Alcohol, Tobacco and Firearms, "Civilian Firearms " Domestic Production, Importation, and Exportation."
8. "Two short guns vie for pocket space; chiefs special and undercover: weapons coveted by discriminating thugs," article reprinted in series titled "The Snub-Nosed Killers, Handguns in America," by Cox Newspaper Services (Fall, 1981), p. 12.
9. Christopher Geehern, "Arms and the Man," *New England Business* (August 1990), vol. 12, no. 8, sec. 1., p. 24.
10. "NRA's Violent Crime Ads Hit Home," *American Rifleman* (January 1988), p. 50. The NRA also marketed a "Principles of Home Defense" video pushing the use of firearms. See advertisement in *American Rifleman* (July 1987), p. 16.
11. "The industry white papers: expert intelligence on the state of the industry; the future of the gun industry," *Shooting Industry* (July, 1993), vol. 38, no. 7, p. 40.
12. "Sure as shootin' — No longer gun shy, Californians discover a new status symbol," *Chicago Tribune*, (Feb. 19, 1993) Tempo section, p. 1.
13. "Second Amendment Message in Los Angeles," *American Rifleman* (July 1992), pp. 32–33.
14. "O.C. pistol sales fell 24% in '94," *The Orange County Register* (March 24, 1995), p. A1.
15. Ibid.
16. "California Gun Sales Climb," *Gun Tests* (Sept. 1994), p. 31.
17. "Under Fire: Guns in Los Angeles County; Proliferation of Guns May be Bloody Legacy of Riots," *Los Angeles Times* (May 17, 1992), p. A-27.
18. "Delays, Chaos Add to Woes in Solving Riot Homicides," *Los Angeles Times* (June 21, 1992), p. A-1.
19. Peter Cummings, MD, MPH, and Thomas D. Koepsell, MD, MPH, et al., "The Association Between the Purchase of a Handgun and Homicide or Suicide," *American Journal of Public Health* (June, 1997), vol. 87, no. 6, pp. 974, 977.

20. Arthur L. Kellerman, MD, MPH, Frederick P. Rivara, MD, MPH, et al., "Gun Ownership as a Risk Factor for Homicide in the Home," *The New England Journal of Medicine* (October 7, 1993), vol. 329, no. 15, pp. 1084, 1090.

21. Arthur L. Kellerman, MD, PHD, and Donald T. Reay, MD, "Protection or Peril: An Analysis of Firearms-Related Deaths in the Home," *The New England Journal of Medicine* (June 12, 1986), vol. 314, no. 24, pg. 1557–1560.

22. "The Changing Faces of America's Shooting Sports Families: Kids, Parents, and our Cultural Heritage," *Shooting Sports Retailer* (May/June 1994), pp. 6, 14.

23. U.S. Department of Justice, Bureau of Justice Statistics, *Guns and Crime: Handgun Victimization, Firearms Self-Defense, and Firearm Theft* (April 1994), p. 1.

24. David Hemenway, PhD, "Survey Research and Self-Defense Gun Use: An Explanation of Extreme Overestimates," *The Journal of Criminal Law & Criminology* (1997) vol. 87, no. 4, pp. 1430–31. Kleck and Gertz defended their methodology and results in the same issue. See, "The Illegitimacy of One-Sided Speculation: Getting the Defensive Gun Use Estimate Down," p. 1446.

25. Philip J. Cook and Jens Ludwig, *Guns in America: Results of a Comprehensive National Survey on Firearms Ownership and Use* (Police Foundation 1996), p. 76.

26. "A Call to Arms: Facing Tough Competition, Smith & Wesson's New CEO Presses Ahead With Sweeping Changes," *BusinessWest* (November, 1992), vol. 9, no. 7, sec. 1, p. 17.

27. "Shot Show Indicates Defense Guns on the Roll," *Shooting Industry* (April 1997), p. 16.

28. Massad Ayoob, "The Defensive Market Today," *Shooting Industry* (February 1997), p. 20.

29. Massad Ayoob, "'Trend Crimes' and the Gun Dealer," *Shooting Industry* (March 1993), p. 18.

30. Philip J. Cook and Jens Ludwig, *Guns in America: Results of a Comprehensive National Survey on Firearms Ownership and Use* (Police Foundation 1996), p. 37–38.

31. "Baby With a Bark," *American Firearms Industry* (June 1995), p. 78.

32. "Beretta keeps going great guns," *The Baltimore Sun* (May 1, 1995), p. 6C.

33. "Smith & Wesson Academy Begins Personal Protection Training for Citizens," *Shooting Sports Retailer* (July/August, 1994), p. 66; "Handguns, revolvers, semi-autos; selecting a weapon," *Sports Afield* (June, 1996), Vol. 216, no. 1, p. 67.

34. "Smith & Wesson Academy Expands," *Guns & Ammo* (January, 1997), p. 23.

35. Reuters News wire (March 30, 1997).

36. See, e.g., "Concealed-Carry Handguns: 10 Best-Kept Secrets!" *Guns & Ammo* (Jan., 1997), p. 42; "Home Defense Handguns: What's Best for You?" *Guns & Ammo* (November 1994), cover; "Self-Defense Rimfires," *Guns & Ammo* (November 1996), p. 54.

37. Massad Ayoob, "Help Your Customers Fashion Their Defensive Handgun Wardrobe," *Shooting Industry* (June, 1996), p. 20.

38. "GunGames publisher wants change in industry," *Firearms Business* (July 1, 1995), pp. 3–4.

39. "Defensive Handgun Ammo," *Shooting Industry* (January, 1996), p. 29.

40. Jan Libourel, "Handgun Stopping Power: The Current Controversy," *Guns & Ammo* (October 1992), p. 40.

41. To protect the inside of the barrel from excessive lead "fouling,"hollow point bullets often have a copper "jacket" around the larger diameter, so that the lead tip (hollow point) does not come into contact with the barrel as the round exits the gun. Such bullets are called "jacketed hollow points."

42. "Update: Stopping Power; A Look at the Latest in High-Performance Handgun Ammunition," *Guns & Ammo* (July 1995), p. 58.

43. "Defensive Handgun Ammo," *Shooting Industry* (January, 1996), p. 29.

44. "Police Ammo Trends Turning," *Firearms Business* (July 1, 1993), p. 3.

45. "9mm Ammunition," *American Rifleman* (November 1989), p. 36.

46. "Update: Stopping Power; A Look at the Latest in High-Performance Handgun Ammunition," *Guns & Ammo* (July 1995), p. 58.

47. "2 Firms Unveil Defense Loads," *Firearms Business* (Nov. 1, 1994).

48. "Self-Defense Rimfires," *Guns & Ammo* (November, 1996), p. 54.

49. "PMC Ultra-Mag Ammo," *Guns & Ammo* (February 1987), p. 70.

50. See, e.g., "The three levels of self-defense: sell your customer the right gun for their experience and threat level," *Shooting Industry* (December, 1993), vol. 38, no. 12, p. 132; "Selling the total home defense handgun package," *Shooting Industry* (June, 1995), vol. 40, no. 6, p. 20; "High Performance Ammo Still Sells," *Shooting Industry* (January, 1997), p. 10.

51. "What Do You Put in Your Handgun? Shooting Industry Ammo Blowout: A Look at the Most Explosive Items You'll Ever Have in Your Stock," *Shooting Industry* (January, 1993), vol. 38, no. 1, p. 18.

52. "Black Talon:Designed for Defense," *American Rifleman* (November 1992), pp. 36-37.

53. "A 'very nasty' new bullet; claw-like slugs, latest in urban arms race, do horrendous damage," *Newsday* (Nov. 8, 1993), p.3.

54. "Police ammo trends turning," *Firearms Business* (July 1, 1993), p. 3.

55. "A 'very nasty' New Bullet; Claw-like slugs, latest in urban arms race, do horrendous damage," *Newsday* (Nov. 8, 1993), p.3.

56. "Black Talon Public Sales Stop," *Firearms Business* (Dec. 1, 1993), p. 1; "Winchester Pulls Black Talon Ammo," *Shooting Sports Retailer* Magazine (Jan., 1994), p. 53; "Winchester Pulls Black Talon," SHOT Business (January/February 1994), p.8.

57. "Black Talon Sales Strong," *Firearms Business* (Dec. 15, 1993), p. 3.

58. "Winchester Plans New High Performance Ammo," *Shooting Industry* (April, 1994), vol. 39, no. 4, p. 14.

59. "Winchester Introduces High-Performance Ammo," *Shooting Industry* (Sept. 1994), p. 14.

60. "Winchester's Hot, New SXT Ammo," *Guns & Ammo* (November, 1995), p. 76, 77.

61. "High-Perforamce Ammo Still Sells," *Shooting Industry* (Jan. 1997), p. 10.

62. "Tinier, Deadlier Pocket Pistols Are in Vogue," *The Wall Street Journal* (Sept. 12, 1996), p. B1.

63. Massad Ayoob, "The Defensive Market Today," *Shooting Industry* (February 1997), p. 20.

64. "CCW bills positive direction for industry," *Firearms Business* (June 15, 1995), p. 1.

65. "Companies Eye Gun Carry Laws," *Firearms Business* (April 15, 1995), p. 7.

66. "More Gun Permits Equal More Gun Sales," *Shooting Industry* (February, 1997).

67. "Don't Be a Victim," *Guns & Ammo* (July, 1992), p. 20–21.

68. "SSR Retailer of the Month: McBride's Guns," *Shooting Sports Retailer* (Jan. 1996), p. 78.

69. "CCW bills positive direction for industry," *Firearms Business* (June 15, 1995), p. 1.

70. "Federal's Personal Defense Ammo," *Guns & Ammo* (May 1997), p. 70.

71. "The Most Profitable Accessories," *SHOT Business* (September/October 1994), p. 20.

72. "Picking a Hideout Holster," *American Rifleman* (September 1993), pp. 42, 43.

73. Violence Policy Center, *License to Kill: Arrests Involving Texas Concealed Handgun License Holders* (1998); *Concealing the Risk — Real World Effects of Lax Concealed Weapons Laws*, (1996); *Concealed Carry: The Criminal's Companion* (November, 1995).

74. Violence Policy Center, *Concealed Carry: The Criminal's Companion* (1995).

75. Violence Policy Center, *Concealing the Risk* (1996).

76. Violence Policy Center, *License to Kill* (1998).

77. Massad Ayoob, "The Defensive Market Today," *Shooting Industry* (February 1997), p. 20.

78. Massad Ayoob, " 'Trend Crimes' and the Gun Dealer," *Shooting Industry* (March 1993), p. 18. See also, "The industry white papers: expert intelligence on the state of the industry; the future of the gun industry," *Shooting Industry* (July, 1993), vol. 38, no. 7, p. 40.

79. "Don't Be a Victim," *Guns & Ammo* (July, 1992), p. 20–21.

80. "Urban Apartment Crime Prevention," *Guns & Ammo* (November 1992), p. 38.

81. "New Handguns Belie Market State," *Firearms Business* (Feb. 1, 1996); "Smith & Wesson .357 M686 now in 7-shot," *Shooting Sports Retailer* (January 1996), p. 89.

82. "First Look! Taurus" New .357 Seven-Shooter," *Guns & Ammo* (August 1995), p. 41.

83. "The New Taurus 'Eightgun'," *Guns & Ammo* (August 1996), p. 28.

84. "Exclusive! S&W's Revolutionary New . . . Air Lite," *Guns & Ammo* (March 1997), p. 44; "High-Capacity .357 Magnum Revolvers: Are They Just a "Flash in the Pan" or the Wave of the Future?" *Guns & Ammo* (October, 1996), p. 78; "The New Taurus 'Eightgun'," *Guns & Ammo* (August 1996), p. 28; "S&W 10-Shot Model 17," *Guns & Ammo* (August 1996), p. 76; "S&W .357 Seven-Shooter," *Guns & Ammo* (March 1996), p. 46.

CHAPTER 11: PLAYING SOLDIER

1. Ailing Gun Industry Confronts Outrage Over Glut of Violence," *The New York Times* (March 8, 1992), sec. 1, p. 1, col. 1.

2. See. e.g., *Gungames* (Feb./Mar. 1997), vol. 3, no. 1.

3. "GunGames publisher wants change in industry," *Firearms Business* (July 1, 1995), pp. 3.

4. "Showdown at the End of the Trail," *Guns & Ammo* (March, 1989), p. 60.

5. "Cowboy Action Shooting: Tombstone Lives; Sixguns, longarms . . . and cash registers are blazing away in this Old West sport that's taking the country by storm!" *Shooting Sports Retailer* (January, 1997), p. 22.

6. "New Fun in the Old West," *NSSF Gun Club Advisor* (Summer 1993).

7. "Cowboy Mounted Shooting; The Action is Wild and Wooly at these Old West Rough-Ridin' and Shootin' Competitions!" *Guns & Ammo* (December 1995), p. 98.

8. "Showdown at the End of the Trail," *Guns & Ammo* (March, 1989), p. 60;"Shoot-Out and the End of the Trail," *Guns & Ammo* (February 1984), p. 42.

9. "The industry white papers: expert intelligence on the state of the industry; the future of the gun industry," *Shooting Industry* (July, 1993), vol. 38, no. 7, p. 40.

10. "Trail's End Magazine's Retailer's Guide to Cowboy Action Shooting" (January 1997), vol. 1, no. 1, p. 46.

11. "Cowboy Mounted Shooting Association at Full Gallop!" *Guns & Ammo* (April 1997), p. 32.

12. "Cowboy Action Shooting: Blazing Sixguns and Thundering Hooves!" *Guns & Ammo* (Nov. 1996), p. 60.

13. "Dealers Reap the Profits as Shooters Relive the Old West," *Shooting Industry* (July 1996), p. 36; "Cowboy Action Shooting: Tombstone Lives; Sixguns, long-arms . . . and cash registers are blazing away in this Old West sport that's taking the country by storm!" *Shooting Sports Retailer* (January, 1997), p. 22.

14. "Wholesalers show reveals market direction; Industry News," *Shooting Industry* (Feb. 1993), vol. 38, no.2, p. 11.

15. "The industry white papers: expert intelligence on the state of the industry; the future of the gun industry," *Shooting Industry* (July, 1993), vol. 38, no. 7, p. 40.

16. "Ruger's Stainless Vaquero," *Guns & Ammo* (January, 1994), p. 73-74.

17. "Trail's End Magazine's Retailer's Guide to Cowboy Action Shooting," (January 1997), vol. 1, no. 1, p. 47.

18. "Cowboy Action Shooting: Tombstone Lives; Sixguns, longarms . . . and cash registers are blazing away in this Old West sport that's taking the country by storm!" *Shooting Sports Retailer* (January, 1997), p. 22, 80.

19. "Cowboy Shootin'", *Shooting Industry* (August 1996), p. 73.

20. "Trail's End Magazine's Retailer's Guide to Cowboy Action Shooting" (January 1997), vol. 1, no. 1, p. 6.

21. "Local gun sales healthy, cowboy shooting booming and Beretta teams with Winchester," *Shooting Industry* (May 1996), vol. 41, no. 5, p. 56.

22. "Winchester John Wayne Commemorative Carbine," *American Rifleman* (August 1981), p. 59.

23. "Colt Memorializes John Wayne," *American Rifleman* (June 1982), p. 37.

24. Dixie Gun Works, Inc. Advertisement, *American Rifleman* (February 1989), p. 88.

25. Advertisement, Gun World (April 1977) p. 76.

26. Richard Slotkin, *Gunfighter Nation: The Myth of the Frontier in Twentieth Century America* (Atheneum, 1992), p.518.

27. Ibid, pp. 514-15.

28. "Sporting Clays: The Newest Shotgun Challenge," *American Rifleman* (January 1988), p. 26.

29. "Random Shots," *American Rifleman* (January 1992), p. 6.

30. "Sporting Clays . . . Fun for Everyone," *Guns & Ammo*, (June 1994), p. 52.

31. "S&W Sponsors NASCAR Report," *Firearms Business* (Aug. 15, 1996), p. 7.

32. "Chevy Truck Sportsman's Team Challenge," *Guns & Ammo* (Dec. 1995), p. 54; "S&W Sponsors Chevy Team Events," *Firearms Business* (Sept. 1 & 15, 1996), p. 7.

33. "Sell the Gun, Freebie the Ammo," *Shooting Sports Retailer* (Nov./Dec. 1996), p. 14, 25–26.

34. "Sturm, Ruger & Co., Inc.," *American Firearms Industry* (February 1993), p. 14.

35. "Industry Looks to the Future at NSSF Summit," *Shooting Industry* (September 1997), p. 8.

36. Ibid.

37. National Shooting Sports Foundation, "A Strategic Analysis of the Shooting Sports Industry: 'Phase One Report'" (undated).

38. Ibid, p. 18.

39. "Historic Summit Looks at Shooting's Future, NSSF Commits $1 Million for Programs," *Shooting Industry* (June 1996), p. 10.

40. "Fun Shoots Support Sales," *Firearms Business* (July 1, 1993), p. 5.

41. National Rifle Association of America, "An Explanation of The Pittman Robertson Funds" (Nov. 21, 1995).

42. International Association of Fish and Wildlife Agencies, *Proceedings of the First National Shooting Range Symposium* (1990), p. 88.

43. "Fun Shoots Support Sales," *Firearms Business* (July 1, 1993), p. 5.

44. See, National Rifle Association of America, "An Explanation of The Pittman Robertson Funds" (Nov. 21, 1995).

45. "Range Upgrades Planned; Shooting Facility Weighs Gun Classes," *The Arizona Republic* (Sept. 6, 1996), p. 1; "Groups Set Shooting Range Talks," *Firearms Business* (February 1, 1996), p. 5; "Building Better Ranges," *Shooting Industry* (April 1996), p. 54; "How to Build Better Shooting Ranges," *Shooting Industry* (October 1994), p. 70.

46. "Taurus Initiates Range Program," *Firearms Business* (Nov. 1, 1995), p. 2.

47. "S&W Offers Sigma Promotion for Ranges," *Shooting Industry* (Shot Show Super Issue 1996), p. 20.

48. "Firms Offer Range Programs," *Firearms Business* (July 1, 1994), p. 3.

49. "Glock, Inc.," *American Firearms Industry* (November 1992), p. 22.

50. "Glock, Inc.," *Shooting Sports Retailer* (January 1993), p. 20; see also Glock Shooting Sports Foundation Web site.

51. "AIMARK launches first shooting range franchise," *Shooting Sports Retailer* (Jan. 1995), p. 86; "Franchising the Indoor Range," *American Rifleman* (May 1989), pp. 36.

52. "Ranges Offer Youth Discounts," *Firearms Business* (Oct. 15, 1996), p. 8.

53. Russ Thurman, "Not in Harm's Way," *Shooting Industry* (October 1994), p. 70.

54. "Firearms Safety Course?", letter from Nick Peluso, *Guns & Ammo* (March 1986), p. 8.

55. "Another Range Gone," *American Rifleman* (February 1992), p. 12.

56. Ibid.

57. "Franchising the Indoor Range," *American Rifleman* (May 1989), pp. 36–37.

58. See, e.g., "Woman shoots herself at indoor firing range," *The Orange County Register* (Jan. 24, 1997), p. B5; "Broad belly protects tot in shooting," *The Denver Post* (Nov. 2, 1996), p. B-2; "Boy accidentally shot at Aurora firing range," *Rocky Mountain News* (Nov. 1, 1996), p. 4A; "Shooting-Range Suicides Trigger Questions on Gun-rental Restrictions," *Los Angeles Times* (Oct. 27, 1996), p. B-4; "Auxiliary Officer is

Wounded at Firing Range," *St. Louis Post-Dispatch* (Oct. 24, 1996), p. 12A; "Man Rents Gun, Kills Himself," *Sacramento Bee* (Oct. 3, 1996), p. B2; "Suicides haunting gun range owners,' *The San Francisco Examiner* (Sept. 23, 1996), p. A-1; "3rd Gun Range Suicide in Bay Area This Month," *The San Francisco Chronicle* (Sept. 18, 1996), p. A13; "Suicides halt gun rentals at 2 ranges," *The San Francisco Examiner* (Sept. 18, 1996), p. A-1; "$500,000 claim filed over errant bullet," *The Orange County Register* (July 26, 1996); "Aurora death ruled a suicide," *The Denver Post* (July 12, 1996), p. 2B; "Shot in head kills man at firing range; inquiry under way," *Rocky Mountain News* (July 6, 1996), p. 34A; "Firing Range Death Investigated as Suicide," *Tulsa World* (June 4, 1996), p. A12; "Big Check in Bizarre Suicide Believed to Be Racial Slur," *Sacramento Bee* (Feb. 29, 1996), p. B3; "Neo-Nazi Wrote Suicide Note to Gun," *The San Francisco Chronicle* (Feb. 28, 1996), p. A2; "Death at Shooting Range in Newton Ruled Accidental," *The Union Leader* (Manchester, NH)(July 13, 1995), p. A-5; "Woman Dies After Firing Range Shooting," *The Columbian* (June 14, 1995), p. A5; "Woman Shoots Herself," *The Columbian* (June 13, 1995), p. A3; "After Shooting, Firing Range Closed," *The Morning Call* (March 31, 1995), p. B2; "Man takes own life at shooting range," *The Orange County Register* (Mar. 28, 1995), p. B-2; "Walnutport Man Guarded" After Cellar Shooting," *The Morning Call* (Allentown, PA)(March 24, 1995), p. B2; "Two Die at Firing Range," *The New York Times* (Feb. 23, 1995), p. A21; "Slaying-Suicide at Firing Range," *Sacramento Bee* (Feb. 22, 1995), p. B3; "Gun Range Suicide," *Scottish Daily Record* (July 20, 1994), p. 12; "Customers' suicides haunt firing ranges," *The Orange County Register* (May 1, 1993), p. B-1; "Man kills himself at firing range," *The Washington Times* (July 7, 1992), p. B2; "Man Rents Gun, Kills Self at Target Range," *Los Angeles Times* (June 14, 1991), p. B-7; "Gunshot wound fatal," *The San Diego Union-Tribune* (Oct. 14, 1989), p. B-3; "Garfield refuses to Allow Shooting Range to reopen," *The Record* (Bergen) (June 13, 1986), p. B-4; "State Police to Investigate Firing Range," *The Record* (Bergen) (May 7, 1986), p. C1; "Accidental shooting," *The San Diego Union-Tribune* (April 17, 1986), p. B-16P.

59. "Gun Ranges Considering New Rules," *St. Louis Post-Dispatch* (July 2, 1989), p. 1B.
60. "NRA Opposes Restrictions Placed on Automatic Weapons," *American Rifleman* (September 1986), p. 55.
61. "Noise and Night Shooting," Letter from John Oppenheimer, *Guns & Ammo* (January 1991).

CHAPTER 12: TARGETING NEW MARGETS

1. "NSSF Board Approves New Programs: New Focus on Women & Youngsters," *NSSF Reports* (January/February 1992).
2. "Smith & Wesson's LadySmith Revolvers," *American Rifleman* (March 1989), p.40.
3. Paul Jannuzzo, vice-president and general counsel for the US arm of Glock, quoted in "The Four-gun Family in Their Sights: US Gunmakers Are on the Offensive," *Financial Times* (March 2, 1996), p. 7; see also, "No Recession for Firearms Industry," *The New York Times* (Jan. 13, 1992), sec. A, p. 12, col. 4.
4. "Compact pistol designed with women users in mind," *International Defense Review — Despatches* (Dec. 1, 1995), vol. 2, no. 12, p. 1.
5. "'Pocket rockets' hit target: buyers; weapons: the market for compact guns has shot

off, thanks to relaxed laws and widespread fear of crime," *The Orange County Register* (Dec. 30, 1995), p. A22.

6. A few selected titles give the flavor of these articles: "Sponsoring Educational and Fun Events Will Increase Your Female Clientele;" *Shooting Industry* (June, 1996), p. 24; "Dealers Profit From Understanding How To Sell A Firearm To a Woman;" *Shooting Industry* (June, 1994), p. 20; "Equipping Ladies For Firearms Training Is Smart Business;" *Shooting Industry* (August, 1994), p. 22;"Guns fit for a queen;" *Shooting Sports Retailer* (Sept./Oct. 1995), p. 24;"A Market Filled with Women . . . Armed, Hunting and $pending;"*Shooting Sports Retailer* (May/June 1993), p. 6.

7. Violence Policy Center, *Female Persuasion: A Study of How the Firearms Industry Markets to Women and the Reality of Women and Guns* (1994).

8. Tom W. Smith and Robert J. Smith, "Changes in Firearms Ownership Among Women, 1980–1994, *The Journal of Criminal Law & Criminology* (Northwestern University School of Law, 1995), vol. 86, no. 1, p. 133; see also, "Reports of rise in women buying guns may be false," *The Orange County Register* (Dec. 4, 1994), p.G6; Tom W. Smith, "Armed and Dangerous Statistic: Media Coverage of Trends in Gun Ownership by Women," *The Public Perspective* (May/June, 1990), vol. 1, No. 4, p. 5.

9. "A Market Filled With Women . . . Armed, Hunting and $pending!", *Shooting Sports Retailer* (May/June 1993), P. 6, 17.

10. "The Changing Faces of America's Shooting Sports Families: Kids, Parents and Our Cultural Heritage," *Shooting Sports Retailer* (May/June 1994), p. 6, 12.

11. Police Foundation, *Guns in America* (1996), p. 31.

12. "Gun Knowledge For Christmas," *American Rifleman* (December 1959), p. 14.

13. Quoted in Violence Policy Center, *Young Guns* (March 1998), Section Two.

14. "Historic Summit Looks at Shooting's Future, NSSF Commits $1 Million for Programs," *Shooting Industry* (June 1996), p. 10.

15. "Special Inserts in Boys" Life and Scouting Help Introduce Millions of Youngsters to the Shooting Sports," *SHOT Business* (November/December 1994), p. 18; "Scouting & 4–H Magazines Bring Shooting Message to 5,000,000 Potential Customers," *NSSF Reports* (September/October 1991), p. 1.

16. "NSSF Board Approves New Programs: New Focus on Women & Youngsters," *NSSF Reports* (January/February 1992).

17. "Farewell '96. Are You ready For a Challenging 1997?" *Shooting Industry* (Shot Show Super Issue 1997), p. 235–236.

18. "Yes, The Industry is Being Noticed," *Shooting Sports Retailer* (May/June 1992), p. 38.

19. "Industry News," *Shooting Industry* (April 1997), p. 14.

20. "NRA Official Journal," *American Rifleman* (June 1993), pp. 76–77.

21. "Even Old Traditions Need New Beginnings," *NSSF Gun Club Advisor* (Summer 1992).

22. New England Firearms ad, *Gun World* (June 1998), p. 14.

23. Harrington & Richardson ad, *InSights*(April 1997), p. 2.

23a. Grits Gresham, "Community Relations: The Schoolchildren of today are the leaders of tomorrow," *SHOT Business* (September/October 1993), p. 9.

24. Violence Policy Center, *Use The Schools,* (1994), p. 3.

25. "CD-ROM Attracts Kids; NEF IIits With Super Light; Bassett Hides Furniture," *Shooting Industry* (April, 1997), p. 42.

26. "Our Children Can Play With Guns," *GunGames* Web site, April 13, 1998.

27. Quoted in Violence Policy Center, *Young Guns* (March 1998), Section Two.

28. Bob Hausman, "Gun industry must become less racist to survive in the 21st century," *Shooting Sports Retailer* (Jan., 1997), p. 86.

29. Carolee Boyles-Sprenkel, "Minorities: How Do You Reach this Untapped Market?", Archery aisle, *Shooting Industry* (January 1997), p. 32, quoting Bill Krentz, vice president of marketing and sales for Bear/Jennings Archery.

30. Police Foundation, *Guns in America* (1996), p. 33.

31. Cooper, Jeff, "Jeff Cooper's Commentaries," Vol. 1, No. 11, December 1993, p. 1.

32. Cooper, Jeff, "Jeff Cooper's Commentaries," Vol. 3, No. 3, February 1995, p. 6.

33. Cooper, Jeff, quoting Paul Kirchner, "Jeff Cooper's Commentaries," Vol. 2, No. 16, December 1994, p. 5.

34. Cooper, Jeff, "Cooper's Corner," *Guns & Ammo*, April 1991, p. 104.

35. Cooper, Jeff, "Cooper's Corner," *Guns & Ammo*, June 1992, p. 103.

36. *Detroit Free Press Magazine*, July 15, 1990.

37. Ibid.

38. Ibid.

39. *Westworld Newspaper*, July 27, 1994.

40. WRIF FM Radio, Detroit, Michigan, September 25, 1991.

41. Transcript of Speech by NRA First Vice President Charlton Heston, delivered at the Free Congress Foundation's 20th Anniversary Gala (December 7, 1997).

CONCLUSION: CLEANING UP THE MESS

1. Erik Larson, "The story of a gun; Cobray M-11/9," *The Atlantic* (January, 1993), vol. 271, no. 1, p. 48.

2. "Bill Ruger's gun company celebrates 45th anniversary," *New Hampshire Business Review* (July 22, 1994), vol. 16, no. 14, sec. 1, p. 1.

3. Ibid.

4. "Two short guns vie for pocket space; chiefs special and undercover: weapons coveted by discriminating thugs," article reprinted in series titled "The Snub-Nosed Killers, Handguns in America," by Cox Newspaper Services (Fall, 1981), p. 10.

5. "Fridley firm boasts a gun 'Dirty Harry' would be proud of," *Star Tribune* (Feb. 1, 1994), p. 1A.

6. "Ailing Gun Industry Confronts Outrage Over Glut of Violence," *The New York Times* (March 8, 1992), sec. 1, p. 1, col. 1.

7. "Gun Maker on Mayhem: That is Not Our Doing," *The New York Times* (March 19, 1994), sec. 1, p. 8., col. 1.

8. Ibid.

9. Ibid.

10. Saltzman, Linda, et al. "Weapon Involvement and Injury Outcomes in Family and Intimate Assaults," *The Journal of the American Medical Association* (June 10, 1992), Vol. 267, no. 22, p. 3043.

11. "Gun Designer Defends 'American Tradition'," *Los Angeles Times* (Sept. 11, 1994), A-18.

12. "Weapon-Carrying Among High School Students — United States, 1990," *Morbidity and Mortality Weekly Report* (October 11, 1991), vol. 40, no. 40, pp. 681–684.

13. Charles M. Callahan and Frederick P. Rivara, "Urban High School Youth and Handguns," *The Journal of the American Medical Association* (June 10, 1992), vol. 267, no. 22, p. 3038.

14. "Smith & Wesson Survives New Age," *The Sunday Gazette Mail* (May 28, 1995), p. 13A.

15. See, e.g., "Rash of Shootings That Have Claimed Children Shakes Miami," *The New York Times* (Feb. 11, 1997), p. A10.

16. "Rates of Homicide, Suicide, and Firearm-Related Death Among Children — 26 Industrialized Countries," *Morbidity and Mortality Weekly Report* (Feb. 7, 1997), vol. 46, no. 5.

17. Violence Policy Center, *Kids Shooting Kids* (March 1997), and sources cited therein.

18. Quoted in "Gun makers have a friend in the NRA," *The Boston Globe* (December 19, 1993), p. 35.

19. "No Recession for Firearms Industry," *The New York Times* (Jan. 13, 1992), sec. A, p. 12, col. 4.

20. "Rambo fad in weapons draws fire; High tech arms and easy access center of debate," *The San Diego Union Tribune* (January 23, 1989), p. A-1.

21. "Weapons Makers' Business Booming," *Pittsburgh Post-Gazette* (June 28, 1994), p. A1.

22. "U.S. Gunmakers: The Casualties Pile Up," *Business Week* (May 19, 1986), p. 74.

23. "Beretta (the Gun) Aims Suit at Beretta (the Car)," *The Washington Post* (July 20, 1988), sec. F, p. 1.

24. "Would you like anything else today? A shelf-load of handgun 'extras' no customer should leave your store without," *Shooting Industry* (February, 1993), vol. 38, no. 2, p. 34.

24a. Violence Policy Center, Cease Fire: *A Comprehensive Strategy to Reduce Firearms Violence* (1994), p. 29.

25. See Bogus, *Pistols, Politics and Products Liability*, 59 Cincinnati L. Rev. 1103 (1991).

26. "Industry Lawyers Track New Suits," *Firearms Business* (August 15, 1994), p. 1; "A Lesson on Liability," *SHOT Business* (July/August 1994), pp. 22, 23.

27. "Why the Firearms Business has tired blood," *Business Week* (Nov. 27, 1978), p. 107.

28. "The industry white papers: expert intelligence on the state of the industry; the future of the gun industry," *Shooting Industry* (July, 1993), vol. 38, no. 7, p. 40.

29. "Lorcin Seeks Chapter 11 Refuge," *Firearms Business* (Dec. 1, 1996), p. 3.

30. "Suit Causes Hellfire Bankruptcy," *Firearms Business* (Nov. 1, 1994), p. 5.

31. "Bill Ruger's gun company celebrates 45th anniversary," *New Hampshire Business Review* (July 22, 1994), vol. 16, no. 14, sec. 1, p. 1.

32. Ted Gest, "Trying to take gun makers to court," *U.S. News & World Report* (Dec. 2, 1996), p. 38.

33. "Repair Policies Cause Concern," *Firearms Business* (Oct. 15, 1993), p. 4.

34. "Are you ready for home security?" *Shooting Sports Retailer* (March/April 1993), p. 24.

35. See, e.g., "Anti gun groups shift concerns from Congress to courts," *Shooting Sports Retailer* (May/June 1995), p. 43.

—Index

Adkins, Jack, 138

Advertising, see "marketing"

AK-47 assault rifle, 8
  Growth in imports from China, 72–73
  Smuggling into United States, 44–45

American Civil Liberties Union, its alliances with gun lobby, 65

American Shooting Sports Council (ASSC), 66–67

Ammunition
  Defensive ammunition, 164–168
  FBI search for more effective service round, civilian market impact, 112–119
  Foreign imports of, 70
  General description of basic types, 33
  Hollow point ammunition, 164–165
  Magazine ("clip") described, 34
  Special loads for cowboy action shooting,177
  "Wildcat," 24

Anderson, Gary (NRA official) and "Rambo factor" in U.S. gun market, 83

Arida, Wally, publisher of *GunGames*, 57, 164, 175

Arms Technology, 25

Assault pistol, see "semi-automatic assault weapons"

Assault rifle, see "semi-automatic assault weapons"

ATF, see "Bureau of Alcohol, Tobacco and Firearms"

Australia, ban on automatic and semi-automatic rifles, and pump action shotguns, 8

Austria, gun exports to United States, 75–78

Automatic firearms (Machineguns), general description, 34

Automobiles, parallels with guns as consumer products, 198–199

Ayoob, Massad (gun writer), 57, 91, 95, 140

"Backup" guns, see "concealable handguns"

BB and pellet guns, how they work, 33

BATF, see "Bureau of Alcohol, Tobacco and Firearms"

Belgium, gun exports to United States, 31

Benaventure, Robert (Beretta official), 82

Beretta and Beretta USA Corporation, 5, 25, 27, 57–58, 61–62, 70, 71, 101, 135, 141, 142, 147, 148
  Development and execution of strategy to penetrate U.S. market, 81–82

Black Talon and other defensive ammunition, design and marketing, 164–168

Brazil, gun exports to United States, 31, 75–77

Bren Ten, 115

Bridgewater, Bill, 48

Britain, 1997 ban on handguns, 8

Browning, 5, 31

Bryco Arms, 25–26, 28

Bureau of Alcohol, Tobacco and Firearms, U.S.
  Acquiescence in "rule-beating" gun designs, 132
  Anemic enforcement of import restrictions, 124
  As unwilling source of data and information about gun industry, 6–7
  Ex parte meetings and communications with gun industry, 5
  Expertise for gun product safety regulation, 199–200, 204–206
  Licensing of gun dealers, 37–38
  Ministerial attitude toward regulation of firearms,12–13
  "Sporting purpose" interpretation and 22 caliber guns, 124
  Tracing of guns used in crimes in United States, 27–30
  Weak inspection of gun dealers, 42–43

Canada, gun exports to United States and strict Canadian gun laws, 32

Census Bureau, U.S., as source of information about gun industry, 6

Century International Arms (gun importer), 39–40, 148

Chain stores and gun market, 91–92

Charter Arms, 86

Children
U.S. deaths and injuries from firearms, 8
Economic impact of firearms violence against, 10
Exploitation as market by gun industry, 129–130, 186–189
Guns in schools, 196–197
Increased gun death and injuries after rise of semiautomatic pistols, 104–105

China North Industries Corp. (Norinco), 72

China, People's Republic of
Export of assault weapons to United States, 71–75
Chinese firms indicted for attempting to smuggle missiles, tanks, etc., 75

Citizens Committee for the Right to Keep and Bear Arms, 65

Colt, Samuel, 19

Colt Delta Elite, 116

Colt Model 1911 45-caliber pistol, 19, 81

Colt (Colt's Mfg. Co., Inc.), 25–29, 139

"Compact" handguns, see "concealable handguns"

Concealed carry laws
Flaws in theory and operation of, 169–171
Impact on handgun market, 137, 168–169

Concealable handguns
And concealed carry laws, 137, 168–169
"Backup" guns, 172–173
Gun manufacturers' emphasis on as product line, 82, 168–174
"Pocket rockets," small guns in high calibers, 134–140
Similarity to Saturday night specials, 137

Assault weapons ban as excuse for marketing "pocket rockets," 138–139

Connecticut Lottery homicides, 27

Congress, United States
And exclusion of firearms from CPSC regulatory authority, 13–14
Failure to examine gun industry, 5–6
Routine introduction of "paper tiger" legislation, 14

Consumer products, firearms as (see also, "public health and safety")
Automobiles, parallels with guns as consumer products, 198–199
NRA description of firearms as similar to other products, 87

Consumer Product Safety Commission
History of exclusion of firearms from regulatory authority, 13–14
Why ATF preferable to for regulation of firearms, 204–205

Cooper, Jeff ("the gunner's guru"),
And Bren Ten pistol, 115
On Delta Elite pistol, 116
On low practical value of high-capacity magazines, 102
On racial and ethnic minorities and women, 190–191
On superiority of big rounds for military and police work, 114

Cowboy action shooting, 175–177

Crime and violence, gun industry exploitation of fears of, 155–160, 162–164

"Crime guns," top 10 traced in United States by ATF,
common appearance of "old line" as well as "Ring of Fire" companies on list, 23
annual lists, 1989–1997, 27–29
limitations in tracing data, 29–30

Cunanan, Andrew, 119

Cummings, Samuel (gun importer), 40, 87

Daniel, Wayne E. (gun manufacturer) 25

Davis Industries, 25, 28–29

Dealers in firearms (see also "Secondary gun market")
Competition between "stocking dealers" and hobbyists, 38

Dealers in firearms (*continued*)
Ethics of retail dealers, 43–47
Federal retail licensing system, 37–39
Importers, 39–41
Weak inspection of gun dealers, 42–43
Weak state licensing systems, 38
Wholesalers (distributors), 41
Deaths and injuries from firearms in
United States (see also "lethality of
firearms," "public health and
safety")
Annual data and comparison to other
countries, 8
Costs of, 9–11
Impact on of rise of semiautomatic
pistols, 103–105
Defense contractors compared to gun
industry (see also "Military market"),
106
Defensive ammunition, see "self-defense
and marketing of firearms"
Delfay, Robert, 66
Dick, Mike (gun dealer), 46
Dingell, John (U.S. Rep.), and Consumer
Product Safety Act, 13
"Dirty Harry" and Smith & Wesson
Model 29 .44 Magnum Revolver, 62
Domestic arms race, see "law enforce-
ment agency sales"
Domestic firearms manufacturers gener-
ally (see also names of specific com-
panies), 23–30
Number of guns manufactured domes-
tically by type, 24 (Table 1)
Top ten manufacturers by type, 25–26
(Tables 2–5)
Dunblane (Scotland) primary school
handgun massacre 8

Empire State Building shootings, 27
Entertainment media and promotion of
guns, 4, 60–64
Ethics of gun dealers, 43–47
Experimentation in gun and ammunition
design, 24

FBI (Federal Bureau of Investigation,
U.S.)
Employment of former agents in gun
industry sales positions, 142
1986 Miami shootout and develop-
ment of .40 S&W pistol, 112–119
Federal Firearms Act of 1938, 21
Firearms, general description of basic
types and how they function, 32–35
The Firearms Coalition, 65
Firearms Importers Roundtable Trade
Group (FAIR), 75
Firearms International (gun importer), 76
Firearms Owner's Protection Act
(McClure-Volkmer), 47–48
Firearms violence, see "Deaths and inju-
ries from firearms"
Fish & Wildlife Service, U.S., 92
Fletcher, C. Hugh, 91
Foreign governments and commercial
interests (see also names of specific
companies)
as parents of major domestic gun
manufacturers, 5
foreign governments as suppliers to
U.S. gun market, 7, 71–80
ownership of U.S. brand names, 20–21
secrecy about operations 5, 31
United States as source of gold in trade
for guns from former Soviet
Union, 78–80
Foreign gun manufacturers (see also,
"foreign governments and commercial interests," "import of guns"),
generally, 30–32
Development of "rule-beater" designs
to evade assault weapons bans, 132
Gun control laws stricter in countries
exporting to U.S., 31–32
Impact of Gun Control Act of 1968, 22
Secrecy of, 31
strategies to penetrate U.S. market,
20–21, 71, 77–78
Former Soviet Union, see "Russia"
Freedom Arms, Inc., 25

Garcia, Carlos, 22
Germany, gun exports to United States,
31–32, 75–76

Glock, 27, 57, 107, 118, 135, 139, 147, 148
  Development and execution of strategy
      to penetrate U.S. market, 77–78
  Litigation involving alleged design
      defects, 112
  New York Department of Environmen-
      tal Conservation sales scandal,
      143–145
Glock, Gaston, 77
Grover, Jim (gun writer), 59, 172–173
Gun battles, involving law enforcement
      agencies, 108–111
Gun Control Act of 1968, 21–22
  Impact on foreign manufacturers 22
Gun Owners of America, 65
Gun press generally, 4, 51–60
  Involvement of gun writer in gun
      designs, ethics and liability
      questions, 58–59
  Manufacturer use of reviews to promote
      specific guns, 57–60
Gun shows, 47–49
Gunsite Raven Corporation, 115
Guthrie, David M., 100

Handguns, general description of types
      (revolver, pistol), 33–35; explanation
      of various handgun operating
      mechanisms, 96–99
  Dominant part of gun imports, 30–31
  Growth of handguns to dominate U.S.
      gun market, 83–84
  Import of high-capacity handguns
      from foreign countries, 75–78
  Marketing of new handgun designs
      to law enforcement agencies,
      106–119
  Minority of Americans who own
      handguns, 11
  Revolver design, increased capacity,
      173–174
  Rise of semiautomatic pistol in United
      States, 96–105
  Standards for imported handguns
      stricter than domestic guns, 70,
      81–82
Heckler & Koch, 71, 107, 127, 135

Heritage Mfg. Co., Inc., 25
Heston, Charlton (NRA board member,
      former movie star), on "cultural
      war," 192
High-capacity magazine
  In pistol, described, 99
  In semiautomatic assault weapons, 121
  And rise of semiautomatic pistol in
      U.S. market, 100
  And increased lethality of handguns,
      101–105
  Debate among gun experts over need
      for in handguns, 102
  Police trade-ins and "grandfathered"
      magazines, 150–152
High-capacity semiautomatic pistol,
  Debate over law enforcement conver-
      sion from revolver, 108–112
  Rise to market dominance over
      revolver, 99–105
  Ruger profits from introduction of, 103
  Marketing to law enforcement agencies,
      106–119
High Standard, 20
H&R 1871, Inc., 25
Hollow point bullets, design and effect,
      164–165
Hopkins, Cameron (gun writer), 92
Hunting, decline of and impact on U.S.
      gun market, 83–84, 92–93

Import of guns
  Chinese assault guns as case study,
      71–75
  Former Iron Curtain exports as case
      study, 78–80
  Growth of civilian gun imports, 30–32,
      69–71
  Handguns as dominant part of gun
      imports, 30
  High-capacity handguns as case study,
      75–78
  Stimulus for domestic sales, 70
  United States as "last great market" in
      world, 69–70
Importers of guns (see also names of
      specific companies), 39–41
Industry organizations, 64–68

Innovation in gun design as key market-
ing device, 91–105
  Compared to nicotine, 95
  Distinguished from need by gun
    experts, 93–94
  Market stagnation as consequence of
    durability of guns, decline of
    hunting, 91–93
  Innovation as response to stagnation,
    93–96
  Lethality increased in U.S. handgun
    market as result of innovation,
    96–105
  Marketing of new gun designs to law
    enforcement agencies, 106–119
Italy, gun exports to United States, 75–76
Interarms (gun importer) 39–40, 76
Intratec, 22
Iron Curtain countries, see "Russia"
Ithaca, 20

James, Garry, (gun writer), 56, 72
Jannuzzo, Paul (Glock official), 57, 92
Japan, gun exports to United States, 31
Jennings complex of firearms companies,
  22
Jews for the Preservation of Firearms
  Ownership, 65
Jonesboro middle school ambush, 27
Jordan, Bill (gun writer), 97
Jorgenson, Ken, 139
Junk guns, see "Saturday night specials"

Kahr Arms, 58, 138, 140
  And Unification Church interest in,
    82–83
Koresh, David, 49, 126

Larson, Erik, 54, 60, 104
Laser sighting devices, seepage into civil-
  ian market from law enforcement
  use and lack of regulation, 135–136
Law enforcement agencies, sales to (see
  also, "FBI,"),
  As driving force in increased lethality
    in civilian market, 106–119
  As wedge to enter broader civilian
    market, 77, 106, 141–142

Conversion from revolver to pistol as
  standard sidearm, 106–112
Conversion from 9mm pistol to .40
  S&W, 148–152
New York Department of Environmen-
  tal Conservation scandal, 143–145
Traded-in police guns used in crimes,
  147–148
Police trade-ins and "grandfathered"
  high-capacity magazines, 150–152
Law enforcement, gun industry exploita-
  tion of ties to generally, 141–152
  Academies for law enforcement
    training,ba 145–146
  Former law enforcement officials in
    sales positions, 142–143
  New York Department of Environmen-
    tal Conservation scandal, 143–145
  Professional associations and special-
    ized publications, 146
Lethality of firearms (see also "deaths and
  injuries," "FBI," "law enforcement
  agency sales," "public health and
  safety")
  Comparative lethality of various
    firearms, 8,
  Increase in lethality as consequence of
    industry innovation, 95–105
  Increase in civilian lethality from law
    enforcement marketing, 106–119,
    148–152
  Increase in lethality from sales of
    assault weapons, 120–134
  Increase in lethality from development
    and sales of "pocket rockets,"
    134–140
Liability of gun dealers and manufacturers
  Growing industry concern about
    dealer liability, 45–46
  New theories developing, 207–209
Liability of gun writers, see "gun press"
Libourel, Jan (gun writer), 32, 56, 101,
  111, 112, 114
  And giving product advice to gun
    manufacturers, 58–59
Long, Duncan (gun expert and writer), on
  semiautomatic assault weapons, 128
Long guns, 33

Long Island Railroad massacre, 27, 61, 195
Lorcin Engineering Co., Inc., 25–29

McVeigh, Timothy, 49
M-1 Garand rifle, 19
Magaw, John, Director of U.S. Bureau of
Alcohol, Tobacco and Firearms, 7
Magnum Research,
And Galil assault rifle, 127
and movie placements of its guns, 63
MAK-90, 74
Manufacturers of firearms (see also,
"marketing of firearms" and indi-
vidual manufacturers by name),
generally 19–35
Domestic manufacturers, 23–30
Foreign manufacturers 30–32, 69–83
Marine Corps, U.S., hosting NRA law
enforcement pistol seminar for gun
industry, 107–108
Market data
Value of wholesale and retail sales,
affiliated equipment sales, etc., 7
Growth and dimensions of U.S. gun
market, 69–84
Marketing of firearms (see also, "innova-
tion in gun design")
Innovation as marketing device, 95–105
Nostalgia and cultural values as
marketing devices, 85–86
Shooting sports as means to develop
new markets, 175–183
To children, 129–130, 186–189
To women, 184–186
To racial and ethnic minorities,
189–192
Marlin (The Marlin Firearms Co.), 20,
26–27, 29
Marshall, Evan (gun writer), 112
Maverick Arms, Inc., 26
McClure-Volkmer, see Firearms Owner's
Protection Act
Miami (Fla.), connection between 1986
FBI shoot-out and 1997 Gianni
Versace homicide, 112–119
Milek, Bob (gun writer), 55
Mil, Inc., 25

Military market,
As wedge to enter civilian market,
81–82
Influence on civilian gun design and
marketing, 135,136
"Mini-guns," see "concealable handguns"
Moffett, Conley L. (U.S. Fish & Wildlife
Service official), 92
Molchan, Andrew, president, National
Association of Federally Licensed
Firearms Dealers,
On extensive tax-cheating by gun
dealers,ba 43
On innovation as marketing device,
94–95
On lobbying movie industry
executives, 63
"Money-making machine," William
Ruger's description of gun
company, 86
Moon, Justin (see "Kahr Arms")
Moon, Sun Myung (see "Kahr Arms")
Mossberg (O.F. Mossberg & Sons, Inc.),
26–29, 61
Movies, see "Entertainment media"

National Alliance of Stocking Gun
Dealers, 48
National Association of Arms Shows, 49
National Association of Federally Li-
censed Firearms Dealers, 43
National Firearms Act of 1934, 21, 33
National Rifle Association (NRA), 64–66
Board members on racial and ethnic
minorities and women, 190–192
Hosting of industry semiautomatic
pistol seminars for law enforce-
ment, 107
National Shooting Sports Foundation
(NSSF), 56, 66
Navy Arms (gun importer), 39–41
Nazi regalia (at gun shows), 48–49
New York Department of Environmental
Conservation, Law Enforcement
Division, gun sales scandal, 143–145
Nicotine compared to innovation in gun
design, 95
Norinco (China North Industries Corp.),
72

North American Arms, Inc., 25
Novak, Wayne, gun designer, 134
Nugent, Ted (NRA board member and rock musician), on racial and ethnic minorities and women, 191–192

Oberg, James L., 86
O'Brien, Bill (gun writer), 100
Oregon Arms, Inc., 26
Ownership of firearms
Declining proportion of American households owning guns 11
Minority of Americans who own handguns 11

Para-Ordnance, Canadian exporter of high-powered pistols to United States, 32, 58, 118, 138, 140
People's Republic of China, 7
Phoenix Arms, 25–26, 28–29
Planned obsolescence, see "Innovation in gun design"
"Pocket rockets," see "concealable handguns"
Police sales (see "Law enforcement agency sales")
PolyTechnologies, 72
Port Arthur (Australia), 1996 semi-automatic assault weapon massacre, 8
Portugal, gun exports to United States, 31
Pratt, Larry, 65
Profit as motivation of gun industry, 85–88
Public health and safety
Firearms and firearms violence as issue of, 9
Lack of federal regulation
Exemption of guns from federal product safety laws, 13–14
Firearms described as similar to other consumer products, 87
Ministerial attitude of ATF, 12–13
Proposal for comprehensive reform and regulation, 199–209

Racial and ethnic minorities,
As marketing target, 189–192
Disparagement by leading industry spokespersons, 190–192

Reagan, Ronald, 47
Remington (Remington Arms Co., Inc.), 20, 26–28
Repeating firearms, general description, 34
Retail trade in firearms (also see "Dealers," "Secondary gun market")
Weak regulation of retail trade in firearms, 36–37, 42–43
Smuggling of AK-47 assault rifles, 44–45
Retail sales figures, see "market data"
Revolver, see "handguns"
Rifles, general description, 33
"Ring of Fire" gun companies
and manufacture of "Saturday night specials," 22
Risdall, John, 63
Rogers, Bob, 15, 96
Rossi (Amadeo Rossi Municoes, gun manufacturer), 76
Rossi, Luciano, 76
Ruger, William B. Sr., 21, 54, 61, 85, 142
Description of gun company as "little moneymaking machine," 86
Rejecting responsibility for gun violence, 194–197
Reported wealth, 87
Theory of innovation as key to marketing, 94
Ruger Old Model Single Action revolver, 55
Ruger P-85 pistol, 94, 141
Rule-beaters, guns designed to evade import restrictions, 132
Russia and other countries of former Soviet Union, gun exports to United States, 78–80

Saeilo, Inc., 82
Sapporito, Mike, 46
Saturday night specials and "junk guns"
General description, 34–35
And "Ring of Fire" companies, 22
As force driving rise of semiautomatic pistols, 99–100
Resurgence as concealable pistols, 137
Secrecy of gun industry, 5–7

Second Amendment (to U.S. Constitution), use by gun industry as false flag, 16

Secondary gun market, 4, 47–49

Self-defense and marketing of firearms in United States, generally, 155–174

    Increased risk that accompanies firearms ownership for self-defense, 160–162

    Industry exploitation of fears of crime and violence, 155–160, 162–164

    "Stopping power" and defensive ammunition, 164–168

Semi-automatic firearms, general description, 34

Semi-automatic assault weapons, generally, 35, 120–134

    automatic or selective fire feature, irrelevance of, 122

    Australian ban on, 8

    China as major exporter to United States, 71–75

    debate over nomenclature, 126–130

    design features of assault weapons and their significance, 120–125

    "after-market" modifications to militarize civilian guns, 123–124

    industry marketing to children, 129–130

    "rule-beaters" designed by industry to evade bans, 132

    specific assault weapons

        AA Arms AP-9, 128, 129

        AB-10, 22

        AK-47, 8, 44–45, 72–73, 122

        AR-15, 130

        Calico M-100, 122, 130

        Commando Mark 9, 126

        Century FAL, 132

        Galil, 127

        HK-94, 130

        MAC 10, 122

        M-16, 19, 130

        MAK-90, 74

        Norinco NDM-86

        Partisan Avenger, 121,122

        Ruger Mini-14, 113, 123

        SKS, 74

        Sten, 125

        Sturmgewehr 44, 122

        TEC-9, 22, 127

        TEC-22 Scorpion, 124

        Uzi, 125

    Survivalist movement and assault weapons, 125–126

    U.S. ban, ineffectiveness of 1994 federal law, 133–134

    Use in police killings and mass murders, 131–132

Shooting ranges,

    As key component of gun industry survival strategy, 179–181

    National Shooting Range Symposium, 92

    Problems and liabilities of shooting ranges, 181–183

"Shooting sports" as means to develop new markets, generally, 175–183

    Cowboy action shooting, 175–177

    Sporting clays, 178–179

Shotguns

    general description, 33

    Australian ban on pump-action shotguns, 8

Shumar, Don (gun writer), 81

Sigarms, 107, 135, 146, 148

Sigma compact pistol, 139

Sig Sauer, 135, 139, 147

Sitton, G., 93

Smith & Wesson, 5, 20, 25–29, 62, 71, 86, 107, 118, 134, 135, 139, 143, 147, 148

    Academy, 145–146

    Development of the .40 S&W round and pistol, 115–119

    Innovation and handgun design, 95, 134–135

    Model 29, .44 Magnum revolver and "Dirty Harry," 62

Sniper rifles, marketing to civilians, 120

Spain, gun exports to United States, 75–76, 118

Sporting Arms and Ammunition Manufacturers Institute, 66–67

Sporting Arms, Mfg., Inc., 26

Springfield Armory, 19

Springfield, Inc., 26

Structure of gun industry generally, 3–5 (see also specific companies and "Manufacturers of firearms,")

Sturm, Alex, 21
Sturm, Ruger & Company, Inc.
    ("Ruger"), 5, 19, 24–29, 54–55, 118,
    141–142
  Description of by founder as "little
    moneymaking machine," 86
  Pistol used in Long Island Railroad
    massacre, 195
  Profitability of, 85–86
  Profitable effect of introduction of
    semiautomatic pistol, 103
  Vaquero pistol and cowboy action
    shooting, 176
Sucher, William, 40
Sundra, Jon, 93
Survival Arms, Inc., 26
Survivalism, and rise of assault weapons,
    125–126

Taurus, 31, 59, 76, 119, 139
TEC-9 assault pistol, 22
Television, see "entertainment media"
Texas Longhorn Arms, Inc., 25
Tobacco products and tobacco industry,
    parallels with 4, 5, 6, 9, 10, 15–16
  Nicotine and enhanced gun lethality
    from industry innovation com-
    pared, 95–96

Tracing guns, see "Crime guns"
Traded-in police guns used in crimes,
    147–148

Unification Church, see "Kahr Arms"
U.S. Repeating Arms Co., Inc., 26, 91

Violent Crime Control and Law Enforce-
    ment Act of 1994 ("Crime Bill")
  Specious use by gun industry as
    excuse for marketing "pocket
    rockets," 138–139
  Weakness of assault weapons ban,
    133–134

Waldorf, Jim, 27
Walther, 147
War Revenue Act of 1919, 21
Wayne, John, and gun culture, 177–178
Weatherby, Inc., 26
Williams, Dick (gun writer), 54
Wilson, Sheriff Jim (gun writer), 112
Winchester Repeating Arms Co., 20
Wintemute, Dr. Garen and study of "Ring
    of Fire" companies, 22
Women, as target market, 184–186
"Wondernine," see "high-capacity semi-
    automatic pistol"